High Anxieties

High Anxieties

Cultural Studies in Addiction

Janet Farrell Brodie
and
Marc Redfield

EDITORS

UNIVERSITY OF CALIFORNIA PRESS
Berkeley   Los Angeles   London

University of California Press
Berkeley and Los Angeles, California

University of California Press, Ltd.
London, England

© 2002 by the Regents of the University of California

Library of Congress Cataloging-in-Publication Data

High anxieties : cultural studies in addiction /
Janet Farrell Brodie and Marc Redfield, editors.
         p.   cm.
Includes bibliographical references and index.
ISBN 0–520–22750–6 (Cloth : alk. paper).
—ISBN 0–520–22751–4 (Paper : alk. paper)
1. Substance abuse—Social aspects.   2. Drugs and literature.
3. Drugs and motion pictures.   4. Alcoholism in literature.
5. Alcoholism in motion pictures.   6. Virtual reality—Social aspects.
I. Brodie, Janet Farrell.   II. Redfield, Marc, 1958–
         HV4998 .H54   2002
         394.1'4—dc21   2002002289

Manufactured in the United States of America
10   09   08   07   06   05   04   03   02
  10   9   8   7   6   5   4   3   2   1

The paper used in this publication is both acid-free and totally chlorine-free (TCF).
It meets the minimum requirements of ANSI/NISO Z39.48–1992 (R 1997)
(*Permanence of Paper*).♾

CONTENTS

    *Alcohol and Native American Identity
    in the Fiction of James Fenimore Cooper* / *109*
    NICHOLAS O. WARNER

PART IV. PLEASURES, REPRESSIONS, RESISTANCES

7. Smoking, Addiction, and the Making of Time / *119*
    HELEN KEANE

8. An Intoxicated Screen
    Reflections on Film and Drugs / *134*
    MAURIZIO VIANO

PART V. TRAUMA, MEDIA, CYBERSPACE

9. Welcome to the Pharmacy
    Addiction, Transcendence, and Virtual Reality / *161*
    ANN WEINSTONE

10. If "Reality Is the Best Metaphor," It Must Be Virtual / *175*
    MARGUERITE R. WALLER

    NOTES / *191*

    ABOUT THE CONTRIBUTORS / *225*

    INDEX / *227*

ILLUSTRATIONS

ACKNOWLEDGMENTS

We gratefully acknowledge the Center for the Arts and Humanities of Claremont Graduate University and the Deans of the Claremont Colleges (Claremont McKenna College, Harvey Mudd College, Pitzer College, Pomona College, and Scripps College) for their generous support of the Addiction and Culture conference at which these papers were first presented. We just as gratefully thank Maureen O'Connor, Sara Patterson, and Catherine Corder, our skilled and diligent research assistants, for the many ways they aided us with this volume.

Introduction

Marc Redfield and Janet Farrell Brodie

Who will ever relate the whole history of narcotica?—It is almost the history of "culture," of so-called high culture.
—NIETZSCHE, *Gay Science*, par. 86.

The essays collected in this volume stem from a conference held at the Claremont Colleges; like most of the presentations at that conference, they argue for connections between our notions of "addiction" and "culture" that go far beyond the commonplace that addiction, like any representable entity or event, is a phenomenon with a cultural side to it.[1] As presented here, addiction and culture become concepts that float and overlap, refer to and interfere with each other. Such a project may at first seem strange, or willfully perverse. The two terms have very different valences—one is negative, the other positive; one evokes medical and legal questions and histories, the other essential human powers of expressivity, memory, and collective existence. On the occasions when they encounter each other, they seem inevitable opponents. Addiction is the sickness, culture the state of health; addiction arrives from outside and elsewhere, as a historical or ontological accident, while culture radiates from the heart of individual, group, or species identity.

On closer inspection, however, these binary oppositions dissolve into more complex affiliations. It is worth pausing at this point to define these terms and sketch their lexical and conceptual history. As Raymond Williams has shown, the term "culture," which derives from the Latin root *colere* ("inhabit, cultivate, protect, honor with worship") via *cultura* ("cultivation, tending"), acquired its contemporary meanings over the last two or three centuries, with the development of Enlightenment humanism, on the one hand, and modern aesthetics, on the other.[2] In its early uses "culture" was "a noun of process: the tending of something, basically crops or animals" (87). Subsequently, by metaphorical extension, it came to mean the tending of the mind; and over the course of the eighteenth century it began to acquire its three principal modern meanings. As a synonym for another keyword of the Enlightenment, "civilization," culture came to signify humanity's "intellectual, spiritual, and aesthetic development"; around the same time, however, it also began to mean the specificity of a local or folk or traditional culture (often in contrast to the globalizing rationalism and technologism of "civilization"), as well as intellectual and artistic activity. Williams suggests that this third meaning is an applied form of the first: "The idea of a general process of intellectual, spiritual, and aesthetic development was applied and effectively transferred to the works and practices which represent and sustain it" (91). The general and particular or aesthetic senses of the word "culture," in any case, have always tended to fold into each other. In Matthew Arnold's *Culture and Anarchy* (1867) the term's double (or triple) duty sums up the text's aesthetic project: "culture" names at once the general accomplishment of humanity, the specific accomplishment of European man, and the aesthetic accomplishment of art, which mediates contradiction by allowing universal truths to radiate from particular acts. We may note in passing that a version of this triple play, ironically enough, marks our contemporary term "cultural studies": the word "cultural" in the phrase "cultural studies" works as a formal universal, even though the "studies" in question usually set out to debunk Arnoldian universalism. All cultures may be different, but they are all cultures. This double bind informs the semantic and ideological history of the term "culture" itself.

"Addiction," in its modern sense, has an even more abbreviated history. The word has intriguing and ancient philological roots: like "diction" or "dictation," it derives from the Latin *dicere* (say, relate), which returns to the Greek *deiknunai*, "show, point out, bring to light." In Roman law the word *addicere* had the more prosaic job of signifying a giving or binding-over of something or someone by sentence of a court: the assignation of slave to master, debtor to creditor. That legal meaning gave rise to a now obsolete English verb, "to addict," meaning "to bind, attach, or devote oneself or another as a servant, disciple, or adherent, to some person or cause"; hence, of course, our modern use of "addiction" to signify a compulsive attachment to a behavior, and in particular the need to ingest a drug. This modern meaning, however, is of remarkably recent vintage. The first entry in the *Oxford English Dictionary* in which "addiction" refers to drug use is dated 1906; its first recorded use of "addict" as a noun is from 1909.[3] Recent scholarship has demonstrated the magnitude and complexity of the history behind these dictionary entries. Like the "homosexual" with whom s/he has often been linked, the addict emerged with the development, a little more than a century ago, of a medico-legal discourse capable of reconceiving human identity in the language of pathology. Throughout much of the history of the United States, Americans drank prodigiously but no one labeled such behavior a disease capable of controlling the drinker's life.[4] A similar understanding of opiate use as a more or less unremarkable behavior or vice, rather than the kernel of a deviant or pathological identity, was the norm in the United States and England until the end of the nineteenth century. Although growing numbers of Americans habitually used opium, morphine, laudanum, cannabis, heroin, and beginning in the 1880s, cocaine, there was little public anxiety and no formal campaign to restrict drug consumption until the early twentieth century. Americans quietly tolerated drug use, associating it primarily with middle class women dosing themselves with opiate-laden patent medicines and with veterans of the Civil War habituated to pain-killers.[5] If the laissez-faire approach to economic regulation did not extend to all private behaviors, as purveyors of "obscenity" and birth control learned in the 1870s, it was not until the early twentieth century that the specter of the drug addict began to loom in American public consciousness and reform rhetoric.[6]

The legal history of the "addictive substance" provides an equally abrupt narrative. In both Britain and the United States the criminalization of drugs has been a twentieth-century phenomenon. No laws regulated opium, marijuana, heroin, or other drug use until campaigns orchestrated by diverse groups spurred the passage of the earliest state laws to curb morphine use in the 1890s, until the Pure Food and Drug Act removed opiates from patent medicines in 1906, and until a 1909 law banned the importation of opium for smoking. Not until 1914 in the United States did the Harrison Act establish the power of the federal government to regulate possession, use, and sale of narcotic drugs; Supreme Court decisions in 1919 upheld its constitutionality, particularly the right of the state to regulate medical prescription of drugs. With the establishment of the Federal Bureau of Narcotics in 1930, the first of the century's "wars" on drugs began, to peak in intensity in the cold war 1950s, decline during the 1960s, only to be expanded and reinvigorated in the last third of the century. Similarly, although opium use began to be regulated in Britain with the 1868 Pharmacy Act, the serious criminalization of drugs dates from the 1916 Defense of the Realm Act and the 1920 Dangerous Drugs Act. In Britain the emergent discourse of addiction was associated, as several chapters in this volume illustrate, with colonialism, with the foreign—especially Asian—"Other," and with a feminized or otherwise "degenerate" nation. Addiction as a concept and a discourse in modern American culture resonated similarly around stereotypes of the opium-smoking Chinese immigrant, the "cocaine-crazed" and sexually threatening African-American male, the marijuana-smoking and violent Mexican youth of the Southwest. In the United States, medical professionals, police and criminologists, government bureaucrats, policymakers, and social reformers harnessed the mass media, the language of statistics and academia, and harrowing descriptions of newly discovered "deviant subcultures" to mount campaigns against the perceived threats of racial minorities, the urban poor, and the foreign born.

Anxieties about addiction meshed with wider American anxieties about lost autonomy and the dangers of the un-American.[7]

Much can be made, then, of this sudden pathologization and criminalization of habit: it occurred as part of the emergence, on the one hand, of a disciplinary society in which typologies of deviance play a significant role in the operations of power, and, on the other hand, of a society of consumption in which identities and desires become attuned to the repetitive seriality of commodity production.[8] For the moment, though, we may pause to digest the simpler and more general point that addiction, like culture, belongs as a concept to the social and technical regimes of the modern era.

How then, to return to the question we posed earlier, are we to conceive of the relations between addiction and culture? A number of considerations suggest that these terms imply each other even more insistently than they oppose each other. We may note first that addiction is marked by the specificity of a culture: besides being a twentieth-century notion, it is also primarily (though by no means simply or entirely) an Anglo-American one. The French language, for instance, has no precisely equivalent word—a French drug addict is a *toxicomane:* a term with its own history and compulsions—and the discourse of addiction in France has developed in ways specific to Francophone culture. (It is partly for this reason that our volume focuses heavily on Anglo-American material.) Addiction, therefore, is nothing if not a cultural concept, despite its affiliations with scientific and medical discourse. But if our notion of addiction is culturally specific, so too is our notion of "culture" (though here the differences among European national traditions are subtler and less decisive: one is better off thinking of "culture" as culturally specific to post-Enlightenment Western capitalism). And within "our culture"—uncertain entity that it is, with undeterminable, unpoliceable borders—addiction seems able to follow the term "culture" wherever the latter drifts. Addiction, that is, appears to belong to culture as culture's own proper disease. Over the past century, both the ruin and the superabundance of culture have been symbolized by the addict, who has proved capable of evoking by turns an urban, racialized underclass, the glitter of jet-set consumption, or the hothouse bloom of Wildean aestheticism. The discourses of both "high" and mass or commodity culture seem inextricable from that of addiction.[9] Even the anthropological concept of culture as a totality of discourses, representations, technologies, and material practices seems—at least in the case of contemporary U.S. culture—to be infiltrated by an equally totalizing spiral within addiction. As Eve Sedgwick notes, in contemporary American society "it has now become a commonplace that . . . any substance, any behavior, even any affect may be pathologized as addictive."[10] One can become addicted to food, to the refusal of food, to exercise—to "health" itself: "Addiction, under this definition, resides only in the structure of a will that is always somehow insufficiently free, a choice whose voluntarity is insufficiently pure" (132).

Like the notion of culture, then, which expands so easily to name the totality of a social group or that of humanity itself, our peculiar, recent, extremely cultural notion of addiction has a generalizing force that needs to be reckoned with. We may hypothesize that this generalizing force is that of culture itself: that the humanist myth of culture contains within it something like what Freud called the "death drive"—a dependence on repetitive process, a need for a certain alterity or intoxication. The roots of this dependence arguably go deep. Jacques Derrida's massive critique of Western metaphysics suggests that something like "addiction" would always have to be posited as inhabiting a concept like "culture," to the extent that repetition and alterity underwrite identity and presence. Derrida's well-known reading of the *Phaedrus* focuses on the figure of the *pharmakon*—a word that means both poison and remedy—to demonstrate the dependence of Platonic philosophy on iterative and differential processes (the dependence, that is, of the logos on what Derrida calls "writing").[11] These large metaphysical issues press heavily on addiction discourse. The question of questions ("what is truth?") echoes in the endless media coverage of drugs and drug addiction, in the hysteria that colors the issue of drug consumption. "We do not object to the drug user's pleasure per se," Derrida comments in a recent interview, "but to a pleasure taken in an experience without truth."[12] Avital Ronell has pressed the question of addiction to the point where addiction becomes a name for "the structure that is philosophically and metaphysically at the basis of our culture," and has shown that even as antimetaphysical a thinker as Heidegger must allow "wish and willing, addiction and urge" to infiltrate the care in which Dasein's Being reveals itself.[13] Sedgwick, for her part, suggests that "so long as 'free will' has been hypostatized and charged with ethical value, for just so long has an equally hypostatized 'compulsion' had to be available as a counterstructure always internal to it, always requiring to be ejected from it."[14] It would seem that what matters, finally, is not the self's particular wishes or acts—not whether it indulges in cocaine, or food, or exercise, or any other object or behavior per se. Rather, what matters is the essential integrity of its will, and the essential truth of its being. The thought of addiction thus spreads to the point of infecting the founding tropes of Western philosophy.

When addiction is at issue, however, metaphysical complications immediately acquire empirical importance. ("You can only," as Ronell comments, "be addicted to what is available" [42].) The modern recasting of addiction as pathology has occurred as a massive institutional and sociohistorical articulation of metaphysical values, tensions, and contradictions. Mark Seltzer has suggested the term "machine culture" to capture aspects of modernity that went into the making of, among other things, the addict. We

noted earlier that the addict emerged as part of the advent of a technolo-
gized, bureaucratized, disciplinary society of consumption, in which power
becomes what Foucault termed "biopower"—power articulated in and
through the surveillance and training of bodies. The disciplined body
becomes at times seductively, at times dangerously similar to a constructed
object or machine; desire becomes geared to the seriality of consumer society; and the subjects whose desires and bodies are so repetitively constructed suffer the possibility of a "fundamental 'leakiness' of the self, a leaking away of agency and identity."[15] Like a number of critics who have written
recently on addiction, Seltzer thus suggests that the notion of the "addict"
pathologizes the predicament of the normative subject of late capitalism.

This century's repeated crises surrounding illegal drug addiction have
been, as always when addiction is at issue, both "real" and rhetorical, an
ongoing cycle of profit and damage in which narcopolitics has gone deci-
sively global, on the one hand, and has become an affair of representations
and words, on the other. The ravages of the epidemics of fear about addiction are only too readily apparent in Britain and the United States.
Although Britain's legal drug maintenance treatment programs (established as early as 1926) met with approval from Americans sympathetic to
prevention and treatment rather than policing models for habitual drug
users, the British government and public turned to harsher drug policies,
beginning in the 1960s and continuing under the Conservative government
of the 1970s and 1980s. New drug laws gave more power to the police to
search and seize, to arrest and prosecute suspected drug abusers; arrests
and convictions for possession of drugs including cannabis soared, the
numbers of convictions for drug manufacture and importation doubled
and tripled in the subsequent drug war. In the United States since the mid-
twentieth century, billions of dollars have been allocated to civilian and military policing of drug users and distributors. Federal and state governments
have passed draconian antidrug laws, upheld as constitutional in state and
federal courts. Possession of cocaine has brought life imprisonment without
possibility of parole; rehabilitation and drug treatment programs have been
steadily dismantled, only to be replaced by "tough drug laws" with mandatory prison sentences that eliminate all alternative sentencing. Since the
reescalation of the antidrug campaign in the mid-1970s, the portion of the
federal budget devoted to drug enforcement has more than quadrupled;
scores of new federal and state agencies with police power over drugs have
been created; the FBI, CIA, the IRS, and all branches of the Armed Services
(formerly prohibited from engaging in civilian law enforcement) have
assumed expanded antidrug police powers. Under the familiar rhetoric of
drug abuse as a "national emergency afflicting both the body and soul of
America" and the necessity of an "all-out global war on the drug menace,"
Americans since the 1970s have acceded to the increased use of wiretaps,

police roadblocks, drug-sniffing dogs, search and seize procedures without customary warrants, mandatory urine and blood tests to detect illegal drug use. These policies, along with the widespread use of undercover drug agents and anonymous informants, represent an erosion of constitutional rights on a scale known earlier only occasionally and briefly during the Civil War and the two world wars. During the last fifteen years, savagely lopsided crack-cocaine sentencing laws and militarized inner-city police tactics have criminalized the nation's black male population so relentlessly as to constitute an indirect near-equivalent of apartheid. Neither the First Amendment's protection of free speech, the Fourth's due process protections, nor the Eighth Amendment's prohibition of cruel and unusual punishment has offered legal recourse in the frenzy of the post–cold war drug witchhunts.[16] It is not an exaggeration to say that the police state runs on drugs.

On the global front, the specter of the drug crisis has also had its obvious uses. The figure of the drug addict rested on constructions in the United States and Britain of a foreign other demonically seeking to weaken the nation. In foreign policy, the association of Latin American and Asian nations as villainous growers and suppliers in international drug cartels has given the Western governments new tools for refashioning old-fashioned gunboat diplomacy into postmodern police violence. Such actions (taken at every step in the name of drugs) are vast and probably irreversible acts of damage; as to the human lives ruined or ended over the course of this latest, massive grab for state power, the count is so high and the individual narratives so painful that "war" becomes an appropriate, if misleadingly grandiloquent, metaphor.[17] Rarely, perhaps, has the drive to protect identity from an "experience without truth" had a more extensive impact on the world.

It may help at this point to herd some of these observations in the direction of a concrete example. In his introduction to *Naked Lunch*, William Burroughs offers a powerfully compact account of the scene of addiction, and a close reading of his text will suggest a few of the ways in which the figure of addiction repeats but also destabilizes the logic of consumer culture: "Junk is the ideal product . . . the ultimate merchandise. No sales talk necessary. The client will crawl through a sewer and beg to buy. . . . The junk merchant does not sell his product to the consumer, he sells the consumer to his product. . . . A dope fiend is a man in total need of dope. Beyond a certain frequency need knows absolutely no limit or control. In the words of total need: 'Wouldn't you?' Yes, you would. You would lie, cheat, inform on your friends, steal, do anything to satisfy total need."[18]

The drug itself, as object of desire, is at once utterly coercive and nugatory: it's junk, the broken residue of useful technology, the leavings of instrumental reason; as an object it no longer makes sense and belongs in a junkyard. Yet it is also the "ideal product." It sells itself; and in doing so it reverses the official relation between consumer and product, to reveal a hallucination that is in fact the truth of consumer capitalism. The consumer is not sold the product but is rather sold to the product. As everyone knows—for this is no secret: children and fraternity men know it as well as anyone—the enlightened magic of advertising consists in making us desire things for no better reason than that they are being advertised. "Junk," to Burroughs, takes the power of the commodity to its limit, stripping the object of any remains of aesthetic glamour or illusions of usefulness, collapsing it into a black hole. The object has become purely and simply the need for the object. In one sense, therefore, it is no longer properly an "object" at all. Yet this nonobject is just as far from being a screen onto which a "subject" projects its desire. The subject of desire has been produced by the product, even though the product is nothing more than a placeholder for desire.

We may briefly recall Marx's famous analysis of commodity fetishism in the first chapter of *Capital,* so as to have more clearly in mind what kind of object a commodity is, and what kind of illusions it generates. "A commodity," Marx comments, "appears at first sight an extremely obvious, trivial thing. But its analysis brings out that it is a very strange thing. . . . As soon as it emerges as a commodity, it changes into a sensible suprasensible thing [*ein sinnlich übersinnliches Ding*]."[19] This doubleness results from the fact that objects become commodities by becoming sensible tokens of abstract (and thus thoroughly suprasensible) human labor power. Only thus can things enter into exchange as commodities possessing quantifiable "value." And there is a further twist: in becoming tokens of quantified labor power, commodities generate the illusion that value inheres in themselves, rather than in the socioeconomic relations that produce them and make them possible. "So far no chemist has ever discovered exchange value either in a pearl or a diamond," Marx comments acerbically (1:177); nonetheless, the commodity glows with value as a poetic symbol shines with meaning, or a fetish with divinity. Two interrelated things have happened: a relation among human beings (the social relations of production) has been transformed into a relation among things (exchange value); and a structural effect (value as a quantity of abstracted human labor) has been transmogrified into the property of a sensuous object. Both aspects of commodity fetishism are summarized and enacted in the trope Marx employs to dramatize the commodity's strangeness—personification: "A table continues to be wood, an ordinary, sensuous thing. But as soon as it emerges as a commodity, it changes into a thing which transcends sensuousness. It not only stands with its feet on the ground, but, in relation to other commodities, it stands on its head, and evolves out of its wooden brain grotesque ideas, far more wonderful than if it were to begin dancing of its own free will" (1:163–64).

It is easy to understand this "personification" of inanimate things as a transfer of attributes from a subject to an object: a self-projection whereby the subject, usually unbeknownst to itself, discovers itself alienated in objectified forms. Versions of this narrative have composed a dominant theme in philosophy since Kant; and humanist versions of Marxism have often characterized capitalist production as entailing the reification of human consciousness and the personification of things. Burroughs's account does not directly contradict such a narrative. Indeed, his fiction is known for exaggerating to a hallucinatory intensity the chiasmic exchange of properties between human and nonhuman, animate and inanimate entities. Yet at the same time, Burroughs complicates our notion of personification by drawing attention to the artificiality of the "subject." If junk is the black hole of need, this need is radically unnatural. No subject ravaged by this need can properly lay claim to it, for the need has been produced by the object, even though the object is a nonobject—pure, uncut "junk." The personification emerges in a context in which no "person" can be found at its origin. One can thus say that in Burroughs's text, addiction names the madness at the heart not just of consumer society but also of desire in Freud's sense, or Lacan's. Desire constitutes the subject and yet remains radically alien to the subject. By noting this desire as "need," Burroughs's text destroys the hint of naturalism made available by the Lacanian distinction between need and desire. The addict, body transformed by (and into) junk, does not "desire" junk, but needs it, as a plant needs water, or a baby milk, at the same time that the naturalness of the need vanishes irretrievably.[20]

One can press the uncanny logic of addiction in Burroughs one step further and suggest that the origin of addiction is, paradoxically, withdrawal, the trace of a sickness and loss prior to health or presence. "Any opiate that relieves pain is habit forming, and the more effectively it relieves pain the more habit forming it is" (241). But the pain here is precisely that of the withdrawal of the drug that, in a viciously (or rapturously) addictive circle, relieves the pain it causes. The drug obliterates any memories of a pain (or pleasure, or relief) that would preexist it: the drug is at once pain and relief, poison and medicine; to be an "addict" is to live this circularity, with nothing at the origin but a sickness that strengthens itself in curing itself. And if we take "drugs" in their role as our society's lurid metonym for "addiction" per se, we may understand Burroughs's text as a narrative about the destruction of identity through addiction, but a story quite different from, and critical of, the official version of this theme—where identity is represented as originally or naturally healthy, and as "addicted" only insofar as it falls victim to an alien force. In Burroughs, addiction destroys identity not by attacking it from the outside, but by usurping the origin or identity of identity itself. This is the predicament Ronell calls "Being-on-drugs." There is no natural identity. Yet there is also no god to set its guarantee on an originary moment of artifice, a "constructedness" that could guarantee the identity of identity.

Burroughs thus encourages us to rethink our very notion of "construction." Another way to put this is to say that his texts render identity historical.

All the essays in this book explore the social construction of addictions. Some focus on particular cultural constructions, others on important periods and themes in the history of addiction discourse, still others on the contemporary politics of addiction. The two chapters in Part I, "Constructions of Addiction," take as their principal object of inquiry either the historical specificity of the discourse of addiction, or the power such discourses have had to position subjects, shape desires, and rechannel anxieties ("constructions of addiction," that is, as a subjective genitive). The links among narrative, addiction, and possession receive sustained attention in Stacey Margolis's contribution, which reads a number of late-nineteenth-century literary texts—a short story by Arthur Conan Doyle; George du Maurier's *Trilby;* Bram Stoker's *Dracula;* and Pauline Hopkins's *Of One Blood*—in order to chart "the emergence of a particularly modern form of desire." The late-nineteenth-century notion of addiction, Margolis argues, names not just a desire proper to a subject or self, but "desire as a circuit that by-passes the subject completely." Margolis identifies this story as a version of the possession narrative, but she draws attention to the cultural work done by the figure of a self liberated from desire: "Imagining individuals who could embody feelings or intentions that were not their own, the possession narrative invented a new kind of subject, one defined not by the depth of its desires but by its permeability." Tracing British and American versions of this narrative, Margolis argues that, in its American form, the story of the permeable self became that of the racial subject—a bypassing of the individual that, ultimately, recuperates and resituates the individual within the continuum of heredity. Arguing against a long and powerful critical tradition that links the notion of addiction to the emergence of consumer capitalism, Margolis suggests that we understand the addicted subject as a figure marking a certain internal limit or alternative to consumerism, opening the possibility of literary, legal, and medical discourses predicated on "identity that cannot be understood in terms of the subject-centered discourse of the market at all."

If Margolis emphasizes the ideological desirability of a desireless subject—the cultural needs and fantasies driving an image of the self as an empty vessel, filled with borrowed cravings—Timothy Melley focuses on the "agency panic" that twentieth-century discourses of addiction at once register, assuage, and perpetuate. Melley sees the omnipresence of addiction discourse in contemporary U.S. culture as the result of this culture's inability to abandon the assumptions of possessive individualism "despite an anxious sense that they fail to explain the unsettling compulsions that seem to be turning us into addicts." Melley centers his essay on the work of William Burroughs, in which he discovers an extreme instance of this double bind.

Although Burroughs's fiction "pressures traditional assumptions about the person in the most radical fashion imaginable," it does so "in the mode of panic—and thus tends to romanticize a traditional view of the individual, a fantasy of the autonomous self isolated from any threat of external invasion or control." Comparing the work of Burroughs with a number of other American texts from the 1950s and 1960s, Melley discovers again and again "a tendency to question whether humans are self-governing agents" and a simultaneous "refusal to modify the traditional model of the agent, which he applies to other, non-human entities." The result is a paranoid style of personification, which Melley identifies as characteristic of addiction discourse from the era of "demon rum" to Burroughs's cold-war fictions.

Part II, "Figures of the Orient," addresses aspects of what is perhaps the most striking characteristic of addiction discourse: its close historical association with Western discourses of the "Orient." If, as Melley suggests, paranoid personification is the style proper to addiction, these essays by Cannon Schmitt and Marty Roth extend considerations of agency panic beyond the realm of the individual self and interrogate the role of addiction discourse in the history of nationalism, racism, and occidentalism. In "Narrating National Addictions: De Quincey, Opium, and Tea," Schmitt explores interwoven representations of self, gender, and nation in the writings of Thomas De Quincey, focusing on ways in which De Quincey's texts redeploy Gothic motifs so as to "gothicize the orient" and "orientalize the gothic," thereby linking individual and national concerns. By representing himself and the English nation as feminized victims, De Quincey both constructs a self "out of helplessness and victimization" and provides "the most powerful nation in the world with a rationale for aggression based, paradoxically, in a sense of itself as the beleaguered heroine of Gothic romance." Motifs of the paranoid Gothic thus serve to structure imperialist rhetoric at the same time that they console a self whose use of opium has called its national and racial identity into question.

Schmitt's close reading of De Quincey's texts is accompanied by a richly textured account of relevant political and economic contexts: the Sino-British trade imbalances that led the British to sanction a covert trade in opium; the subsequent Opium Wars. In "Victorian Highs: Detection, Drugs, and Empire," Marty Roth nominates the British opium trade as the prime mover behind a "collective Anglo-Saxon fantasy" at work in Victorian detective fiction. If historical fact suggests that the British forced opium on the Chinese in order to defray the costs of British addiction to tea and of running the empire in India, Victorian detective fiction effected a fantastic, compensatory reversal by representing the Chinese as foisting opium on an innocent British public. Examining texts by Poe, Dickens, Collins, Conan Doyle, and other lesser-known writers, Roth documents in detail the ubiquity of drugs and drug-taking in early detective fiction, arguing that these texts are steeped in an "anxiety of empire," and are obsessed with the motif of "imperial rule returning to pollute the metropolitan homeland." The genre's connections with empire and narcotics only began to disappear, Roth suggests, when detective fiction became a fully-fledged genre system in the 1920s.

In Part III, "Demon Drink," we include three essays that focus on aspects of the rich discursive tradition on alcohol and alcoholism in the nineteenth and twentieth centuries. In "The Rhetoric of Addiction: From Victorian Novels to AA," Robyn R. Warhol compares Alcoholics Anonymous stories to narratives about alcohol abuse in Victorian novels, arguing that "the ideas about alcoholism that shape the recovery and the identity of the contemporary real-world alcoholic are created and circulated through narratives that have had currency in our culture for at least 150 years." Warhol notes that in AA discourse, alcoholism is at once an identity ("Hi, I'm Bill and I'm an alcoholic") and an incurable disease; recovery occurs as the endlessly repeated telling of a story—the alcoholic's story of his own identity. Warhol points to ways in which this reliance on storytelling can be traced back, on the one hand, to a "Victorian emphasis on communitarian values," and, on the other hand, to "the ambiguous status of alcoholism in early twentieth-century culture": an era during which alcoholism could be regarded both as a disease and as a moral failing. Warhol demonstrates that the redemptive power of a conversion narrative is already present in Victorian narratives of alcoholism, but draws attention to ways in which mid-nineteenth-century constructions of alcoholism as a "behavior" (rather than an "identity") also led to narratives very different from that proposed by AA discourse. Warhol's chapter thus provides a focused account of the historical and cultural construction of one sort of addiction and one influential model of "recovery."

In "Firewater Legacy: Addiction and Native American Identity in the Fiction of James Fenimore Cooper," Nicholas O. Warner examines the discourse about Native Americans and drinking that began in the seventeenth century and saw full tide during Cooper's era, in the first half of the nineteenth century. This discourse had two competing but intertwined strands: on the one hand, drink was understood to be the catalyst that unleashed the violence of the "savage"; on the other hand, drink was recognized as a tool for the destruction of native cultures. Underlying both strands is the notion that Native Americans were fated to self-destruct. Cooper, in Warner's reading, seems torn between "the firewater myth of inevitable Indian degradation, and his own sense of the ways that social convention and cultural expectations can blind even the best-intentioned of persons." Cooper found Native American life "at once alien and profoundly admirable"; his work encapsulated a remarkable number of white stereotypes and assumptions about Native American drinking. Cooper also exhibited reserves of complexity and sensitivity, as when, for example, "he invests Chingachgook's personal addiction with tragic dignity and with broader meaning as he connects that addiction to the fragmentation of Native American racial identity and, by extension, of an entire way of life."

The essays in Part IV, "Pleasures, Repressions, Resistances," overtly engage the eudaemonic and political dimensions of addiction in contemporary society. In "Smoking, Addiction, and the Making of Time," Helen Keane revisits and radicalizes themes treated by Richard Klein in his influential *Cigarettes Are Sublime*. If Klein attends to ways in which a puritanical culture disavows the darkly aesthetic—that is, sublime—pleasures of smoking, Keane insists that "the virtues of cigarettes and the appeal of addiction cannot be excluded, even from the discourse of nicotine addiction." And while Klein's book studies ways in which smoking constitutes and reconstitutes time, Keane develops these themes in a different direction by juxtaposing Klein's insights with "the economies of time and risk which operate in health promotion and anti-smoking discourse." "If the attractions of cigarettes are taken seriously and thought of in relation to temporality," Keane suggests, it becomes possible to construct a relationship between smoking and time different from that presupposed by health-management calculation: a relationship in which "the smoker emerges as an active and skillful producer of time and pleasure." Controversial and bold, Keane's paper provides a powerful reminder of what is meant by the cultural construction of addiction, not least by reminding us of ways in which what we call health is culturally constructed.

An impassioned call to arms, Maurizio Viano's "An Intoxicated Screen: Reflections on Film and Drugs" surveys the synergistic relationship among drugs, cinema, history, prohibition, and war. The representation of drugs in film has been coextensive with the history of cinema, and Viano suggests that cinema itself may be conceptualized as the "intoxicated screen." He surveys ways in which drugs have been associated with film and draws attention to a persistent cinematic fantasy: the "fantasy of drugs as a virus coming from outside to corrupt an otherwise healthy body." Woven into this history and analysis of the intoxicated screen are "communiqués" that Viano launches like missiles against U.S. drug policies: the criminalization of the distribution of clean syringes to heroin addicts; the laws against hemp production; the difficulty patients have in obtaining marijuana on medical grounds.

The concluding essays in Part V, "Trauma, Media, Cyberspace," examine aspects of the long and complex links between addiction discourse and modern technology. In her "Welcome to the Pharmacy: Addiction, Transcendence, and Virtual Reality," Ann Weinstone argues that the long established connection in Western tradition between addiction and transcendence (especially transcendence as acquisition of new and powerful knowledges, dis- or reembodiment, life extension, or other special powers) provided a "constitutive, founding rhetoric for discourses concerning VR [virtual reality]." Weinstone imaginatively ranges across VR novels, cyber-graphics, advertisements for cyberspace games, and even the relatedness of molecular biology and cybernetics/information theory to explore the impli-cations of the cyberspace/addiction linkage. As with other contributions in this volume, her conclusions accentuate the centrality of addiction in the production of subjectivities in the late-twentieth-century West.

Finally, in "If 'Reality is the Best Metaphor,' It Must Be Virtual," Marguerite Waller draws attention to the ways in which the virtual reality world, in spite of expectations to the contrary, has replicated the real world in its reification of self/other, truth/untruth, difference/identities, and gender/power relations: "The flow of subjectivity into the 'visual pixel dust' of cartoon avatars . . . permits us to carry on with business as usual." Waller's critical examination of the model of electronic communication argues that three-dimensional, online, interactive cyberactivities do not decenter the old, destabilize binary opposition, subvert ontologies or reorder gender; they provide, rather "a seductive new phallicism," an intoxicated phallicism deriving its power not from demarcation and dominance, but from "weight-less, transparent interactivity." Her essay focuses, as well, on the gender pol-itics of virtual reality spaces, particularly the state's efforts to police illicit sex and drug references on the Internet: "As usual," she notes, "sexuality, espe-cially as signified by women's bodies, is being constructed by the state for the production of conventional, centralized power."

As stories about the historical contingency of identity, subjectivity, and desire, narratives of addiction potentially have great critical power, and thus should be—and have been—of interest to cultural critics. For all their dif-ferences in methodology and content, the essays collected here testify to the weight of particular questions and themes within the gravitational field cast by the figure of addiction. The two concluding essays by Weinstone and Waller focus on a dialectic of transcendence and embodiment that returns us to issues raised at the beginning of the book by Melley and Margolis and, indirectly, by most of the other writers in this collection. Addiction, it seems, is bound up with discourses and figures of embodiment and disembodi-ment, on the one hand, and with questions of will, intention, and desire, on the other. Addiction thus insinuates itself into the fabric of what we call "identity" and becomes inseparable from the history of the individualized, pathologized subject, and from that of collective or systemic (national, racial, sexual, and so on) forms of identification and subjection. Further-more, whether this addicted subject displays a will to power or, as in Margolis's reading, a desire to escape desire, it seems doomed to under-mine or exceed its own consolations. There is always desire left over; and there is always the possibility that this excessive, addicted desire—including, of course, the desire to stop desiring—comes from elsewhere: from foreign parts; from something not altogether human, a monster, a "substance." The salience of personification in addiction discourse may be understood as a defense against this foreignness—but also as a repetition of the threat against which personification defends. The compulsiveness with which we render the inhuman human (and vice versa) in addiction discourse suggests the fragility of conventional notions of personhood and the necessity of thinking the "construction" of persons in new ways. "Thinking the body as constructed demands a rethinking of construction itself," Judith Butler observes, since constructedness is not something one chooses or controls.[21] Indeed, if we take "addiction" as a trope for a being-constructed that disrupts oppositions between determinism and freedom, we might at times find it helpful to claim that we are "addicted" to our genders, our sexualities, our bodies, and our "selves."

The body, therefore, that returns, stubbornly and excessively, in addiction discourse, does not return us to a stable human identity or natural being, but rather testifies to a materiality that resists these categories. If the essays collected here reveal that one can only be a modern subject by running the risk of addiction, they also show that this subject of addiction is what Donna Haraway would call a cyborg: inhumanly technical in its constructed humanity; always already embodied, but never substantially enough to be able to police its borders and be sure of its form.[22] Culture itself, under the pull of addiction, becomes cyborgian: addiction calls the thought of culture toward the difficult thought of a technicity ungrounded in culture's organic root. Such ontological instability is not easy to endure. Anguish and ecstasy color addiction discourse, and a deep repetitiveness marks it. Repetition can signal control or the loss of control, and the figure of addiction is lodged ambivalently in between, signifying both and neither. Addiction, consequently, explains both too much and too little; but we seemingly cannot do without it. Our culture's addiction to addiction constitutes one of the fault lines that cultural studies most urgently needs to explore, and the essays collected here demonstrate some of the benefits of pursuing a topic on which we are, in any case, hooked.

PART I

Constructions of Addiction

Addiction and the Ends of Desire

Stacey Margolis

The striking thing about Miss Penelosa, the mesmerist in Sir Arthur Conan Doyle's short story "The Parasite" (1894), is not that she can make her subjects perform certain actions, but that she can make them, against their will, experience certain desires. Engaged in a series of mesmeric experiments with Miss Penelosa, Professor Paul Gilroy discovers to his horror that she has made him fall in love with her: "Again, tonight, I awoke from the mesmeric trance to find my hand in hers, and to suffer that odious feeling which urges me to throw away my honour, my career, everything, for the sake of this creature who, as I can plainly see when I am away from her influence, possesses no single charm upon earth."[1] But to suggest that the problem of mesmerism is that it both enables and enforces an unaccountable desire in the victim only raises a more fundamental question about the nature of desire in this text. For the threat that Doyle illustrates here—that one could find oneself ("in a moment of reasonless passion" [124]) desiring something one wants not to desire—is not so much a frightening exception to the logic of desire as it is the fulfillment of that logic. As this story makes clear, one cannot decide whether to be passionate. Even before he meets Miss Penelosa, Gilroy acknowledges the fact that desire is, by definition, involuntary; confronted with "rich, silent forces of nature" he experiences an echoing "ferment in [his] blood" that makes him, despite his position as a staid and respectable man of science, want to "dance about" in the sunshine "like a gnat" (111).

What is truly striking, then, about Miss Penelosa is not that she can make her subjects feel desire against their will, but that she can make the ordinary mechanisms of desire seem like the terrifying effects of magic. Gilroy explains this magic as a kind of monstrous "influence," a condition he compares to being helplessly under the influence of a drug: "Perhaps," he thinks at one point, "there is a mesmeric craze as there is an opium craze, and I am a victim to it" (125). At the time that Doyle was writing, however, these two kinds of "crazes" were hardly synonymous. Mesmerism, which at midcentury had been considered a form of mind control (enabling unscrupulous practitioners to enslave their victims), had become by century's end a way of liberating the subject's true desires.[2] Taken up as a form of "mind cure," mesmerism promised to help individuals transcend what was inauthentic in themselves and discover their own "divine nature."[3] And yet, Miss Penelosa's version of mesmerism, far from bringing to light Gilroy's hidden self, makes possible a desire that can bypass the self altogether.[4] While he begins by entertaining the possibility that his unaccountable desire stems from "something in [him], something evil, something [he] had rather not think of" (125), he discovers in the end that his love for Miss Penelosa cannot be understood as his at all: "'If ever you heard me speak of love,' said I, 'you know very well that it was your own voice which spoke, and not mine" (135). Rather than defining himself in terms of his desires, Gilroy here defines himself *against* a desire that he feels but cannot identify as his own. By imagining that Miss Penelosa replaces Gilroy's desires rather than uncovers their truth, "The Parasite" charts the emergence of a particularly modern form of desire, a desire better understood in terms of opium than in terms of mesmerism, the emergence of addiction.

THE RISE OF ADDICTION

At the turn of the century, the term "addiction" actually encompassed both of these forms of desire, the desire ascribed to the victim and the desire ascribed to the drug itself. Our own notion of addiction as unbridled consumption is indebted to the first model, in which the user is imagined to suffer from an uncontrollable desire. This kind of excessive desire became known as a disease because the user was believed to be unable to act freely against his urges; the addict feels a desire so strong and has a will so weak that he is literally forced to continue using the drug: he is "a victim to it." As early as 1829 one temperance advocate argued that "drunkenness is itself a disease. . . . When the taste is formed, and the habit established, no man is his own master," and by the late nineteenth century addiction-as-disease had become the dominant paradigm.[5] As Virginia Berridge and Griffith Edwards have argued in their influential book, *Opium and the People*, by the last quarter of the nineteenth century the medical profession had successfully transformed habitual drug use into a disease "defined in terms of 'moral bankruptcy'" and "a paralyzed control over a craving for drink, or opium, or cocaine."[6] Although it is true that "moral bankruptcy" looks more like a version of sin than a version of disease, this idea worked at the time to highlight the unhealthy imbalance between the user's will and her desires. The turn of the century was, of course, an era noteworthy for constructing identities out of what were perceived to be illnesses (the homosexual is perhaps the best-known example). And it was in this context that the victim of a diseased will, the individual who is defined by her inability *not* to act on her own cravings for a drug, becomes known as the addict.

For most contemporary critics, this rhetoric of addiction-as-desire becomes especially relevant for turn-of-the-century culture because it perfectly emblematizes the workings of consumerism.[7] Just as the addict is enslaved to his endless desire for the drug, they argue, the consumer is enslaved to a system of advertising and merchandising that creates an endless desire to consume. According to Harry Gene Levine, for example, it is no accident that addiction was "discovered" and popularized as a disease at a time of unprecedented market expansion; drawing an explicit analogy between the excesses of the addict and the everyday experience of the consumer, he claims that "the idea of addiction 'made sense' not only to drunkards, who came to understand themselves as individuals with overwhelming desires they could not control, but also to great numbers of middle-class people who were struggling to keep their desires in check—desires which at times seemed 'irresistible.'"[8] Mark Seltzer attempts to complicate this easy connection between consumerism and addiction by stressing the horrifying "permeability" of the addict's self: "From the turn of the century on, the living dead subject . . . is at once generalized and pathologized. And it is generalized and pathologized precisely as the subject, or quasi-subject, of addiction." But if Seltzer shifts the focus of analysis from the addict's excessive desire to his excessive drive for a kind of mindless repetition and substitution, he nevertheless concludes that the "substitution mania" that grips the addict is "epitomized in . . . exchanges of money."[9]

Yet there was a powerful, competing model of addiction at work at the turn of the century, one that cannot be understood in terms of the competition between the individual's desires and her will, one that in fact helped to create an identity that cannot be understood in terms of the subject-centered discourse of the market at all. Indeed, according to a common description of inebriety, alcohol, once ingested, does not evoke a monstrous desire in the drinker so much as replace the individual agent with its own monstrous agency. Benjamin Ward Richardson, speaking at the 1893 World's Temperance Conference in Chicago, compares alcohol with fire in its ability to devour the drinker: "But here is the difference. A man cannot swallow fire, and he can swallow alcohol, which latter being swallowed, he does cry out for more, until he is slowly or quickly consumed."[10] The substitution of desiring object for desiring subject is made even more explicit in Henry Cole's *Confessions of an American Opium Eater* (1895), in a passage in which the newly recovered Cole casts a critical eye on a confirmed opium user, a person who seems to him to have become merely the phantasmatic body of the drug itself:

A lean, wan face, belonging to a creature who is just arousing himself from his long drugged sleep, stares out upon us with terrible eyes. . . . This is the gaze of what is called an 'opium devil'—one who is supremely possessed by the power of the deadly narcotic on which he has leaned so long. Without opium he cannot live; though human blood runs in his veins, it is little better than poppy juice; he is no longer really a man, but a malignant essence in forming a cadaverous human shape.[11]

From this perspective, the problem with the addict is not that he desires too much or too freely, but that he stops desiring altogether. Since the user is actually replaced by the drug, addiction here is constituted not by the self that wants the drug, but by the drug that wants itself.

It is this model of addiction-as-substitution that Doyle takes up in "The Parasite." Like the addict whose desire has been replaced by the stronger desire of the drug for itself, Gilroy discovers that what he took to be his own love for Miss Penelosa was actually her own love acting through him: "It was your own voice which spoke, and not mine." What this discovery makes visible is the fact that this kind of substitution does not represent the horror of desire so much as it represents an escape from desire. Since what frightens Gilroy about his desires is that they create a "hideous" self—so that when he claims that his feelings for Miss Penelosa stem from "something evil in me," he in fact means some evil part of himself—this displacement of his desires turns out to be a boon rather than a curse. In other words, if Miss Penelosa's presence evokes the problem of desire, her ability to "[creep] into [his] frame as the hermit crab does into the whelk's shell" (127) effectively solves it, transferring the "hideous" responsibility from Gilroy to the mesmeric "parasite" and rewriting "something evil in me" as "something evil that has possessed me." Through the mechanism of Miss Penelosa's mesmerism, he becomes free—not free to indulge in his dangerous or forbidden desires, but free not to have any desires of his own. As Gilroy admits, "There is some consolation in the thought, then, that those odious impulses for which I have blamed myself do not really come from me at all. They are all transferred from her, little as I could have guessed it at the time. I feel cleaner and lighter for the thought" (127). Thus, when Gilroy imagines that "a peculiar double consciousness possessed me," he describes not a single consciousness divided but a literal doubling: "There was the predominant alien will, which was bent upon drawing me to the side of its owner, and there was the feebler protesting personality, which I recognized as being myself" (131). Of course, this reading denies the possibility that Doyle's tale allegorizes the unconscious, representing a form of disavowal in which these alien desires turn out to be Gilroy's own hidden desires after all. In the context of the turn-of-the-century obsession with addiction, however, Doyle makes a much more radical assertion about the self: not that it can have unconscious desires (and thus a more complicated psyche) but that it can have desires that cannot be understood in terms of psychology at all.[12]

Elaborating on the logic of substitution being worked out in the rhetoric of addiction, "The Parasite" transforms a social crisis into a cultural fantasy. For, revising my earlier formulation, addiction in this text doesn't create a new form of desire so much as it creates selves that are free of the burden of having any desires of their own. Rather than emblematizing the way that the subject is constituted in consumer culture, addiction becomes a way of exploding the subject of desire, a way of imagining modes of desire that neither require nor sustain subjectivity. If the ability to replace one's own desires is exemplified in stark terms by the addict, however, this logic of substitution is certainly not limited to the world of drug addiction. Indeed, as "The Parasite" suggests, this logic finds one of its most perfect expressions in the "possession" narrative, a genre that reached the height of its popularity during the period and that comprised a wide range of Anglo-American fiction from George Du Maurier's wildly popular *Trilby* (1894) and Bram Stoker's *Dracula* (1897) to tales by Frank Norris and Pauline Hopkins. Moreover, by giving the role of the drug to a person with designs of her own—an evil mesmerist, a vampire—the possession narrative actually literalizes the mechanism of addiction, exploring what it would mean for an object of desire to enact the desire for itself. Representing desire as a circuit that bypasses the subject completely, the possession story creates a world in which it is possible to have a desire outside the organizing framework of the self, to experience a self without the burden of desire.

In emphasizing both the rise of dynamic psychology (the growing belief that individuals were motivated by unconscious desires) and, especially in the American context, the consolidation of a national market (in which selfhood was established through the mechanism of contract), critics have made desire the constitutive feature of modern subjectivity. It is not surprising then that the addict, who is defined by his endless and exaggerated desires, has become emblematic not only of the consumer but of the modern subject in general. My point in examining a competing model of addiction is not to dispute the fact that turn-of-the-century Anglo-American culture created psychological and contractual subjects, individuals who thought of themselves as having wants and who thought of the social realm as the place where these wants could be fulfilled. Instead, I am arguing that there was, during this period, a significant discourse of desire that not only dismantled these modes of subjectivity, but that enabled individuals to invent forms of identity that had nothing to do with their desires and to imagine social relations that had nothing to do with contract. Thus the possession narrative not only reveals the limits of desire but also suggests how this nonpsychological, noncontractual way of thinking about the self became an important social technology in its own right. Imagining individuals who could embody feelings or intentions that were not their own, the possession narrative invented a new kind of subject, one defined not by the depth of its desires but by its permeability.

In examining both British and American versions of the possession narrative, we find that the British version reveals the commitment to replacing the individual's desire with an alien desire, while the American version's commitment to ancestry translates this form of self-erasure into a way of creating new social formations. In this regard, Pauline Hopkins's fantasy of racial identity in *Of One Blood; or, The Hidden Self* (1902–1903) is the most striking example of the American possession narrative, for the novel's insistence on replacing the individual's desires with collective memory ultimately produces the modern racial subject. It is the path that leads from the British model of "possession" as supernatural fantasy to the American model of "possession" as social technology that the rest of this chapter explores.

VAMPIRES IN LONDON

Like the addict, the vampire has typically been understood as a product of consumer culture. Of course, the reading of the vampire as capitalist goes back, at least, to Marx, and finds one of its most powerful expressions in Franco Moretti's well-known reading of *Dracula*.[13] But the real evidence of Dracula's modernity, according to a number of recent readings, is not that he represents the capitalist (or even capital), but that he represents the system of consumer culture itself. From this perspective, the vampire stands in for the "cultural technologies" of desire encountered "in the department store, on the billboard, in the nickelodeon parlor, at the newsstand or the telegraph office"; he "consumes but thereby turns his victims into consumers" "directed by invisible longings and compelled by ghostly commands to absorb everything in sight."[14] George Du Maurier's *Trilby*, another popular tale of "psychic vampirism," would seem to take the vampiric construction of consumerist desire one step further. For this novel about a mesmerist who creates a desire for himself in his helpless victim became a remarkably effective advertisement for itself. Indeed, the novel proved so popular when it was finally released in book form that it sparked its own "craze" in the United States—"*Trilby* mania"—that lasted until Du Maurier's death in 1896. The first modern "best-seller," *Trilby* unleashed an unprecedented wave of merchandising; fans of the novel saw productions of *Trilby* on the stage, bought ice-cream and brooches in the shape of Trilby's famous foot, sang songs based on the novel, read parodies like *Thrilby* and *Drilby Re-Versed*, and participated in countless other *Trilby*-related activities.[15] What the novel seems to make visible, then, is the truth of the vampiric metaphor found on its pages; in creating and perpetuating an insatiable desire for itself in the mass reading audience, *Trilby* enacts the vampiric construction of desiring subjectivity.

At the level of the narrative, however, *Trilby* seems to have quite a different investment in the technologies of psychic vampirism. For it is not the job of the mesmerist/vampire Svengali to evoke Trilby's desires, but rather to save her from them. Accordingly, the bohemian Trilby, an artists' model in the Latin Quarter of Paris, begins with a miraculous "unconsciousness" of desire, an unconsciousness that makes it possible for her to pose naked in front of an audience of men and still maintain her innocence. In the end, the party responsible for bringing her hidden desires to consciousness is the band of bourgeois artists led by Little Billee. It is, after all, only when she witnesses Little Billee's horrified reaction to seeing her in the "altogether" that Trilby begins to imagine intention where there had been none ("I never thought anything about sitting [for the figure] before") and to imagine a desire for Little Billee where there had been only a kind of unthinking affection for everyone ("In the caressing, demonstrative tenderness of her friendship she 'made the soft eyes' at all three indiscriminately").[16] Furthermore, if Little Billee and his friends rebuild Trilby on the model of the consumer, they also insist on the immutability of this desiring self; Trilby finds that she is imprisoned in a self made legible by desire. Thus every transformation she undergoes is read as "a new incarnation of Trilbyness"; every action, no matter how uncharacteristic, becomes evidence of her "irrepressible Trilbyness" (62–63). The central problem of the novel, then, is that Trilby's newfound desires at once require her to change ("to live straight for the future" [82]) and make it impossible for her to change (she is, after all, "irrepressible"). No wonder that Trilby, forced to leave Little Billee, complains that her character "can't be righted!": "Of course I could never be a lady—how could I? though I ought to have been one, I suppose" (128).

If Trilby can only dream of becoming another person, however, it is Svengali who transforms this metaphor into reality. A practiced mesmerist, Svengali at first seems to be working squarely within the consumerist model. As the Laird warns Trilby, mesmerists can "get you into their power, and just make you do any blessed thing they please—lie, murder, steal—anything!" (50). But what gives Svengali (like Miss Penelosa) his real power over his subject is that he has no interest in "making" her do anything; he neither convinces his victim to act against her desires nor evokes her own hidden desires, but makes her desires irrelevant by acting through her. To hear Trilby "sing the 'Nussbaum,' the 'Impromptu,'" was actually to hear "Svengali singing with her voice" (288). Thus the mesmerized Trilby becomes "the unconscious voice that Svengali sang with" (288). If this possession is at first understood to create a kind of doubling, so that "there were two Trilbys" (287), the one who sings and the one who cannot, Du Maurier's account of mesmerism ends up describing not the multiplication but the systematic erasure of Trilby: when La Svengali sang, "*our* Trilby had ceased to exist . . . *our* Trilby was fast asleep . . . in fact, *our* Trilby was *dead*" (289). Since Trilby is, initially, something akin to an empty vessel—Svengali describes her mouth as "the dome of the Panthéon; there is room in it for 'toutes les gloires de la France,' and a little to spare!" and her throat as "the middle porch of St. Sulpice when the doors are open for the faithful" (48)—by the end she can literally contain other people.

Far from creating the ideal modern consumer, Svengali here instigates an opposing model of subjectivity, for insofar as the mesmerized Trilby becomes a desiring subject, she can only be understood as the subject—rather than the object—of *Svengali's* desire. Transformed into Svengali's "instrument," Trilby is not only able to sing without actually singing, but to love without actually loving:

> He had but to say '*Dors!*' and she suddenly became an unconscious Trilby of marble, who could produce wonderful sounds—just the sounds he wanted, and nothing else—and think his thoughts and wish his wishes—and love him at his bidding with a strange, unreal, factitious love . . . just his own love for himself turned inside out—*a l'envers*—and reflected back on him, as from a mirror . . . *un écho, un simulacre, quoi! par autre chose!* . . . It was not worth having! (288)

Whether or not Svengali loves Trilby, the fact that he has literally replaced her means that there can be no answering desire on her part. If their relationship is the most sexually charged in the novel, the charge is clearly autoerotic; Trilby is reduced to a mirror, one component of the circuit of desire that begins and ends with Svengali. *Trilby* ultimately creates a fantasy world in which the subject/object relation is elided in favor of an object/object relation—the relation of an object to itself. Vampirism, then, cannot be understood to evoke the subject's own desires (or even to create a desiring subject); instead it creates a hollow subject, a subject without desire. And thus the competition between Little Billee and Svengali over Trilby—one wins her love and loses her, the other replaces her love and keeps her—enacts in miniature the competition between the consumerist subject created by the novel as cultural artifact and the vampiric subject created by the narrative. Whereas one creates a version of market subjectivity by making the object irresistible to consumers, the other elides subjectivity altogether by making the object irresistible to itself.

At the same time, however, one might argue that Little Billee's "panic" when Trilby leaves him, far from merely representing the consumerist model of desire, seems to be motivated by the Trilby-like desire to get rid of his desires. His panic grows out of his discovery that, after suffering a terrible shock, he no longer feels anything for anyone: "For some mysterious cause his power of loving had not come back with his wandering wits," a power of loving that "would never come back again—not even his love for his mother and sister, not even his love for Trilby—where all that had once been was a void, a gap, a blankness " (132). According to Eve Sedgwick, Little Billee functions here as one example of a late-nineteenth-century cultural stereotype—the "bachelor." And if, according to Sedgwick, the bachelor "popularized by Thackeray," "felt no urgency about proving" he could love a woman, the bachelors who populate turn-of-the-century literature, a literature that was confronting the "ever greater visibility across class lines of a medicalized discourse of—and newly punitive assaults on—male homosexuality," find that "even that renunciatory high ground of male sexlessness has been strewn with psychic land mines." The terrible feeling of "blankness" Little Billee experiences is, in other words, the late-nineteenth-century version of male homosexual panic that is "acted out as a sometimes agonized sexual anesthesia that was damaging to both its make subjects and its female non-objects."[17]

Against such a reading stands the fact that Trilby is not exactly a "non-object" to Little Billee. Indeed, he spends quite a bit of time in fetishistic admiration of her feet; at one point he notes, "with a curious conscious thrill that was only half-aesthetic," that their perfect form has "ennobled" her "shapeless" slippers "into everlasting classic shapeliness" (30). Thus, "reversing the usual process," Little Billee proceeds to "[idealize] from the base upward" (34). And yet this fetishistic desire for Trilby does not necessarily invalidate Sedgwick's claim about the novel's investment in homosexual panic since Trilby is meant to be, at the very least, androgynous—she has "a portentious voice of great volume and that might almost have belonged to any sex"—and at times, unmistakably masculine—wearing "the gray overcoat of a French infantry soldier" and "a huge pair of male slippers," she, according to the narrator, "would have made a singularly handsome boy . . . and one felt instinctively that it was a real pity she wasn't a boy, she would have made such a jolly one" (12–13). In fact, given Little Billee's infatuation, it is more likely that what provokes the real sexual "panic" in the text is not that he discovers that he feels nothing for Trilby, but that he feels too much for the boy-Trilby. His hysterical reaction when he sees her posing naked in an artist's studio—"I saw her, I tell you! The sight of her was like a blow between the eyes, and I bolted! I shall never go back to that beastly hole again!" (76)—seems to suggest that he is not, as his friends imagine, shocked by the impropriety of her action so much as he is shocked by the fact that she is not a boy after all. Attempting to idealize "from the base upward," Little Billee suddenly discovers the ghastly truth of Trilby's anatomy—a "beastly hole." In light of such a shock, it seems more likely that his "sexual anesthesia" serves as one possible antidote to his sexual panic than it serves as evidence of that panic. Little Billee, then, mirrors Trilby's problematic relation to desire as much as he counters it.

If in *Trilby* the vampire enacts a reflexive desire, in *Dracula* the vampire seems to have no reflection at all. In one famous scene, Jonathan Harker looks into his shaving glass, expecting to see Dracula standing behind him: "But there was no reflection of him in the mirror! The whole room behind me was displayed; but there was no sign of a man in it, except myself."[18] Critics have repeatedly turned to this scene, in which Dracula's reflection seems to take on the form of his victim, to argue that what the victim really fears in the monster are his own hidden desires; what the mirror reflects is not so much an absence as the presence of a "repressed" desire that "returns . . . disguised as a monster."[19] Following this line of reasoning, an amazing number of critics have read this novel as an explicit fable of sexual repression, an attempt to come to terms with desires that lurk beneath Victorian proprieties. In these readings, scenes of vampires draining and sucking blood become "masked and symbolic" representations of, among other things, sexually predatory women, homosexuality, rape, group sex, forced fellatio, and incest. More generally, critics claim that these "emanations of irresistible sexuality" that "break through into consciousness in fantastic and grotesque forms" perform a kind of cultural work in the late nineteenth century by creating "a fantasy world that would have provided escape from many of the sexual and psychic restraints prevalent in Victorian culture."[20]

If these readings have been set in opposition to the consumerist model (indeed Moretti, unable to reconcile the sexual reading and the economic reading, calls them "different signifieds"), from the perspective of *Trilby* they look exactly the same.[21] For, in terms of Du Maurier's vampiric subject, what counts in such readings is not the conscious or unconscious nature of the subject's desires, but only that the desires are imagined to define the subject. To this way of thinking, the fact that Lucy Westenra's chaste exterior seems to hide a dangerous sexuality ("Why can't they let a girl marry three men, or as many as want her?" [76]) suggests that her emergence as a "wanton" and "voluptuous" vampire represents the monstrous truth of Lucy's self. But this kind of commitment to desire as the foundation of the self—the representation of Lucy's truth—cannot account for the radical mobility of desire in this novel, the fact that selves do not seem to produce desire so much as they come into *relation* with desire. Desire, in other words, comes from outside the self.[22]

Although the novel from the very beginning suggests that Lucy is not as demure as she appears to be, that she feels desires that are barely containable, Dracula's arrival does not liberate Lucy's desires so much as herald a series of strange absences: her fall into her "old habit" (91) of sleepwalking, the beginning of her mysterious "long spells of oblivion" (at one point she describes "the harsh sounds that came from I know not where and commanded me to do I know not what" [164]). Indeed, when she finally confronts Van Helsing's army she is imagined to be dead. The most telling mark of her effective absence, however, is that the vampiric Lucy has become nothing but surface, a surface that the novel has already put in competition with any kind of interiority; as Lucy writes to Mina, "'Do you ever try to read your own face? I *do,* and I can tell you it is not a bad study, and gives you more trouble than you can well fancy if you have never tried it'" (71–72). Seward makes this distinction between surface and depth clear by calling the vampire "the foul Thing which had taken Lucy's shape without her soul" (256). In the terms the novel sets up, Lucy's ability to embody this "foul Thing" without becoming one herself suggests that if she is a cipher for repressed desires, these desires must have been repressed by someone else. Given the fact that Lucy has been transfused with blood from all of her suitors and the fact that blood is continually equated with desire in this text, it seems likely that her "wantonness" when she becomes a vampire does not represent her own hidden desires so much as it represents the sexual fury of this band of rejected lovers. In fact, Lucy-as-vampire is more like a mirror image of her pursuers than their opponent; witnessing Lucy's "angry snarl," Seward admits that "had she then to be killed, [he] could have done it with savage delight" (253). What is interesting about Lucy, then, is not the perverse content of the desires she figures but the hollowness that allows her to contain desires that are not her own. Like the mesmerized Trilby, Lucy in her vampiric state is not reduced to her desire but saved from it.

Dracula uses blood as a metaphor for desire precisely because of blood's mobility. Circulating from one body to another (from Lucy's suitors to Lucy, from Lucy to Dracula, from Dracula to Mina) and animating these bodies, blood marks the difference between the self and what is imagined to constitute it. Nowhere in the novel is this bloodlike mobility of desire made more explicit than in Dr. Seward's accounts of his mental patient Renfield: "My homicidal maniac is of a peculiar kind. I shall have to invent a new classification for him, and call him a zoophagous (life-eating) maniac; what he desires is to absorb as many lives as he can, and he has laid himself out to achieve it in a cumulative way" (90). Renfield defends his unusual practice of collecting, documenting, and eating the small creatures that populate his cell at the asylum (flies, spiders, even sparrows) by claiming that each one "was life, strong life, and gave life to him" (88). Yet Renfield's habit is not, as Jennifer Wicke would have it, simply "a pun on the tremors of consumption," a desire to consume for its own sake.[23] Instead, according to Seward it follows a curious pattern, "some scheme of his own" (87). That Renfield not only keeps meticulous records of the tiny ecosystem he has established (the flies eat the sugar, the spiders eat the flies), but is more concerned with creating the system than with eating any one individual within the system, suggests that he doesn't want the flies or the spiders or the sparrows for themselves, for the "life" they offer; he wants them for their relation to one another. He swallows not the spiders, but the spiders' desire for the flies, not the sparrows, but the sparrows' desire for the spiders. What is significant about Renfield, then, is that his odd eating habit is not an act of consumption so much as it is an attempt literally to *ingest* the process of consumption. More forcefully, the Renfield chapters provide a model of subjectivity in direct competition with that of the consuming subject, for in this account what you want is not to fulfill your desires but to replace them.

AMERICAN GENEALOGIES

American writers were just as interested as their British counterparts in writing tales of possession, investigating the ways in which one could experience a feeling or an impulse that seemed to originate outside the self. What they were not interested in, however, was writing vampire stories. Although this distinction might seem to be purely thematic, it actually signals a profound difference in the way that these structures of displacement were used in the American context. For when American authors from Henry James to Pauline Hopkins imagined possession, they did not imagine a self invaded by something as exotic as a vampire, but rather by something much closer to home. Indeed, if in British vampire stories the individual is replaced by a lover, in the American possession story the individual is, more often than not, imagined to be replaced by her grandfather. This insistence on the "sameness" of the possessor and the possessed (figured as the claims of ancestry) marks the crucial difference between American and British versions of the addiction allegory. When blood emerges in the British tales, it is not as a way of characterizing an individual's identity so much as it is a way of disrupting identity, a way of insisting on the difference between the individual and her desires. Thus whereas "The Parasite," *Trilby*, and *Dracula* all feature vampires who are racially "tainted"—Miss Penelosa is West Indian, Svengali is (in Taffy's words) "a filthy black Hebrew sweep" (46), and Dracula is not only Eastern European but also "of criminal type" according to the classifications of "Nordau and Lombroso" (406)—their victims are unmistakably English. Or, to revise the point slightly, they are unmistakably white. The fact that Trilby seems to be as much French as she is English highlights the insignificance of actual ancestry in these tales—what counts about Trilby is not the fact that her father was Irish (and a drunk) but that her "delicate, privet-like whiteness" (13) could never be confused with Svengali's "filthy" blackness. These contrasts between black and white certainly can (and often have) been read in terms of England's own racial conflicts and the dynamics of empire.[24] But in terms of the problematics of desire traced here, this contrast between black and white in the British version of the possession tale works as a purely formal difference, as a way of highlighting the noncoincidence of the self and the desire it embodies. Race is crucial here because the force of "possession" as an escape from the self depends on this rhetoric of absolute difference. It is, by contrast, the commitment to "sameness" that leads, in the American context, to the transformation of the possession narrative into a technology for producing new forms of identity. American tales of possession were interested not only in using race to evacuate subjectivity but also in creating, out of this permeable self, a form of racial identity.

In "A Reversion to Type," a story published in the San Francisco *Wave* in 1897, Frank Norris tells a version of the possession story. "Two months and a day after his forty-first birthday," a respectably employed man named Paul Schuster experiences an "unfamiliar" desire that "came upon him with the quickness of a cataclysm, like the sudden, abrupt development of latent mania."[25] Submitting to this impulse to "get drunk," to "bolt," the respectable Schuster is soon performing actions that are "counter to every habit, to every trait of character and every rule of conduct he has been believed to possess" (44). Acting out this unfamiliar desire gives Schuster a new identity housed in a new, phantasmatic body: "At the beginning of that evening he belonged to that class whom policemen are paid to protect. When he walked out of the Cliff House he was a free-booter, seven feet tall, with a chest expansion of fifty inches" (46).[26] Yet unlike Lucy or Trilby, Schuster's actions actually reveal (as the title suggests) a continuity that runs even deeper than "character" or "habit"—the continuity of blood (44). As the narrator is quick to note, "Schuster, like all the rest of us, was not merely himself. He was his ancestors as well. In him, as in you and me, were generations—countless generations—of forefathers. Schuster had in him the characteristics of his father, the Palace Hotel barber, but also he had the unknown characteristics of his grandfather, of whom he had never heard, and his great-grandfather, likewise ignored" (45).

Taking on the phantasmatic body of his outlaw grandfather, Schuster cannot really be understood as acting, since he only "[comes] to himself" (49) after robbing the superintendent of the Little Bear mine. But unlike the vampire's relation to his victim, the consciousness that possesses Schuster, that performs the robbery through him, cannot really be understood as another person's. His grandfather, though not exactly Schuster, is quite clearly imagined to be an integral part of him, both someone who helped create him and someone who is still alive in him. Thus the kind of heredity argument made by Norris's story is only partially assimilable to the logic of substitution articulated by writers such as Stoker and Du Maurier. Although it is true that in the model of heredity endorsed by Norris the victim experiences someone else's desire, the fact that this "someone else" is imagined to have produced the victim means, in "Reversion to Type" at least, that the alien desire is *not* entirely alien after all. The desire, in other words, can be attributed not to the vampire that invades the self, but to the grandparent who forms a part of the self.

From the perspective of the vampire story, then, the American version of possession (in which the victim is replaced, but only by a version of himself) looks like a failed attempt to displace desire. This failure to get out of one-self seems to be the point of Henry James's unfinished novel, *The Sense of the Past* (begun in 1900), in which Ralph Pendrel exchanges identities with one of his ancestors. He begins this adventure into the past by confidently claiming, "I'm not myself . . . I'm somebody else."[27] At first it does appear that taking on another identity might save him from his own failed relationship with Aurora Coyne by enabling him to live out his ancestor's successful courtship of Molly Midmore. What James ends up stressing, however, is not the difference between the living man and the dead ancestor that makes this exchange worthwhile—Pendrel's desire for the Past, his ancestor's desire for the Future—but the sameness that makes it possible; the ancestral portrait that sets this interaction in motion presents Pendrel with a face that "miracle of miracles, yes—confounded him as his own" (88). If the problem that James was working on at his death, then, was not how to get Pendrel back into his own identity but how to get him back to his "native temporal conditions," it is perhaps because Pendrel, in becoming his ancestor, had not completely ceased to be himself. Indeed, in this novel the ancestor is so much a part of the self that they are virtually indistinguishable. Thus when Pendrel ventures back into the past, it is not as if "he had lost himself, as he might have done in a deeper abyss, but much rather as if in respect to what he most cared for he had never found himself till now" (66). As Pendrel concedes, his ancestor is in his own right "just exactly by the amazing chance, what I was myself—and what I am still, for that matter," so that "the strangest part of all" is that becoming his ancestor "doesn't interfere nearly as much as you might suppose" (99) with being himself. So long as becoming "somebody else" means becoming your ancestor, you are, as Pendrel discovers, "in fact not nearly so different" (99).

When possession moves from the exotic world of the vampire to the domestic realm of the family, then, it does not explode the subject-of-desire, but reproduces it. In other words, if the vampire stories use blood to replace an individual's desires, the American possession tales use blood to recuperate them. In terms of Norris's project, this insistence on the sameness of the possessed self makes sense, since he was not setting out to replace the self but to define it, not trying to displace desire, but to explain it. To the question, How can one account for Schuster's unaccountable desires? Norris answers that he has those desires because he was born with them. But the American investment in blood as a form of possession did not necessarily lead to the continual reproduction of the desiring self. In *Of One Blood*, for example, Pauline Hopkins, unlike Norris, recognizes that the power of the possession model lies not in its ability to explain the self, but in its ability to produce a new kind of self.

Thus, if Hopkins was interested in the model of possession based on blood, she wasn't concerned with the family that creates the individual, but with the race that organizes individuals into the collective. If the point of *Of One Blood* is to uncover the truth of the hero's identity, then this identity is not based on the family into which he was born, but instead resides in the race to which he belongs.

In this novel, blood counts not because it connects you to your ancestors, but because it makes possible a peculiar kind of collective memory. Thus Reuel Briggs, visiting Africa on an anthropological expedition, suddenly discovers that he can remember things he's never experienced: listening to the "musical language" of the people of Telassar, Reuel finds "to his own great surprise and delight" that he can speak their language "with ease." Looking out on the "hidden city" he claims, "I am surprised to find that it all seems familiar to me, as if somewhere in the past I had known just such a city as this."[28] Unlike "Reversion," these memories do not repeat the experiences of his grandparents; instead, they connect him to a whole racial community that comprises past and present, America and Africa. Indeed, every character of African ancestry in this novel is marked by a kind of impossible familiarity; the first time Reuel sees Dianthe Lusk—she is singing in a public concert—he realizes that it is not the first time he's seen her. Having appeared to him as a vision in his solitary room, Dianthe is familiar to him at the very moment that he meets her. And if Dianthe feels only a "slight, cold affection" (492) for Reuel after he befriends her, her attachment to him is based on the same kind of familiarity: "Oh, it is you; I dreamed of you while I slept" (470), she claims at their first meeting. Accordingly, whereas Reuel's relation to Dianthe—she is both his sister and his wife—underscores the power of family bonds by doubling them, this tie to Dianthe is finally (and, in the logic of the novel, inevitably) replaced by his tie to Candace, the Queen of Telassar, a woman to whom he is not related but whom he also seems to remember. That she appears to be the incarnation of Dianthe ("She reminded him strongly of his beautiful Dianthe; in face, the resemblance was so striking that it was painful" [568])—rather than, as Norris might have imagined, the reincarnation of her own grandmother—only emphasizes the way that in *Of One Blood* the sentimental bonds of family are systematically replaced by the mystical bonds of race. Inheritance, in other words, does not move diachronically from parents to children, but synchronically among the members of a group that it defines as racial.

This insistence throughout the novel on blood as the creator of collective memory works against Hopkins's ostensible purpose, to demonstrate the irrelevance of blood to questions of identity and the injustice of the "one-drop rule": "Who is clear enough in vision to decide who hath black blood and who hath it not? Can any one tell? No, not one; for in His own mysterious way He has united the white race and the black race in this new continent" (607). After centuries of racial amalgamation, she argues, "no man can draw the dividing line between the two races, for they are both of one blood!" (607). But being "of one blood" in this novel means not that individuals share a common humanity, but that they belong to particular races.[29] Blood both emerges on the surface of the body (in the shape of Reuel's "lotus lily" birthmark) and ultimately makes the appearance of the body inconsequential by announcing itself through memory. An outsider may not "know" that Reuel is black, but Reuel, surrounded by the evidence of racial inheritance, cannot help but know. In the end, race—by which Hopkins means the blood ties that produce and enforce collective memory—becomes such a powerful indicator of identity in this novel that it actually assumes the burden of selfhood. According to the philosophy of Telassar, for example, the "Ego" not only "preserves its individuality" even "after the dissolution of the body" (562), but is itself only the incarnation of the "One Supreme Being," the great racial "Unity." Thus Reuel's claim that "life is not dependent upon organic function as a principle" but "may be infused into organized bodies" (468) works not only as an account of the individual's relation to her body but also as a more general account of identity itself. For identity in this text is collective before it can be individual; it organizes groups on the model of the self. From this standpoint, Hopkins's account of race is notable not for claiming that the self must always be understood within a system of "organized bodies," but for insisting that the race be understood as one self, one "Supreme Being," one "organized body."

Two compelling readings of *Of One Blood* acknowledge that Hopkins is working with notions of blood that were most often used in the racialist literature of the period. Susan Gillman argues that, by making the characteristics evoked by black blood positive, by "recovering the hidden self and history of the race, that is, both the kinship relations obscured by American slavery and an African ancestral spirit or race soul," Hopkins actually works against a racist American culture. In other words, "To make 'blood' thus speak out of school is to deconstruct an idiom by exposing the competing contexts and conflicting narratives, in which the term was regularly used."[30] Along the same lines, Thomas J. Otten claims that the "hidden racial self" Hopkins describes enables "the self to move outside the bounds of its own consciousness and its own history," describing "a hidden 'power' that hearkens back to ancient Africa and to a moment in African history centrally formative of Western culture," a power that "is here substituted for the savagery and degeneracy that many whites saw as the hidden self of the black personality."[31] And yet, while it is true that Hopkins makes African-American identity into a positive force in this novel, she neither "deconstructs" the idea of blood that she shared with her racist adversaries, nor does she imagine that she is freeing the self from its own "history" (a history she insists is racial). In order to reverse the affect of racial identity, she must adhere to the same ideas of blood and racial history that produced and enforced the "one-drop rule."

Indeed, this claim that blood has the power to enforce racial identity, that blood carries certain racial "markers" (like memory) that work within a self that takes shape prior to intentionality also grounds the overt racism of Benjamin Rush Davenport's *Blood Will Tell: The Strange Story of a Son of Ham* (1902). In this novel, Walter Burton's "drop" of "negro blood" (one of his grandparents is black) eventually makes itself known as a kind of vampiric presence:

> Sometimes there seems to come a strange, inexplicable spell over my spirit— a something that is beyond my control. A madness seems to possess my very soul. Involuntarily I say and do that, during the time that this mysterious influence holds me powerless in its grasp, that is so foreign to my natural self that I shudder and grow sick at heart at the thought of the end to which it may lead me.

But by the end, Davenport makes clear that it is this "mysterious influence" rather than the repulsion it provokes that reveals Burton's "natural self":

> I have abandoned useless effort to rehabilitate myself in the misfit garments of a civilization and culture for which the configuration of my mental structure, by nature, renders me unsuited. . . . My conduct, following natural inclinations, since my return to Boston, has demonstrated how little control civilization, morality, or pity have over my inherent savage nature.

The point of the novel, then, is to get Burton to admit to himself (and to the reader) that he "really" is, and has always been, "a negro."[32] The fact that this book was published in the same year that Hopkins began serializing *Of One Blood* thus seems to indicate more than just "how prevalent the matter of African cultural origins was in writing about race at the time," as Otten points out; it reveals that both Hopkins's positive and Davenport's negative attitudes toward African-American identity depended on the same structure of "possession."[33] Although it is true that Davenport's model of blood, unlike Hopkins's, does not produce racial memory, it nonetheless insists that racial identity is a "natural inclination," an inherited quality that counts as more truly "you" than any experience you have actually had.

Despite the fact that imagining blood as a carrier of memory is in direct opposition to the vampiric model (in which blood, figured as a kind of mobile, alien desire, replaces memory), it nevertheless ends up serving as an equally powerful displacement of desire. It is, after all, Reuel's blood ties to both Dianthe and Candace that make his desires irrelevant; one woman can easily replace the other because it does not matter, in the end, which one he loves. By displacing desire with memory in this way, Hopkins produces a model of racial identity and racial experience that rivals the notion of racial double-consciousness made famous by W. E. B. DuBois in *The Souls of Black Folk* (1903):

> It is a peculiar sensation, this double-consciousness, this sense of always looking at one's self through the eyes of others. . . . One ever feels his two-ness,— an American, a Negro; two souls, two thoughts, two unreconciled strivings; two warring ideals in one dark body, whose dogged strength alone keeps it from being torn asunder.[34]

In DuBois's account, what marks the racialized subject is a sense of conflicted desire ("two unreconciled strivings"), the belief that race provides one self with "two souls." *Of One Blood* begins with a similar premise, with the suggestion that race constitutes the individual's "hidden self." Indeed, as the novel opens, Reuel is reading an article on the "new discoveries in psychology" called "The Unclassified Residuum" (442) (he attributes the article to Binet, known at the time for his important work on the unconscious and multiple personality; the actual quotations are taken from William James's essay, "The Hidden Self," which Hopkins uses as her subtitle). In the end, however, what distinguishes Hopkins's model from DuBois's is that the hidden self of race is, in her account, not established through desires that divide the individual, but rather through memories that transcend him. If almost everyone in this novel experiences a kind of double consciousness, then, it is not because they are also their ancestors, but because they are also part of the racial self. Thus the racial group emerges as a powerful organizing principle in Hopkins's novel precisely because it has nothing to do with what one wants or rejects; it replaces the burden of conflicted desires with the truth of memory.

Race, as Hopkins depicts it, reveals not only how "possession" works, but more importantly, what it can do; it can connect seemingly unrelated persons into a collectivity by inventing an identity that both transcends and defines them. Like addiction, which imagines a desire that originates outside the self, the racial collectivity that Hopkins imagines depends on a subject who cannot be understood in terms of what he wants. That this kind of noncontractual subject played a crucial role in turn-of-the-century American culture seems clear not only because both race and addiction were powerful ways of organizing experience, but because of the variety of different contexts in which this model of subjectivity emerges. In the realm of the law, for example, the "right to privacy" was (according to one influential version of the argument) imagined to protect an aspect of the self that one could not, in principle, own or sell. It was, as Samuel Warren and Louis Brandeis claimed, the privilege of the "inviolable personality."[35] In the realm of medicine, the expansion of the therapeutic model of self maintained that what was important about one's deepest desires was not that they be fulfilled, but that they be cured. Rather than describing an escape from the world constructed by the market, these ways of imagining the nondesiring, noncontracting self describe the limits of the market, the limits of desire, in the reproduction of modern culture. If addiction opens a window onto turn-of-the-century culture, then, it reveals neither the capaciousness of consumerism nor the transcendence of its perils, but rather the production of a realm in which one's desires are finally irrelevant.

A Terminal Case

William Burroughs and the Logic of Addiction

Timothy Melley

The panic of the alcoholic who has hit bottom is the panic of the man who thought he had control over a vehicle but suddenly finds that the vehicle can run away with him. Suddenly, pressure on what he knows is the brake seems to make the vehicle go faster. It is the panic of discovering that it (the system, self plus vehicle) is bigger than he is. . . . He has bankrupted the epistemology of "self-control."
—GREGORY BATESON, "The Cybernetics of 'Self'"

BAD HABITS

"Addiction," remarked social psychologist Stanton Peele in 1975, "is not, as we like to think, an aberration from our way of life. Addiction is our way of life."[1] By all accounts, this view has gained remarkable popularity in America. Not only are estimates of traditional substance abuse significantly higher, despite declining narcotic and alcohol consumption, but treatment is being mandated for, and sought by, dramatically larger numbers of Americans. More significantly, medical institutions have adopted increasingly flexible definitions of addiction, creating vast numbers of new addicts and whole new categories of addiction.[2] The most striking feature of America's general discourse on addiction, in other words, is just how general it has become: Americans now account for all sorts of ordinary human behavior through the concept of addiction.

In part, this impulse stems from the work of addiction specialists such as Peele, whose *Love and Addiction* advanced the thesis that "addiction is not a special reaction to a drug, but a primary and universal form of motivation" and that "there are addictive . . . ways of doing anything" (59). The increasing popularity of this view would be unremarkable if it signaled merely a growing belief that the compulsion to repeat certain behaviors is a normal human tendency, rather than a sign of disease. But many Americans seem to have adopted Peele's thesis while also retaining the idea that *any* habit, drive, or compulsion indicates a lack of self-control so dangerous it merits medical attention.[3] In his encyclopedic account of America's addiction to addictions, *Infinite Jest,* David Foster Wallace catalogues some of these "exotic new" maladies. At a rehab center, his narrator explains, one learns:

> That sleeping can be a form of emotional escape and can with sustained effort be abused. . . . That purposeful sleep-deprivation can also be an abusable escape. That gambling can be an abusable escape, too, and work, shopping, and shoplifting, and sex, and abstention, and masturbation, and food, and exercise, and meditation/prayer. . . . That most Substance-addicted people are also addicted to thinking, meaning they have a compulsive and unhealthy relationship with their own thinking. . . . That it is possible to abuse OTC cold and allergy remedies in an addictive manner. . . . That anonymous generosity, too, can be abused.[4]

The bizarre logic of this view—the contradictory sense that addiction is utterly normal *and* dangerously pathological—explains why so many Americans now claim to be addicted to behaviors that once epitomized individual autonomy. As Eve Kosofsky Sedgwick has suggested, the relatively new illnesses known as "exercise addiction," "workaholism," "shopaholism," "sexual compulsiveness," and "codependency" or "relationship addiction" all stem from a sense of insufficient free will. "Under the searching rays of this new addiction-attribution," she observes, "the assertion of will itself has come to appear addictive."[5] Paradoxically, the compulsion to sort addictions from freely willed acts increasingly erodes the distinction between those terms; this erosion, meanwhile, feeds the frenzy to separate will and compulsion once and for all. To put the same thing another way, the national tendency toward addiction-attribution stems from what I call "agency panic," serious anxiety about the autonomy and individuality of persons.

The question, then, is not just how to account for the growth of addiction as an explanatory concept in America, but how to account for the more pervasive anxieties about agency and personhood that encourage its growth. To begin, it is worth observing that basic human activities such as shopping, sex, and work, can only appear to be unwanted "addictions" if one makes several assumptions about persons. First, one must believe individuals *ought to be* rational, motivated agents in full control of themselves. This assumption, in turn, entails a strict metaphysics of inside and outside; that is, the self must be a clearly bounded entity, with an *interior* core of unique beliefs, memories, and desires easily distinguished from the *external* influences and controls that are presumed to be the sources of addiction. Finally, one must view control as an indivisible property, something that is possessed either by the individual or by external influences.

Only in the context of these assumptions—all of which undergird longstanding American models of self-reliant or "possessive" individualism—can *any* less than perfectly willed behavior seem to be the product of dangerous external controls.[6] It is the continuing popularity of these assumptions that has encouraged Americans to view drugs, in the words of one observer, as "a power deemed capable of tempting, possessing, corrupting, and destroying persons without regard to the prior conduct or condition of those persons—a power which has all-or-none effects."[7] One of the things at stake in the current discourse on addiction, in other words, is the model of possessive individualism so dear to Americans. Addiction discourse is governed by a refusal to abandon the assumptions of possessive individualism, despite an anxious sense that they fail to explain the unsettling compulsions that seem to be turning us into addicts. Indeed, the matter can be put more pointedly. The apparent existence of multifarious, powerful addictive threats shores up and revivifies the embattled national fantasy of individual autonomy.

Anxiety about such powerful external controls and diminished individual autonomy extends well beyond the substances popularly viewed as "drugs." It is not hard to locate this sense. Narratives depicting individuals in the grip of powerful technologies and social controls have been a staple feature of postwar American culture. Numerous sociologies of the American character, such as David Reisman's *Lonely Crowd* (1950) and William Whyte's *Organization Man* (1956), to name just two, argued that Americans are no longer as autonomous as they once were. Prominent texts by Thomas Pynchon, Don DeLillo, Margaret Atwood, Norman Mailer, Joan Didion, Philip K. Dick, William Gibson, Kathy Acker, Kurt Vonnegut, Joseph Heller, Ken Kesey, and William Burroughs have focused on individuals who are intensely nervous—or paranoid—about their capacity for autonomous action. These characters often suspect that their bodily responses are being governed by someone or something else—usually a large social organization. Some believe that their most individuating traits and desires have been socially constructed and "implanted" in them. The organizations they suspect are sometimes concrete agencies, such as the CIA, but they are more often vague entities, such as Pynchon's "Them," Burroughs's "junk virus," or the general "system" of postwar political rhetoric.[8]

This pervasive sense of agency panic—with its fear of communication systems and technologies in general—is inextricably linked to contemporary discourse on addiction, particularly the sense that addiction has itself become epidemic. Americans, Peele observes in his more recent *Diseasing of America*, "seem to feel that they are more out of control of their lives than they have felt in the past. . . . The addiction industry expresses the sense of loss of control we have developed as a society."[9] *Diseasing of America* rails against the growth of the "addiction treatment industry" and its disease-based concept of addiction, yet ironically it was Peele's earlier hypothesis ("anything can be addictive") that helped to legitimate the growth of an addiction culture. After all, *Love and Addiction* argues that we live in an "addicted society" and that "our vulnerability to addiction" is a direct result of our "transition to the modern age" (151). This assertion, with its subsequent focus on "lost . . . internal self-assurance" (151), echoes David Riesman's narrative of the fall from rugged individualism (or "inner-direction") to postindustrial uniformity (or "other-direction")—a now-familiar story about how modern technological rationality has produced less autonomous individuals who are highly susceptible to external forms of control.[10]

And addiction literature is not the only source of anxieties about the American tendency toward addiction, for the latter has epitomized waning individuality in an array of cultural criticism. It is instructive to see, for instance, how readily the Unabomber's narrative of dwindling human autonomy—itself a recapitulation of popular critiques of "postindustrial society"—invokes models of addiction to account for the dangers of technological rationality:

> Imagine an alcoholic sitting with a barrel of wine in front of him. Suppose he starts saying to himself, "Wine isn't bad for you if used in moderation. Why, they say small amounts of wine are even good for you! It won't do me any harm if I take just one little drink. . . . " Well you know what is going to happen. Never forget that the human race with technology is just like an alcoholic with a barrel of wine.[11]

Such warnings help to explain the all-or-nothing logic that leads the author to recommend a regimen of *total abstinence* from advanced technology—a remedy that, in his view, would require a strict diet of masculinist self-reliance, a return to the individualist frontier, and (of course) "regeneration through violence."[12]

It would be possible to cite any number of links between addiction and more pervasive anxieties about agency, but I want to focus my attention on the postwar American writer whose work most obsessively draws such connections—William Burroughs. Burroughs not only writes about his lifelong preoccupation with drug addiction, but also uses the concept of addiction to represent other postindustrial conspiracies against human agency and uniqueness. The characters of his fiction are usually addicted to junk, but as early as *Naked Lunch* (1959) they are also addicted to commodities, images, words, human contact, and even control itself. They are also the subjects of sadistic forms of mass control, Pavlovian conditioning, and medical or psychological torture. In short, their existence represents a terminal case of agency-in-crisis.[13] Although these characters and scenes have often been read as representations, or products, of an intoxicated imagination, I will show that they have widespread cultural roots. Indeed, some of the most bizarre control scenarios in Burroughs are taken, virtually unmodified, from more sober and popular nonfiction texts. My intention in these pages, then, is not so much to illuminate Burroughs himself as to unravel the mystery of a highly individualist culture that believes itself beset by threats to individual autonomy.

I want to begin this task by examining the problems of subjectivity created by Burroughs's disease-based model of addiction—his view of addiction as "virus." According to this model, addictive substances are agents powerful enough to erode human subjectivity. Not only do they exhaust the addict's will, but they also become "characters" of a sort, part of a phantasmagorical landscape where it is difficult to tell one person from another and even harder to tell persons from nonpersons. The fluid and uncertain subjects of these scenes are often labeled "schizophrenic" and "postmodern," but they are a direct result of attempts to conserve a traditional model of individualism. Burroughs's nervousness about the erosion of individual autonomy stems from the same contradictions that have produced the contemporary culture of addiction: only by assuming that individuals should owe *nothing* to the "outside" for their actions and identity can Burroughs sustain a panic-stricken vision of the individual as a total addict and the world as a hostile place full of controlling agents.

CONTROL ADDICTS

In the preface to *Naked Lunch*, Burroughs claims that his novel is a study of the "junk virus"—though it is never quite clear whether this term refers to addictive drugs themselves or the larger drug economy in which they move.[14] A 1957 letter to Allen Ginsberg explains further that the "real theme of the novel is Desecration of the Human Image by the control addicts who are putting out the . . . addicting virus."[15] Neither of these remarks gives an accurate description of *Naked Lunch*, but both hint at the anxiety about agency that runs through it. First, Burroughs views junk less as an inert *commodity* (something that must be bought and consumed by active agents) than as a parasitic *organism* (something that invades and controls the bodies of unwitting individuals). Second, while he imagines a worldwide conspiracy producing the junk virus, he views the conspirators themselves as "control *addicts*." This tautological concept—the "control addict"—embodies precisely the tendency identified by Sedgwick, in which assertions of will or control are understood as addictions. But it extends the general implications of that tendency even further. The more radical idea of an *addiction to control itself* liquidates the concept of control altogether—at least insofar as control is a capacity of human beings.

For Burroughs, this sort of thinking leads to a series of novels in which ideas of control are at once absolutely central and, at the same time, utterly vexed. In 1955, he explained to Ginsberg that in the "vast Kafkian conspiracies" of *Naked Lunch*, "agents continually infiltrate to work on other side [*sic*] . . . ; more accurately, agents rarely know which side they are working on" (*Letters,* 269).[16] If the first part of this explanation gives the impression of conspirators who are rational, motivated individuals, the second part contradicts that impression by portraying them as pawns in a larger, more obscure plot. This reversal reopens the questions of control that the remark seemed designed to resolve: Who governs and controls the conspiracies afoot, and who or what counts as an agent? In a text where the very *conspirators* are unaware of the plots they conspire to carry out, something has gone haywire in the idea of personhood. It is in *this* sense that *Naked Lunch* is about "the desecration of the Human Image." The novel's addicts and "agents" alike are all under the sway of powerful external controls, and individuals who cannot control themselves are not persons—at least not in the discourse of possessive individualism.[17]

Junk, by contrast, *is* something like a person in Burroughs's work. One reason junk addiction is dehumanizing, for example, is that in the junk-junkie relationship only junk retains human attributes. The addict, says Burroughs, "needs more and more junk to maintain a human form" (*Naked Lunch,* vi)—as if junk were an injection of humanity itself. "Junk is the ideal product," he adds, because "the junk merchant does not sell his product to the consumer, he sells the consumer to his product" (*Naked Lunch,* vii). This passage relies on the same reversal of human agency found in Marx's discussion of commodity fetishism: junk merchants are instruments of their powerful commodity and junkies are merely objects to be sold. As long as a product "is a value in use, there is nothing mysterious about it," says Marx. "But, so soon as it steps forth as a commodity, it is changed into something transcendent. . . . It stands on its head, and evolves out of its wooden brain grotesque ideas."[18] In Burroughs's junk economy, junk takes on human qualities for two reasons: first, because it "steps forth" into something like pure exchange-value—it is "quantitative and accurately measurable . . . like money" (*Naked Lunch,* vii); and second, because although it has no *productive* use (it is *junk*), its use-value to the addicted consumer is almost infinite. It is "the mold of monopoly and possession," says Burroughs, because it reduces the body to a single and "*total need,*" which "knows absolutely *no limit or control*" (*Naked Lunch,* vii, emphasis added). In Burroughs's world, junk produces a terminal capitalist subject, a "grotesque" consumer whose needs and desires have all been replaced by one simple but overpowering bodily need. As the narrator of *Junky* puts it, "Life telescopes down to junk, one fix and looking forward to the next."[19]

Burroughs represents the telescoping effect of junk in shocking bodily terms. His addicts literally have "grotesque" bodies and "wooden brains"— body parts that have mutated so as to do nothing but detect and consume junk. Willy the Disk, for instance, has "a round, disk mouth lined with sensitive, erectile black hairs. He is blind from shooting in the eyeball, his nose and palate eaten away sniffing H, his body a mass of scar tissue hard and dry as wood." Willy "only functions at night" when his "blind, seeking mouth" leads him anywhere there is junk (*Naked Lunch*, 7). Not all of Burroughs's junkies are so fantastically embodied, but almost all have a modified natural body. They have "undreaming insect eyes" (*Naked Lunch*, 58), "black insect laughter" (*Naked Lunch*, 51), and bizarre, nonhuman organs specially suited for sensing what Burroughs calls the "silent frequency of junk" (*Naked Lunch*, 7). They are forever extruding "rancid ectoplasm" (*Naked Lunch*, 19) and undifferentiated cellular material in biologically primitive attempts at consumption.

Why does Burroughs represent the addict in this way? Within the discourse of possessive individualism, addicts do not meet the criteria for personhood because they are not wholly autonomous, rational agents. In representing the addict, Burroughs merely literalizes this notion. Not only do his addicts' desires telescope down to the solitary desire for junk, but their bodies follow suit. As William Lee, the sometimes narrator of *Naked Lunch*, puts it, "The addict regards his body impersonally as an instrument to absorb the medium in which he lives" (67). This view of the body as a technology for finding and consuming junk helps account for Burroughs's phantasmagorical representations of addicts as limited insectoid creatures with special sensory organs for detecting junk:

> "You know how old people lose all shame about eating . . . ?" asks Lee. "Old junkies are the same about junk . . . all their guts grind in peristalsis while they cook up, dissolving the body's decent skin, you expect any moment a great blob of protoplasm will flop right out and surround the junk." (*Naked Lunch*, 5)

This final suggestion is not just a figure of speech; in Burroughs's bodily economy of addiction, junkies *do* extrude protoplasm, because they *are* simpler life-forms—usually single-celled organisms and insects. Junk, in other words, makes the *human* body unnecessary—except as an increasingly efficient (and grotesque) tool for locating junk.

To be more precise, junk consumption generates a dynamic of embodiment and disembodiment in Burroughs. Grotesque embodiment only occurs when junkies become sober and desire more junk. When high, by contrast, the addict is virtually disembodied and lacking in desire. As Burroughs explains, the intoxicated junky is a "terminal" subject, with "metabolism approaching absolute ZERO" (*Naked Lunch*, xiv) and "flesh that fades at the first silent touch of junk" (*Naked Lunch*, 8). Again, Burroughs renders these notions bodily. Lee, for instance, lives in "varying degrees of transparency" (*Naked Lunch*, 71) and (like Burroughs himself) becomes known in Tangier as "The Invisible Man." On a three-day high, his flesh becomes "so soft that he [is] cut to the bone by dust particles" (*Naked Lunch*, 70). Like other junkies, he often has an "anonymous, grey and spectral" (*Naked Lunch*, 15) look about him. When he shoots heroin into a friend's arm, the friend's "misshapen overcoat of flesh" turns "colorless in the morning light" and falls "off in globs onto the floor" (*Naked Lunch,* 70). If this evanescent bodily matter resembles the "ectoplasm" so often extruded by Burroughs's *sober* junk-hungry addicts, that is precisely what it will become when the high wears off. Ectoplasm, of course, is not only undifferentiated cellular matter but also the material residue of a ghost. And the *intoxicated* junkie is a quasi-immaterial, spectral subject—a ghost.

This strategy of literalization helps to explain the phantasmagoria of Burroughs's surreal junk universe. It also depicts, in a graphic way, the paradox of bodily control inherent to addiction. The addict, in Burroughs, is always taking junk to resist reembodiment and the problems it brings. When Lee senses his own impending incarnation, for instance, he shoots up again in order to "refuel the fires that burned through his yellow-pink-brown gelatinous substance and kept off the hovering flesh" (*Naked Lunch,* 70). The reason Lee and others want to prevent the return of their "hovering flesh" is not that they don't want bodies. In fact, the opposite seems true. As one addict says, "I am a ghost wanting what every ghost wants—a body" (*Naked Lunch,* 8). Yet, the problem is that the body of the addicted junky can only return in an undesirable form, since (in Burroughs's bodily economy) addiction *means* possession of a grotesque and uncontrollable body. In the junk-starved addict, Lee observes, "viscera and cells, galvanized into a loathsome insect-like activity, seemed on the point of breaking through the surface" (*Junky,* 58). Oddly enough, then, while junk creates the initial problem, junk is also the antidote to it. "The *pharmakon*" (drug, poison, magic charm), notes Jacques Derrida, "will always be understood both as antidote *and* as poison."[20] For Burroughs, junk intoxication is the only way the junky can avoid hideous reembodiment.

Addiction thus emerges as a paradox of embodiment: addicts who wish to have a functional and controllable body must kick the junk habit, yet, in going off junk, they find themselves imprisoned in a grotesque and uncontrollable body. They can only ward off this obscene instrument of consumption by staying high, yet staying high means surrendering the body to junk—which then intensifies the initial problem. The addict's dilemma, in other words, is whether to risk a struggle with his or her own body in order to regain control of it. Crucially, then, Burroughs's representation of the addict's dilemma presumes a Cartesian dualism in which the "self" or spirit remains the site of identity, while the body is external to the self—mere matter controlled from without. As Jean Cocteau puts it in *Opium: The Diary of a Cure,* "It is not I who become addicted, it is my body."[21] In this view, addiction results in "smaller" subjects who are embattled, struggling against a controlling environment that includes even their own bodies. This is not the only way to theorize addiction, and thus its central feature is quite telling: it willingly splinters the subject to retain the idea that control is a property, parceled out *either* to oneself or to one's environment but never a mixture of the two.

THE JUNK VIRUS

If addiction offers a radical challenge to personhood—a challenge Burroughs envisions at the most basic, bodily level—this challenge is all the more severe given its pervasiveness. As is the case in contemporary America, narcotics are not the only kind of debilitating addiction in Burroughs's fiction. The junk economy operates because of a complex system of mutually reinforcing addictions. "Selling is more of a habit than using," admits one dealer. "Nonusing pushers have a contact habit, and that's one you can't kick. Agents get it too" (*Naked Lunch*, 15). The narcotics agent in *Naked Lunch* who gets this "contact habit" is Bradley the Buyer. Bradley is famous for being the "best agent in the industry," but the better he gets the more he comes to look like a junky: "He can't drink. He can't get it up. His teeth fall out. . . . The Buyer takes on an ominous grey-green color" (*Naked Lunch*, 15). Before long, he assumes the familiar protoplasmic form of the addict and his unruly amoebalike body engulfs the district supervisor of narcotics (*Naked Lunch*, 18). Eventually, when he is caught "digesting the Narcotics Commissioner," a court rules that he has "lost his human citizenship" and condemns him for being "a creature without species" (*Naked Lunch*, 18). Here again, Burroughs specifically represents the addict as a nonperson. Even more significant, however, is that "addiction" of Bradley's sort afflicts individuals at every level of the junk economy—including makers, sellers, and even law enforcement "agents."

This representation has a good deal in common with the concept of addiction currently popular in America. Bradley the Buyer, moreover, possesses a personal quality that more clearly reveals the implications of popular views of addiction. "Fact is," says the narrator, Bradley's "body is making its own junk or equivalent. The Buyer has a steady connection. A Man Within" (*Naked Lunch*, 15). This notion—that Bradley is producing an addictive substance *within his own body*—troubles the idea of addiction, which suggests that an external substance has taken control of the subject. In order to understand Bradley's situation, we must resort to one of two alternative explanations. The first would require us to view his body as wholly external to (or separate from) his "self," the sort of Cartesian dualism mentioned earlier. This solution would retain a traditional concept of addiction—the all-or-nothing logic that locates control either in the self or in a source outside the self—but it would do so only by redrawing the line between self and world so that the body is no longer considered a part of the self. The second type of explanation, by contrast, would understand the tendency toward addiction as *internal* to the subject. This explanation would jettison traditional notions of addiction and, in doing so, would challenge liberal individualism by viewing dependencies as an essential part of subjectivity. That Bradley's body produces an addictive substance, in other words, might only indicate that he is human—that, like all humans, he possesses the capacity for addiction. The fact that Bradley eventually loses his "human citizenship" indicates how reluctant Burroughs is to endorse this second solution.

The rivalry between these two ways of accounting for less-than-clearly-willed behavior has troubled many accounts of subjectivity. As Avital Ronell observes, addiction is one of the human tendencies most disruptive to Heidegger's ontology of Being.[22] The problem with addiction, for Heidegger, is that it is neither clearly internal nor external to Being. On the one hand, it seems to transfer the essential qualities of Being to external sources. The addict, says Heidegger, is "'lived' by the world." On the other hand, Heidegger concedes that addiction is internal to Being—so close in nature to other *essential* drives (like the urge to live) that it "is not to be rooted out."[23] This is precisely the problem that governs the contemporary rhetoric of addiction, which seeks endlessly to "root out" addictions—only to discover that they have grown, multiplied, changed shape, and taken root everywhere.

It is also the problem at work in Burroughs's fiction, which insistently represents addiction as *virus* and *parasite,* entities that can be viewed as both internal and external to the self. "Like any good parasite," remarks Derrida, the *pharmakon* "is at once inside and outside—the outside feeding on the inside. And with this model of feeding we are very close to what in the modern sense of the word we call drugs, which are usually to be 'consumed'."[24] In fact, the problem I have been tracing here may be reformulated as a difficulty in conceptualizing parasitism. If one accepts the assumptions of liberal humanism, the parasite must be regarded as an external invader of an integral self. By contrast, poststructuralist approaches—particularly deconstruction ("a discourse 'on parasite' and in the logic of the 'super-parasite'" ["Rhetoric," 6])—have held that parasites occupy a complex position between inside and out, neither wholly supplementary nor essential to the subject. In this view, technologies (including drugs) cannot simply be viewed as hostile invaders of a clearly bounded self. The "natural, originary body does not exist," says Derrida, "technology has not simply added itself, from outside or after the fact, as a foreign body," but "is 'originarily' at work and in place in the supposedly ideal interiority of the 'body and soul'" ("Rhetoric," 15).

Burroughs frequently presents scenarios that demonstrate this view. A tape recorder, he once wrote, "is an externalized section of the human nervous system you can find out more about the nervous system and gain more control over your reactions by using the tape recorder than you could find out sitting twenty years in the lotus posture."[25] In moments like this, Burroughs pressures traditional assumptions about the person in the most radical fashion imaginable. Yet he often does so in the mode of *panic*—and thus tends to romanticize a traditional view of the individual, a fantasy of the autonomous self isolated from *any* threat of external invasion or control. Much like the disease model of addiction, his writing presents junk as a "possessing" demon, a destructive "evil virus" with extraordinary powers of control (*Naked Lunch*, vii). And, as I have already suggested, junk is not the only such danger for Burroughs. Indeed, it will be easier for me to demonstrate the exceptional nature of his anxieties about control by focusing on his attitude toward a technology that few contemporary Americans would view as a danger—writing.

Like Derrida, Burroughs explicitly views writing as an "organism" and a *pharmakon*—a technology that supplements human memory. Yet, Derrida and Burroughs understand the implications of this view quite differently. Derrida's account of the druglike quality of writing comes in his analysis of Plato's *Phaedrus*. In Plato's text, writing is presented to the king as a way of extending the human capacity to remember events. The king, however, rejects this offering on the grounds that writing will act as a "drug" of sorts, a technological supplement making human memory unnecessary. One of the many problems with the king's position, according to Derrida, is that it "implies that the living being is finite" and projects a fantasy in which the "perfection of a living being would consist in its having no relation at all with any outside."[26] This fantasy—the dream of a self hermetically sealed from the external world—is central to the contemporary American logic of addiction. In fact, Derrida has recently connected it to both prohibitionist *and* liberationist rhetorics of drugs.[27] What is significant for our purposes, then, is the extreme way in which Burroughs embraces this view. Like Plato's king, he views writing and other forms of communication as dangerous supplements to human memory and self-control. "The word is now a virus," warns the narrator of *The Ticket that Exploded:* "The word may once have been a healthy neural cell. It is now a parasitic organism that invades and damages the central nervous system" (*Ticket,* 49). This panic-stricken account of control suggests that, like drugs, communications are enemies of the self. Like other postwar treatments of agency, this one has a historical component: although language was once part of our internal control system (a "neural cell"), it is now a threatening competitor, an alien presence that damages our capacity for self-control.

The most notable feature of this view is its melodramatic rendering of the idea that communications can influence human identity and action. No doubt, ideological effects can be disturbing when revealed, yet the general effectivity of messages, covert and overt, should hardly come as a surprise. Social relations would be impossible if communications did not influence human behavior. Indeed, communications can only seem dangerously parasitic if one has an exceptionally romantic ideal of selfhood—an expectation of radical human autonomy and a nostalgia for the days when messages were in harmony with the self, instead of bent on its destruction. As Derrida suggests, such a view mistakenly associates the "perfection of a living being" with an absolute isolation from "any outside."

This ideal governs much of Burroughs's writing. And because it is made impossible by basic social activities, it continually leads to expressions of agency panic. How else, for instance, can we explain the famous "cut-up technique," the strategy of arbitrarily chopping up and reassembling written and spoken passages by which Burroughs sought to break the controlling power "the word"? This method of resistance—which Burroughs developed into a full political program in his essay "The Invisible Generation"—presumes that any text (even one's own) can be a dangerous instrument of control. The point of using cut-ups is to reintroduce the accidental into what appears determined and determining, thereby short-circuiting the power of social messages.[28] When hearing a cut-up, Burroughs explains, it is "as if the words themselves had been interrogated and forced to reveal their hidden meanings" ("Invisible Generation," 206). Broadly employed, this technique could no doubt disable all kinds of external influences. Yet, if we follow the idea to its logical conclusion and keep in mind that all messages are suspect, then it is clear that a successful program of cut-ups would effectively isolate the individual from communications and thus social relations in general. The cut-up promotes a form of hyperindividualism—a defense of atomistic selfhood against a "penetrating" and controlling social order. If the technique's fundamental exhortation—"everybody splice himself in with everybody else" ("Invisible Generation," 212)—seems to generate a fragmented, postmodern subjectivity, it does so only to defend the individual (and individualism itself) from social systems that humans have "no control over."[29] In this world of powerful control technologies, *everyone* is an addict, "lived by the world," because messages of any sort constitute mind-altering drugs that undermine the individual's self-control. The "subject," a doctor tells Lee, "is riddled with parasites."[30] The goal, for Burroughs, is to exterminate them. "When it comes to bedbugs," writes the one-time exterminator, the "only thing is to fumigate."[31]

CELLULAR PANIC

Here, then, is the problem confronting Burroughs. When he attempts to understand addiction or control on the model of the parasite, he generates an uncontrollable proliferation of agency problems. His response to these problems is agency panic. Rather than accepting the less strictly bordered, and less rationally centered, subject implied by his own representations, he worries in hysterical terms about external invasion and control of the self. At the same time, he attributes agency to nonhuman entities and depletes it from humans until it is no longer clear who, or what, counts as an agent.

The result is a view of the world in which subhuman components and large social organizations appear to behave like rational, motivated individuals, while human beings are merely "soft machines":

> The soft machine is the human body under constant siege from a vast hungry host of parasites. . . . What Freud calls the "id" is a parasitic invasion of the hypothalamus. . . . What Freud calls the "super ego" is probably a parasitic occupation of the mid-brain where the "rightness" centres may be located and by "rightness" I mean where "you" and "I" used to live before this "super ego" moved in.[32]

What might once have been considered components of the self are here regarded as independent agents, parasitic entities no longer integral to the subject. This view imagines something like the decentered, fragmented subject of postmodern theory, the vision of "deterritorialized" schizophrenic desiring machines advanced by Deleuze and Guattari. Yet, Burroughs's view does not really do away with centered subjectivity. Rather, it leaves intact a smaller core of rationality (or "rightness") by way of what I earlier called a Cartesian splitting of the subject. Burroughs thus salvages a vestige of autonomous subjectivity, removing from it both that which is determined (the superego or conscience) and that which is irrational (the id).

But this view has a second effect: it populates the world with entities that once constituted the self but are now autonomous. In one sense, this newly spawned hoard of "parasites" presents a major challenge to individualism. Yet it also depends on that concept since these entities themselves behave as if they were rational, autonomous, bounded individuals. Consider, for example, Burroughs's belief that "kicking a habit involves the death of junk-dependent cells and their replacement with cells that do not need junk" (*Junky*, 23). In this "cellular equation," each cell of the body is imagined as a tiny addict or nonaddict, and addiction becomes a matter of "cellular decision" (*Junky*, 151) and "cellular panic" (*Naked Lunch*, 57). At the same time, the individual addict becomes a sort of social body, a miniature version of the junk economy. What might once have been called the addict's attributes—qualities like decision making and emotion (panic)—have been transferred to his or her component parts. Addiction thus occurs not at the level of the human being, but at the level of the cells, which are themselves *miniature individuals*. This bizarre view epitomizes the logic of addiction, which has always personated the world with powerful substances (for example, "the demon rum") while construing humans as powerless.

Because this view also has much in common with posthumanist models of the subject, it is important to see precisely where Burroughs departs from posthumanism. Postmodern biology provides a good example of the latter because, as Donna Haraway has shown, it privileges "biotic components" over the traditional, integrated organism.[33] In the new biology, she explains, "what counts as a 'unit', a one, is highly problematic, not a permanent given" because "single masterly control" of the biological organism has given way to a "postmodern pastiche of multiple centres and peripheries."[34] This conception of subjectivity is similar to what Deleuze and Guattari have called "the body without organs," a fantasy of subjectivity that resists the totalizing concept of the organism. It is also similar to recent views of the mind as a "society" of independent agents.[35] Like postmodern biology, these theories attribute traditionally human qualities to biotic components or "organ-machines": Deleuze and Guattari speak of intelligent blood cells and "the molecular unconscious." As a result, their subject "is not at the center, which is occupied by the machine, but on the periphery, with no fixed identity, forever decentered."[36] Within such posthuman theories, "even the most reliable Western individuated bodies . . . neither stop nor start at the skin" and "individuality is a strategic defence problem."[37]

When this postmodern view is coupled with a vestigial form of possessive individualism, the result is agency panic. In Richard Dawkins's version of evolutionary theory, for instance, "selfish" genes are privileged over whole organisms, which Dawkins describes as "partially bounded local concentration[s]" and "machines for the production of single-celled propagules." Since the "parasite genes" have their own "selfish" desires (for example, they would "'like' to reduce capital investment" in the total organism), Dawkins foresees an "evolutionary 'arms race.'"[38] What is most striking about this theory is that its conservation of intentionality—albeit at the level of the gene—generates a rhetoric of invasion and self-defense, an anxious sense that the individual is under attack and needs protection. In Dawkins's scheme, Haraway notes, "'We' can only aim for a defended self. . . . Within 'us' is the most threatening other—the propagules, whose phenotype we, temporarily, are."[39]

This is just the sort of biotic struggle Burroughs imagines. But we can now specify the conflict that animates it. On the one hand, Burroughs exhibits a radical, posthumanist tendency to question whether humans are self-governing agents. On the other hand, he exhibits a humanist refusal to modify the traditional model of the agent, which he applies to other, non-human entities. The result is a defensive—or paranoid—conception of the world as a place full of motivated, parasitic entities whose capacity to control individuals, should they gain entry, is total and complete. "I live," Burroughs admits, "with the constant threat of possession, and a constant need to escape from possession, from Control."[40] In such a world, individuals are not responsible for their actions, which can always be traced to a larger entity. Thus, to explain the 1951 "accident" in which he put on a "William Tell act" with his wife and shot her in the head, killing her instantly, Burroughs claims he was possessed by an evil entity.[41]

My concept of possession is closer to the medieval model than to modern psychological explanations, with their dogmatic insistence that such manifestations must come from within and never, never, never from without. (As if there were some clear-cut difference between inner and outer). I mean a definite possessing entity. And indeed, the psychological concept might well have been devised by the possessing entities, since nothing is more dangerous to a possessor than being seen as a separate invading creature by the host it has invaded. (*Queer,* xix-xx)

In this passage, Burroughs suggests that the difference between the inside and outside of persons is not clear cut, but then he goes on to insist vigorously that he was subject to invasion and external control. It is no accident that this contradiction arises as he accounts for the act that epitomizes the misogyny running through his writings, since the very terms of the description are already gendered.[42] Nothing worries Burroughs so much as relinquishing an atomistic masculinity for a more fluid, socially connected subjectivity. It is as if, once employed, the logic of parasitism becomes immediately intolerable and induces a state of panic in which *any* sign of diminished voluntarity seems to indicate a *complete* transfer of agency from self to social order.

Burroughs so needs to believe this transfer is real that he deems psychology itself a trick of the "possessing entities." Psychology, of course, has always taken the opposite route, deeming possessing entities a trick of the psyche. "When human beings began to think," writes Freud,

they were, as is well known, forced to explain the external world anthropomorphically by means of a multitude of personalities in their own image; chance events, which they interpreted superstitiously, were thus actions and manifestations of persons. They behaved, therefore, just like paranoiacs, who draw conclusions from insignificant signs given them by other people.[43]

On the surface, this account diametrically opposes the one offered by Burroughs. Freud explains compulsion and coincidence via the paranoid mechanism of *projection,* while Burroughs explains these events via the *introjection* of external agents. On a deeper level, however, these accounts are similar. Both posit a core of rational will that is subject to a determining agency. They disagree only about the location of that agency. As Freud puts it, anthropomorphism "*is nothing but psychology projected into the external world.*"[44] And if Freud believes that there are no accidents in the unconscious, Burroughs believes that "there are no accidents in the junk world" (*Naked Lunch,* x) and, more dramatically, that "there is no such thing as a coincidence."[45]

Ultimately, however, Burroughs so radically projects psychology into the outer world that the world *in general* seems to possess a psyche—a psyche whose most consistent quality is malice. He believes in magic, and magic, he says, "is the assertion of *will*, the assumption that nothing happens in this universe . . . unless some entity *wills* it to happen" ("On Coincidence," 101). He thus defends the "so-called primitive" tendency to blame *all* apparent accidents on a malicious agent ("On Coincidence," 102). In his antipsychology, all events are motivated, because the qualities of the subject (motive, desire, understanding) reside *everywhere*. This is the logic of postmodern transference writ large. "Take a walk around the block," Burroughs advises his writing students:

> Come back and write down precisely what happened with particular attention to what you were thinking when you noticed a street sign, a passing car or stranger or whatever caught your attention. You will observe that what you were thinking just *before* you saw the sign relates to the sign. The sign may even complete a sentence in your mind. You are getting messages. Everything is talking to you. ("On Coincidence," 103–4)

If a sign can complete one's thoughts, and thinking is something done only by persons, then the "person" having thoughts in the passage is not a human individual. It is a much larger communication system, extending well beyond the individual's borders. This radical conception of subjectivity, however, cannot last for long. Soon enough, it induces the familiar panic response ("the students become paranoid" [104]), which is a defensive attempt to consolidate the self by separating it from external "messages."

The pattern I have been describing—in which a radical challenge to individualism elicits an anxious defense of individualism—typifies the paradoxical logic of addiction. By some accounts, in fact, addiction is sustained by this habit of mind and can be cured if the addict learns to *accept* a feeling of compromised autonomy rather than retreating into hyperindividualism. The notion that a larger system is controlling one's actions, for instance, is essential to twelve-step programs, which function in part by converting the source of the addict's paranoia into the very gateway to recovery. In his "cybernetic" theory of addiction, anthropologist Gregory Bateson suggests that the Alcoholics Anonymous program works because it correctly understands the self as part of a larger system, which the alcoholic is "powerless" to control. Indeed, Bateson argues, the reason alcoholics drink in the first place is to surrender to such a "systems view" of themselves, thus giving up the more popular but "absurd" idea that they are autonomous agents with the capacity for self-control. In a state of intoxication, the addict's "entire epistemology changes." "His self-control is lessened" and he is able to "see himself as and act as *a part of* the group."[46] Unfortunately, drinking only provides this feeling temporarily. To overcome the need for alcohol, the addict needs to develop a "systems-based" or "cybernetic" view on a more permanent basis. Here, as in postmodern biology, the "self" as ordinarily understood is only a small part of a much larger trial-and-error system which does the thinking, acting, and deciding. This system includes all the informational pathways which are relevant at any given moment to any given decision. The "self" is a false reification of an improperly delimited part of this much larger field of interlocking processes.[47]

A person, in other words, is not a material individual, but a socially dispersed system of communications.

A similar conclusion might be drawn from the writing exercise Burroughs gives his students. Yet, Burroughs cannot simply stop there. Like Bateson's alcoholic, he relinquishes this postmodern or "cybernetic" epistemology for the "epistemology of self-control." And he does so, I believe, because he does not share Bateson's positive view of communicative systems. For Bateson, such systems are akin to the "higher spiritual power" of Alcoholics Anonymous. "There is," he writes, "a larger Mind of which the individual mind is only a sub-system. This larger Mind is comparable to God and is perhaps what some people mean by 'God,' but it is still immanent in the total interconnected social system and planetary ecology."[48] For Burroughs, by contrast, social systems are a continual source of terror: "Brainwashing, psychotropic drugs, lobotomy and other more subtle forms of psychosurgery; the technocratic control apparatus of the United States has at its fingertips new techniques which if fully exploited could make Orwell's *1984* seem like a benevolent utopia."[49] In a world where the "higher powers" are in the business of mass-producing mindless, pliant subjects, a surrender to external control seems less like a cure to addiction than the cause of it.

RECONDITIONING CENTERS

Nothing makes Burroughs's view of technological systems more clear than the "control addicts" who populate his novels. These individuals are usually scientists with a strictly instrumental view of persons, and they are often in the employ of shadowy states who want to use postindustrial technologies for purposes of mass social and political control. The most famous control addict, Dr. Benway, operates a "Reconditioning Center" for the Freeland Republic. His center uses sadistic techniques—including drug "therapy," compulsory psychoanalysis, and torture—to restructure the identities of his subjects. One of his more telling products, for instance, is the "latah," an individual who compulsively imitates human actions on command and thus exhibits the "Automatic Obedience Processing" Benway's scientists seek to perfect (*Naked Lunch*, 28).

The most telling feature of these reconditioning "routines" in Burroughs's writing is how many of them concern sexual identity. Benway frequently uses violent psychotherapy to redirect human sexual desires.

"You can make a square heterosex citizen queer with this angle," he says (*Naked Lunch,* 27). Burroughs's interest in Pavlovian "sexual conditioning," like Pynchon's, lies partly in its depiction of a subject whose "deepest" self and "most personal" desires are open to external control—a subject epitomized by the addict. "Admittedly," he writes, "a homosexual can be conditioned to react sexually to a woman, or to an old boot for that matter. In fact, both homo- and heterosexual experimental subjects *have* been conditioned to react sexually to an old boot, and you can save a lot of money that way."[50] The humor of this remark belies Burroughs's other interest in the nightmare of sexual conditioning: his own experience during psychoanalytic treatment. Like his friend Ginsberg, he was treated for homosexuality, was "cured," and turned, however briefly, to a heterosexual lifestyle.[51]

An uneasy connection between addiction and homosexuality haunts Burroughs's work. These two identities—addict and homosexual—have long been associated with one another, not only because they emerged at the same historical moment, but because they have historically been viewed as expressions of "unnaturalness." As Sedgwick notes, that the two are now associated with HIV seems horribly to have "ratified" the connection between them and marked them "as unnatural, as unsuited for survival, as the appropriate objects of neglect."[52] It is all the more uncanny, then, that Burroughs should bring together the categories of homosexuality, addict, and "virus" so forcefully. Consider, for instance, the explanation he gives for his first two novels, the very titles of which evoke the twin identities he struggled with throughout his career: *Junky* and *Queer.* In the retrospective preface to *Queer,* he explains how junk addiction functions as a "cure" for homosexual desire:

> Lee on junk is covered, protected and also severely limited. Not only does junk short-circuit the sex drive, it also blunts emotional reactions to the vanishing point, depending on the dosage. . . . When the cover is removed, everything that has been held in check by junk spills out. . . . And the sex drive returns in full force." (xii-xiii)

The opening lines of the novel clarify this relation between junk and homosexuality in stark economic terms. "The first time he saw Carl, Lee thought, 'I could use that, if the family jewels weren't in pawn to Uncle Junk'" (*Queer,* 1).

This dynamic explains more fully why Burroughs views addiction as a way of "keeping off the flesh" and its (homosexual) desires. What is odd about this view, however, is that it associates junk not with the lost autonomy of addiction, but with a newfound self-control. "While it was I who wrote *Junky,*" Burroughs explains,

> I feel that I was being written in *Queer.* I was also taking pains to ensure further writing, so as to set the record straight: writing as inoculation. As soon as something is written, it loses the power of surprise, just as a virus loses its advantage

when a weakened virus has created alerted antibodies. So I achieved some immunity from further perilous ventures along these lines by writing my experience down. (*Queer*, xiv)

Both writing and junk use offer Burroughs a paradoxical form of self-control: they ward off uncontrollable sexual urges, which are here conceptualized as an invading virus. As a result, Lee in *Junky* is "integrated and self-contained" while in *Queer* he is "disintegrated" and "unsure of himself" (*Queer*, xii)—or, to put it differently, in *Junky* he is a liberal subject, while in *Queer* he is a "postmodern" or decentered subject. Junk use appears then to be a self-defeating method for preserving a liberal selfhood against an enervating and penetrating homosexuality—a conception that only underscores the masculinist biases of liberal individualism. We may now further specify the paradoxical logic of addiction as Burroughs experiences it: not only is junk an evil addicting substance but it is also a welcome relief because it short circuits the internal virus of "uncontrollable" sexual desire. Like any good *pharmakon*, it is both poison *and* antidote. The paradox is that Burroughs cannot become an "integrated and self-contained" self without the use of an *external* technology. We have thus arrived at another conundrum of selfhood, a splintering of the addict into a host of smaller components, each of which may be called on to regulate the crises of self-control generated by the others.

It is within the context of this ever-receding and ever-embattled internality that Burroughs understands mass cultural technologies and psychiatric "cures" as the ultimate invaders of the self. In one scene from *Naked Lunch*, a doctor claims to have turned a former homosexual into a "healthy" subject. His lab technician, however, challenges this claim. "What I'm getting at, Doc," says the technician, "is how can you expect a body to be healthy with its brains washed out? . . . Or put it another way. Can a subject be healthy *in absentia* by proxy already?" (139). To the technician, the idea of health is incompatible with the normalizing efforts of techno-medicine. What Burroughs suggests, in other words, is that reconditioning cannot produce a healthy subject—not only because its violent methods and normalizing ideology are unhealthy, but also because there will literally be no subject left when the process is complete. "It is highly questionable," he writes, "whether a human organism could survive complete control. There would be nothing there. No persons there. *Life is will* (motivation) and the workers would no longer be alive, perhaps literally" ("Limits of Control," 118).

One version of the subject whose brains have been washed out—who is "*in absentia* by proxy," so to speak—is the addict. Indeed, for Burroughs, nothing captures the effects of postwar technocracy so well as the addict. This is why drug addiction and other technological controls are intertwined throughout his writing. As Benway remarks wistfully, "Pending more precise knowledge of brain electronics, drugs remain an essential tool of the interrogator in his assault on the subject's personal identity" (*Naked Lunch*, 25).

Given such connections, it should come as no surprise that Burroughs represents the effects of mass culture in a bodily fashion because this is also how he represents addiction. Consider his description of the "political parties of Interzone," the global village he modeled on Tangier. Each of these "political parties" represents a radically reimagined idea of individuality, and except for "Factualism"—the party Burroughs aligns himself with—all of them are hostile to liberal selfhood. The "Liquefactionist" party, for instance, favors "the eventual merging of everyone into One Man by a process of protoplasmic absorption" (*Naked Lunch*, 146). The "Divisionists," by contrast, "cut off tiny bits of their flesh and grow exact replicas of themselves in embryo jelly" (*Naked Lunch*, 164). While these practices are diametrically opposed, their effects would be largely the same: they would destabilize the traditional self in the same way as posthuman biology and Burroughs's animistic theory of addiction.

Yet, the "Senders" party offers the clearest index of how Burroughs feels about mass culture and technology. According to Lee, they are the most dangerous party. Their goal, as one Sender proclaims, is to reestablish a Mayan form of telepathic control. Their system, however, will draw on new technologies to achieve "control of physical movement, mental processes, emotional reactions and *apparent* sensory impressions" of persons "by means of bioelectric signals injected into the nervous system of the subject" (*Naked Lunch*, 162). "Shortly after birth," the Sender explains,

> a surgeon could install connections in the brain. A miniature radio receiver could be plugged in and the subject controlled from State-controlled transmitters. . . . The biocontrol apparatus is prototype of one-way telepathic control [*sic*]. The subject could be rendered susceptible to the transmitter by drugs or other processing without installing any apparatus. . . . Now one sender could control the planet. (*Naked Lunch*, 163–64)

Here, the link between drugs and electronic culture is made rather explicit, much as it was in popular postwar descriptions of television as "the plug-in drug." The Senders' bizarre human engineering project is designed to produce an entire population of addict-subjects.

But what is most bizarre about this fantasy of control is that it was presented as a serious possibility at the 1956 National Electronics Conference in Chicago. The speaker was an electrical engineer named Curtiss R. Schafer, of the Norden-Ketay Corporation. His subject was "biocontrol"— the great achievement of which, according to Schafer, would be "the control of unruly humans" through electronics—an idea Schafer based on the (cybernetic) premise that since "planes, missiles, and machine tools already are guided by electronics, . . . the human brain—being essentially a digital computer—can be, too."[53] Burroughs has appropriated the scenario from Vance Packard's *Hidden Persuaders*. In Schafer's words,

> The ultimate achievement of biocontrol may be the control of man himself. . . . The controlled subjects would never be permitted to think as individuals. A few months after birth, a surgeon would equip each child with a socket mounted under the scalp and electrodes reaching selected areas of brain tissue. . . . The child's sensory perceptions and muscular activity could be either modified or completely controlled by bioelectric signals radiating from state-controlled transmitters.[54]

Schafer ended, Packard observes dryly, with "the reassuring thought that the electrodes 'cause no discomfort.'"[55]

It is no accident that Packard's central claim is that psychologically savvy advertisers had begun to turn consumers into addicts of a sort—an association already implicit in the historical concept of the consumer. He describes the "hooks" of the admen as "*prescriptions* for our secret distresses" and "*cures* for our hidden aversions," and he views hapless consumers as "adult-children," highly susceptible to what Riesman terms "other-direction" and what Jacques Ellul calls "involuntary psychological collectivization."[56] In one description of a typical motivational experiment, Packard argues that even product labels can tranquilize shoppers, stripping them of self-control. As shoppers walked by a surreptitiously videotaped supermarket display, he explains,

> Their eye-blink rate, instead of going up to indicate mounting tension, went down and down, to a very subnormal fourteen blinks a minute. The ladies fell into what Mr. Vicary calls a hypnoidal trance. . . . Interestingly many of these women were in such a trance that they passed by neighbors and old friends without noticing or greeting them. Some had a sort of glassy stare. They were so entranced as they wandered about the store plucking things off shelves at random that they would bump into boxes without seeing them and did not even notice the camera.[57]

Confronted by the magically intoxicating packages, these consumers become something less than willful agents ("in this generation," says one adman, echoing Marx's account of commodity fetishism, "the products say 'buy me, buy me'").[58] The subliminal seduction is so powerful that when these tranquilized "babes in consumerland" sober up, they often find they do "not have enough money to pay for all the nice things they [have] put in the cart."[59]

No doubt, then, one reason Burroughs found *The Hidden Persuaders* so attractive was that it implied the connection between mass psychology and drugs central to his own writing. Burroughs strengthens this connection when he turns the real electrical engineer and biocontrol advocate, Curtiss R. Schafer, into *Naked Lunch's* Dr. Curt "Fingers" Schafer, the Lobotomy Kid.

To Dr. Schafer, "The human body is scandalously inefficient. Instead of a mouth and an anus," he asks, "why not have one all-purpose hole to eat *and* eliminate?" (*Naked Lunch*, 131). "Why not one all-purpose blob?" replies Dr. Benway (*Naked Lunch*, 131). This brings us back to where we began, because the all-purpose blob is the model of the junkie, the figure whose protoplasmic body has been rationalized so as to have but one purpose—the consumption of junk. Dr. Schafer is busy producing just such a subject. His self-described "Master Work" is "*The Complete All American Deanxietized Man*" (*Naked Lunch*, 103), an individual whose nervous system has been "reduced" to relieve him of human feelings such as angst. To his horror, however, just as Schafer unveils this new and improved individual for his colleagues it turns into a "monster black centipede" (*Naked Lunch*, 104)—again solidifying the link between the insectoid subjects of junk addiction and the similarly "empty" subjects of mass culture.

These scenarios, finally, explain why Burroughs chooses the single-celled organism and the insect as the models for the addicted subject. Tony Tanner has suggested that "matter returning to lower forms of organization" is Burroughs's "version of that entropy which is such a common dread among American writers."[60] This interpretation is helpful if we recall that the postwar literary interest in entropy stemmed from the writings of Norbert Wiener, which characterized entropy as an "evil" tendency, because it moves us "from a state of organization and differentiation in which distinctions and forms exist, to a state of chaos and sameness."[61] Wiener, moreover, explicitly associates insects with fascism and mass culture. Like the totally "conditioned" (51) subjects of fascism, he claims, the insect is a "cheap, mass-produced article, of no more individual value than a paper pie plate to be thrown away after it is once used" (51). This is what Burroughs suggests about the addict-subjects of postwar technocracy. Indeed, what could describe Burroughs's work better than Wiener's argument that while we have the technical capacity to "organize the fascist ant-state with human material," to do so would mean "a degradation of man's very nature" (52)? Wiener develops this defense of human uniqueness for the same reason that Burroughs so often defends the "Human Image": his central thesis casts such doubt on human uniqueness and autonomy that it quickly becomes intolerable and must be counteracted by an impassioned humanism. The larger point of Wiener's text, after all, is that "if we could build a machine whose mechanical structure duplicated human physiology, then we could have a machine whose intellectual capacities would duplicate those of human beings" (57). Only in the context of this daring, materialist thesis does Wiener feel compelled to prove, at considerable length, the rather absurd point that "the human individual . . . is physically equipped, as the ant is not for . . . the most noble flights" (51–52).

Such a humanist retreat repeats the gesture I have been tracing here. In

Burroughs, the gesture is dramatic because his model of pervasive addiction offers radical challenges to liberal humanism. Burroughs finds himself so deeply enamored of liberal humanism that his own attacks on it continually propel him into a state of panic. It is in this sense that his writing dramatizes the tensions in the contemporary culture of addiction. It depicts persons as "soft machines," addict-subjects "lived by" a world of technologies that have themselves appropriated the qualities of rationality, integrity, and self-control supposedly lost to human beings.

PART II

Figures of the Orient

3

Narrating National Addictions

De Quincey, Opium, and Tea

Cannon Schmitt

In the work of Thomas De Quincey, the most immediately recognizable form of national self-definition is that of triumphant England vociferously announcing its supremacy. Consider, for instance, what is perhaps the most affect-laden such moment in De Quincey's corpus, a dream-vision related in the final section of "The English Mail-Coach":

> Tidings had arrived . . . of a grandeur that measured itself against centuries; too full of pathos they were, too full of joy, to utter themselves by other language than by tears, by restless anthems, and *Te Deums* reverberating from the choirs and orchestras of the earth. These tidings we that sat upon the laurelled car had it for our privilege to publish amongst all nations. . . . We waited for a secret word, that should bear witness to the hope of nations as now accomplished for ever. At midnight, the secret word arrived; which word was— *Waterloo and Recovered Christendom!* The dreadful word shone by its own light; before us it went; high above our leaders' heads it rode, and spread a golden light over the paths which we traversed.[1]

Englishness here takes the form of proclamation, and it does so not simply as one nationality among others but rather as the epitome of nationality, set apart both geographically and temporally: England's victory over Napoleon achieves "the hope of nations . . . for ever." Military triumph, declarations of national superiority, a destiny at once earthly and sanctioned by heaven ("*Waterloo and Recovered Christendom!*"), displays of patriotic fervor balancing masculine aggressivity with maudlin tears—such is the familiar stuff of the nationalist imaginary. If anything surprises it must be the very completeness of the inventory: with characteristic De Quinceyan excess, the passage gathers together nearly all possible permutations of the rhetoric of the nation-state in one dense outpouring of sentiment.

As the ecstatic vision unfolds, however, it is unsettled by a feature seemingly at odds with the unalloyed triumphalism of national victory: victimized womanhood. De Quincey discovers that the coach on which he rides, the coach that bears the "secret word," is rolling through an immense cathedral. Suddenly "a female child, that rode in a carriage as frail as flowers," appears in its path. The coach does not slow in its progress, and De Quincey can neither stop it nor warn the child. Immobile, mute, and resigned to the inevitability of a collision, he laments inwardly: "'Oh, baby! . . . Must we, that carry tidings of great joy to every people, be messengers of ruin to thee?'" (13:324). Apparently so: victorious nationhood—and De Quincey's own participation in such victory as its privileged mouthpiece—demands the sacrifice of a young girl.

This construction of national identity by way of threatened womanhood invokes what Claudia Johnson has termed "the Burkean concept of the nation as a fragile body."[2] It does so by drawing on the generic resources of the Gothic—for the young girl who is to be crushed beneath the wheels of the coach bearing news of national victory resembles nothing so much as the victimized heroine characteristic of the fictions of Ann Radcliffe and other Gothic novelists.[3] "The English Mail-Coach" is only one of many autobiographical texts in which De Quincey borrows from the Gothic in order to lend substance and shape to his experiences. The first and most enduringly successful of these attempts at self-representation, *Confessions of an English Opium-Eater* (1822; 1856), can accurately be described as a Gothic autobiography—a text that organizes its material, the life and times of Thomas De Quincey, on the model of a Gothic novel. And like "The English Mail-Coach," *Confessions* suggests that De Quincey found in Gothic narrative a useful way to represent not only the struggles of the self, but the travails and triumphs of the English nation as well. This double function of the Gothic is explained by a fatality at the heart of *Confessions* that inexorably binds De Quincey to the fate of the nation: his addiction to opium.

Opium, the substance to which De Quincey turned for relief from pain and which eventually tormented as much as it soothed him, lay behind two of Britain's most far-flung imperial conflicts, the Opium Wars with China (1839–42 and 1856–58). Contemporary accounts of these wars by British opium traders and military officers illustrate the expanding currency of the Gothic narrative of victimization in explaining Britain's imperial and mercantile relations with the rest of the globe. De Quincey's own journalistic writings on the subject, however, most fully demonstrate the uses to which such a Gothicization of history and geopolitics might be put. Moreover, in the context of these writings the national implications of this expansion of Gothic narrative become particularly clear: his essays on the Opium Wars suggest that to be English is of necessity to be frail. National identity is not secured through triumphant proclamation, with its "restless anthems" and "*Te Deums* reverberating from the choirs and orchestras of the earth."

Rather, Englishness is constructed as a state of dependence, and the English as inevitably, eternally subject to victimization.

> *Si bene calculum ponas, ubique naufragium est.*
> *[If you think it over properly, there is shipwreck everywhere.]*
>
> PETRONIUS, *Satyricon*

For De Quincey, catastrophe is omnipresent. The past is comprised of misfortune and suffering, "the deep, deep tragedies of infancy," the "infinite iteration" of the "aboriginal fall" (13:304). The future holds only despair, for "if from some secret stand we could look *by anticipation* along [life's] vast corridors . . . what a recoil we should suffer of horror!"[4] The present, too, causes dismay, for it "offers less capacity for [humanity's] footing than the slenderest film that ever spider twisted from her womb" ("Suspiria," 13:361). De Quincey's writings attempt to find an adequate expression for the catastrophic and an adequate explanation for its ubiquity. As the digressiveness and prolixity of the writings indicate, the demands of such an attempt could only be met by a restless and exhaustive search for appropriate language.

The Gothic provides one solution to that search. Although not the only generic mold with which De Quincey shapes his experience, the Gothic is one of particular power and significance.[5] De Quincey was steeped in the Gothic: he produced journal entries replete with dark Romantic materials, made clichéd references to Radcliffe as "the great enchantress" (see, for example, *Confessions*, 1856, 282), and wrote his own Gothic novel, *Klosterheim* (1832), a tale of secrecy and vengeance set during the Thirty Years War.[6] So far reaching an effect did the genre have on his imagination that his writings constantly borrow from it in order to give form to his life, his ideas, and, in perhaps the strangest case, his understanding of international relations. "As an essayist and autobiographer," Eve Kosofsky Sedgwick has written, "Thomas De Quincey was a great Gothic novelist."[7]

Sedgwick substantiates this claim by identifying in De Quincey's writings a full catalogue of Gothic conventions—a constellation of related thematic elements that includes "sleep, dreams, live burial, the unspeakable, [and] the sublime of privation."[8] In keeping with her formalist reading of the genre, she surveys these elements only to find in all of them a primary "dynamic structure" dominated by the correspondence between two spaces: "within" and "without."[9] Such a structure is indeed evident in De Quincey's writings. The more interesting and significant kinship to the Gothic found there, however, has to do with an obsessive recourse to the genre not, as Sedgwick would have it, in search of the formal structure of inside and outside, but for the promise of a paranoid narrative involving unjust and inexorable persecution.

The centrality of the Gothic as an organizing presence in De Quinceyan autobiography is not evident on the surface of his works. *Confessions of an English Opium-Eater* presents De Quincey's life up to the time of his opium addiction in order to justify that addiction and to explain the origin and contents of his sleeping and waking visions. As such, its overt structure—clearest in the 1856 revision, but already present in 1822—is at once geographical and medical. Geographically, the text traces a series of spatial relocations: from home and family, to Manchester Grammar School, to Wales, to London, to Oxford, and, ultimately, to the drug that constitutes its own peculiar landscape, opium. The organization of *Confessions* is medicalized as well, for each geographic locale is important in its connection to the stomach ailment that leads to the initial need for opium and, in turn, to De Quincey's addiction and dreams.[10] "Suspiria de Profundis," one of several pieces written as sequels to *Confessions,* carefully articulates the rationale for this pattern: "The work itself [*Confessions*] opened with the narration of my early adventures. These, in the natural order of succession, led to the opium as a resource for healing their consequences; and the opium as naturally led to the dreams" (13:336).

Covertly, however, *Confessions* organizes itself around recurrent scenes of threat to a helpless victim—often female, always feminized—and the unavailing efforts of a would-be savior to provide aid. In most of these scenes De Quincey represents himself as an ineffectual Gothic hero, the character Joanna Russ has called the genre's "Shadow-Male": like Valancourt in Radcliffe's *The Mysteries of Udolpho* (1794) or Vivaldi in *The Italian* (1797), he repeatedly encounters a woman in danger whom he cannot protect.[11] This situation is not unique to *Confessions;* on the contrary, it is played out again and again in De Quincey's writings. In the passage from "The English Mail-Coach" cited above he watches but cannot act as his carriage bears down on the doomed girl (13:324); in the *Autobiography* he recounts standing by helplessly at that "ineffable" affliction, the death of his sister Elizabeth (54); in "On Murder Considered as One of the Fine Arts" he dwells for pages on the vulnerability of a "young girl" stalked by her would-be killer (13:111). Indeed, this scenario dominates his work—and, if the work is to be believed, his life: the appearance of a "lost Pariah woman," "some shadowy malice which withdrew her . . . from restoration and from hope," and his own incapacity to ward off that malice (*Autobiography*, 346–47).

De Quincey encounters the central "Pariah woman" of *Confessions* in London, a city whose terrors are so forceful that the text adumbrates them well before De Quincey's actual arrival there. The menace of certain architectural arrangements is a familiar feature of the works of Radcliffe, Matthew Gregory Lewis, and other Gothicists; their novels frequently invoke the aura of malevolent power given off by passages that lead through Inquisitorial dungeons or Apennine castles. De Quincey invests London with the same aura in his vision of that city in the 1856 version of *Confessions*. He has stopped at Shrewsbury and must await the Holyhead mail coach in a large, unoccupied ballroom. This ballroom, transmogrified by night and imagination, foreshadows the dangers to be found in the English Babylon to which he travels:

> But now rose London—sole, dark, infinite—brooding over the whole capac-
> ities of my heart. . . . This single feature of the rooms—their unusual altitude,
> and the echoing hollowness which had become the exponent of the
> altitude— . . . threw me into the deadliest condition of nervous emotion
> under contradictory forces, high over which predominated horror recoiling
> from that unfathomed abyss in London into which I was now so willfully pre-
> cipitating myself. (46–47)[12]

This nebulous but ominous threat is made good on arrival, for in London De Quincey encounters two young girls victimized by circumstance. The first of these girls is the nameless waif with whom he shares poor lodgings and poorer meals. The second, remembered with "far deeper sorrow," is the London prostitute, Ann.

De Quincey's account of Ann and his inadvertent loss of contact with her, like that of the dark vision of London's streets as imagined from an empty ballroom in Shrewsbury, makes use of the Gothic to body forth an episode from his life and, in doing so, to construct a self out of helplessness and victimization. After spending months in London on the brink of starvation, surviving by means of Ann's companionship and aid, De Quincey at last determines to borrow money against the future inheritance specified in his father's will (1822, 54–56). He sets out for Eton to follow up on this determination, parting from his friend and benefactress but arranging to meet with her on his return and include her in any success he might have. Subsequently, however, their arrangement proves fruitless: despite days of earnest searching, he is unable to locate her. The loss of Ann leads to a powerful fantasy of radical contingency and anonymity, clearly related to fears of mass society, but, if we recall the pervasive opacity of Radcliffe's and Lewis's convents, castles, and dungeons, just as clearly derived from the conventions of the Gothic:

> This, amongst such troubles as most men meet with in this life, has been my
> heaviest affliction.—If she lived, doubtless we must have been sometimes in
> search of each other, at the very same moment, through the mighty labyrinths
> of London; perhaps even within a few feet of each other—a barrier no wider
> than a London street, often amounting in the end to a separation for eternity!
> (1822, 64; 1856, 375)[13]

This "separation for eternity" from Ann reenacts the separation from his sister Elizabeth that De Quincey suffered as a child. In the first volume of the *Autobiography* he describes his feelings after Elizabeth's death, comparing his situation to that of the Wandering Jew—both fated to live out a "doom of endless sorrow," the Jew expelled from Jerusalem and De Quincey cut off from the presence of Elizabeth (43). In the case of De Quincey, though, separation occurred not once but repeatedly. The loss of Ann, whom De Quincey refers to as his "sister" (just as he describes other London prostitutes as his "sisters in calamity"), pointedly repeats the loss of Elizabeth (1856, 359). And, as "Suspiria de Profundis" refers to Ann as the original for the "lost Pariah woman" of his opium visions (13:222), Elizabeth lies at the base of these as well. But the question is not one of origins; whether Elizabeth's death set the terms for all the other losses in De Quincey's life or whether those losses inspired in him the need for an original that he found, after the fact, in his sister is impossible to determine— and finally, perhaps, unimportant. The certainty is that, in De Quincey's self-representations, loss and the constant threat of loss constitute existence.[14]

This loss, which might at first glance appear to be a free-falling melancholy, in fact takes the specific form of a structure of persecution consisting of three positions: persecutor, victim, and impotent onlooker. As Michelle Massé argues in *In the Name of Love: Women, Masochism, and the Gothic,* such a structure is typical of Gothic fictions. Moreover, it corresponds closely to the beater/beaten/spectator (or sadist/masochist/voyeur) triad described by Freud in "Instincts and Their Vicissitudes" (1915) and "'A Child Is Being Beaten'" (1919). Massé questions Freud's notion of this triad insofar as, for Freud, the inhabitants of at least two of the three positions are predictable and static: men are sadists, women masochists.[15] In his meditations on Elizabeth, Ann, and other women in danger, De Quincey reproduces this fixed form of victimization, for frequently he looks on as women suffer at the hands of men. But elsewhere the inhabitants of these positions are in fact quite volatile. In particular, his sympathy for victimized women often results in an identification with them so complete that he takes their place, suffering for them—or, more accurately, as them—the torments of a lost pariah.[16] This inhabitation of the position of feminized victim is crucial to De Quincey's portrayal of himself: the English opium-eater is, above all, one who suffers.[17] Moreover, this construction of autobiographical subjectivity lays the groundwork for a similar construction of English national identity.

A notable instance of De Quincey's victimization appears in the 1856 *Confessions* and has to do with his decision to leave Manchester Grammar School. In 1822 he devotes only a few paragraphs to his time there and is vague about his reasons for running away. In 1856, though, the section detailing this episode has been greatly expanded. According to De Quincey, bad food and lack of exercise reduced him to a state of illness so severe that he determined to leave school against the wishes of his mother and guardians. This decision to "elope," as he calls it, although based in his sense of himself as an outcast, is also an assertion of independence, a refusal to suffer. Suffering comes in the attempt to account for this act to his mother. With this aim in mind he travels from Manchester to his mother's house in Chester. When he confronts her, however, he is incapable of explaining himself—and the effort to explain to the reader this inability to explain to his mother requires the invocation of an Ur-victimization, an archetype of self-betrayal:

> If in this world there is one misery having no relief, it is the pressure on the heart of the *Incommunicable*. And, if another Sphinx should arise to propose another enigma to man—saying, What burden is that which only is insupportable by human fortitude? I should answer at once—*It is the burden of the Incommunicable*. . . . Just so helpless did I feel, disarmed into just the same languishing impotence to face (or to make an effort at facing) the difficulty before me, as most of us have felt in the dreams of our childhood when lying down without a struggle before some all-conquering lion. (316)[18]

In positing an aboriginal dream of "languishing impotence" common to humanity, De Quincey expresses his sense of human life as fundamentally catastrophic. More than this, though, he constitutes the autobiographical subject as victim, and specifically as helpless in the face of the need to speak. By elevating "*the Incommunicable*" to the one affliction without succor, the passage exemplifies De Quincey's self-representation, not as a "Shadow-Male" unable to help a swooning, speechless woman, but as that woman herself. Further, in making the curious analogy between prostrating oneself before a lion and facing the inability to explain to one's mother why one ran away from school, De Quincey connects Gothic victimization to the familial in a way that will recur throughout *Confessions* and elsewhere. The ineffable, which Radcliffe and other Gothicists reserve for the most inexpressibly alien elements of cruel and distant lands, now takes up residence at home, at the feet of an English mother.

There are many other moments in *Confessions* in which the autobiographer dwells on his own status as victim, emplotting his life as if it were a Gothic novel and he the novel's heroine. In the passage on London cited above, for instance, it is the opium-eater himself who cowers before an image of the "unfathomed abyss" of the metropolis (1856, 47). (If, in the event, London torments two young women as well, this fact only confirms De Quincey's identification with female sufferers.) The most remarkable passages of victimization in *Confessions*, however, are those often-discussed accounts of the opium dreams involving the Malay. The final section of *Confessions*, entitled "The Pains of Opium," documents these dreams in great detail. In them the Gothic pattern of victimization returns, but this time with a significance that, in light of De Quincey's subsequent role in Britain's relations with the Far East, can properly be understood as proleptic. For these dreams not only continue the portrayal of De Quincey as victim but also identify the Orient as the source of persecution. In this regard, the following brief excerpt from the "Malay dream" of May 1818 is exemplary:

> Under the connecting feeling of tropical heat and vertical sun-lights, I brought together all creatures, birds, beasts, reptiles, all trees and plants, usages and appearances, that are found in all tropical regions. . . . I ran into pagodas: and was fixed, for centuries, at the summit, or in secret rooms; I was the idol; I was the priest; I was worshipped; I was sacrificed. . . . I was buried, for a thousand years, in stone coffins, with mummies and sphinxes, in narrow chambers at the heart of eternal pyramids. I was kissed, with cancerous kisses, by crocodiles; and laid, confounded with all unutterable slimy things, amongst reeds and Nilotic mud. (1822, 109)

The strange mélange of Near, Middle, and Far Eastern imagery in this dream illustrates an Orientalizing imperative that would turn all concomitants of "tropical heat" into signs of a dismaying and persecutorial East. It also specifies the nature of the danger posed by the Orient: a pollution that amounts to deracination.[19]

Throughout *Confessions* De Quincey undertakes a self-fashioning wherein he presents himself as helpless in the face of persecution—either powerless witness to a woman menaced by some "shadowy malice" or himself a target of such malice. This dream and others like it at the end of *Confessions* lend substance to that shadow. What horrifies De Quincey is the swirling multiplicity of selves he experiences: "I was the idol; I was the priest; I was worshipped; I was sacrificed." Such horror is tied to opium: dependence on the drug promotes a destabilization of identity in the autobiographical subject.[20] And the nature of this destabilization is quite specific: De Quincey's dismay derives from being an "I" that is also an "it," an Englishman "confounded with all unutterable slimy things, amongst reeds and Nilotic mud." To fear being "confounded" with all that lives and dies at the bottom of the Nile is to fear being mixed with, taken for, indistinguishable from what one cannot—for De Quincey, what one must not—be: an Oriental.

The East, in the eyes of nineteenth-century Europe, was the special province of opium use (De Quincey on the Malay: "To him, as an Orientalist, I concluded that opium must be familiar" [1822, 91]).[21] Despite the widespread availability of opium in England, to be an occidental user of the drug could call the integrity of one's national and racial identity into question. The very title *Confessions of an English Opium-Eater* declares as much—though that title may be taken in at least two ways. On the one hand, it may serve to render the threat of Orientalization harmless by proclaiming from the start the Englishness of this particular consumer of opium. On the other hand, it may just as well amount to an admission of contamination: the very necessity of including "English" in the title suggests that those who eat opium ordinarily hail from a different part of the globe. This titular rhetoric of simultaneous innocence and guilt serves as a stylistic analogue for the simultaneous refutation and confirmation of contamination by the foreign evident throughout *Confessions*—of the possibility that, as John Barrell writes of De Quincey, "He *was* Chinese; he *was* the Malay that haunted his dreams."[22] Put another way, the anxiety surrounding addiction to opium concerns an insuperable bodily dependence on—and hence conflation with—a presence alien to the self but also, more horribly, alien to the nation.[23]

> *Thinking the body is thinking social topography and vice versa.*
>
> PETER STALLYBRASS AND ALLON WHITE,
> *The Politics and Poetics of Transgression*

Even in the 1822 edition of *Confessions*, De Quincey was nervously warding off the potentially deracinating implications of his drug habit and his decision to write about it. Structurally, this defensiveness appears in an accumulation of preludes to the actual drug "confessions" themselves. The opium visions treated in Part II of the book are preceded by no fewer than three introductory sections. Part II itself begins with a few pages of introduction; these, in turn, are preceded by Part I, entitled "Preliminary Confessions." And even before these preliminaries, an address "To the Reader" appears, the burden of which is to sketch De Quincey's "apology for breaking through that delicate and honourable reserve, which, for the most part, restrains us from the public exposure of our own errors and infirmities" (29).

The pronouns "us" and "our" refer, as the next sentence makes clear, to the English, to whom "nothing, indeed, is more revolting . . . than the spectacle of a human being . . . [openly displaying] his moral ulcers or scars" (29). Such display is best left to "French literature, or to that part of the German, which is tainted with the spurious and defective sensibility of the French" (29). The reference here is specific: as Marilyn Butler notes, the Tory De Quincey "is careful to begin by disassociating his *Confessions* from those of Rousseau, the archetypal apologist for himself, who moreover made self-realization and fulfillment a potentially liberal cause."[24] The defensiveness evident in the address "To the Reader," though, attempts a distancing from other nationalities more general than the allusion to Rousseau suggests. Certainly De Quincey wishes to avoid being associated with the valorization of the self characteristic of sansculottic Frenchmen and their English Jacobin sympathizers. At the same time, he is concerned to combat the appearance of involvement with the foreign understood more broadly as the source—and perhaps therefore the proper domain—of his addiction.

A passage in "Suspiria de Profundis" that directly addresses opium addiction clarifies the relation among autobiography, the Gothic, and the anxiety about association with and dependence on the foreign intimated in the prefatory sections of *Confessions*. Early on in "Suspiria," De Quincey gives an account of the realization that he no longer has any hope of overcoming his opium habit. No fewer than three descriptions of this realization are required adequately to depict it and to convey the despair to which it gives rise. First, De Quincey recounts a dream in which gates that once provided an exit from "vast avenues of gloom" are now not only closed and barred against him but also, as if to insist that what seems to be merely enclosure is actually live burial, "hung with funeral crape" (337). This dream, in turn, he compares to "the situation of one escaping by some refluent current from the maelstrom roaring for him in the distance, who finds suddenly that this current is but an eddy wheeling round upon the same maelstrom" (337). The dream represents permanent addiction as the imprisonment of a solitary wanderer in a barren, crepuscular landscape; the analogy to drowning in a whirlpool retains and intensifies this sense of immurement but adds the anguish attendant on hopes of salvation suddenly revealed to be unfounded. Finally, both dream and analogy are glossed with reference to "a striking incident in a modern novel":

> A lady-abbess of a convent, herself suspected of Protestant leanings, and in that way already disarmed of all effectual power, finds one of her own nuns (whom she knows to be innocent) accused of an offence leading to the most terrific of punishments. The nun will be immured alive if she is found guilty; and there is no chance that she will not,—for the evidence against her is strong, unless something were made known that cannot be made known, and the judges are hostile. All follows in the order of the reader's fears . . . the judgment is delivered; nothing remains but to see execution done. At this crisis, the abbess . . . considers with herself that . . . there will be one single night open, during which the prisoner cannot be withdrawn from her own separate jurisdiction. This one night, therefore, she will use, at any hazard to herself, for the salvation of her friend. At midnight . . . the lady traverses the passages which lead to the cells of prisoners . . . . Suddenly she has reached the door; she descries a dusky object; she raises her lamp; and, ranged within the recess of the entrance, she beholds the funeral banner of the holy office, and the black robes of its inexorable officials. (337–38)

As in the dream of gates shut and hung with "funeral crape," addiction here is likened to a permanent imprisonment that amounts to being "immured alive" (hence the "funeral banner" of the Inquisition). As in the analogy to the swimmer and the maelstrom, hopes of escape are raised only to be undercut at the last instant. This "striking incident," however, not only echoes but also expands on the representations of addiction that precede it, primarily by dilating a moment of realization to the extent that it becomes a narrative. De Quincey initially presents a tableau: a figure in a landscape. From this tableau he moves to a scene of drowning that constitutes a narrative in miniature (hopes of escape found to be baseless) and that may imply a larger narrative structure (shipwreck, or perhaps—given De Quincey's predilection for classical texts—a revision of Odysseus's encounter with Charybdis). In the tale of the abbess and the nun, what began as tableau swells into an entire novelistic episode, complete with characterization, suspense, and a tortuous plot.

This narrativization, in addition to reinscribing what was at first an instant of dismay as a temporal and developmental sequence, also shifts the story of addiction from the realm of male heroism (the Homeric shipwreck) to that of female victimization. The opium addict is divided into spectator and victim, both women: the abbess, "suspected of Protestant leanings, and in that way already disarmed of all effectual power," and the blameless nun, unfairly "accused of an offence leading to the most terrific of punishments." Elsewhere De Quincey expresses his loathing of the possibility of "find[ing] housed within himself . . . some horrid alien nature" ("The English Mail-Coach," 292n). Here, however, positing the existence of a dual (and female) nature within provides a strategy of disavowal that allows him the luxury of denying responsibility for his own addiction.[25] According to the logic of this episode, that is, one part of the self watches in horror as a second part, innocent but incapable of proving as much, is tried, found guilty, and punished by "inexorable officials."

As mid-nineteenth-century readers of "Suspiria de Profundis" surely recognized, the "modern novel" from which De Quincey claims to have taken this incident, if indeed it existed at all, must have been a Gothic one. Especially remarkable about the appearance of generically Gothic thematic materials in "Suspiria" is that the displacement which is for Gothic novelists themselves a more or less deliberate and cultivated exoticism, here—and also in *Confessions*—provides De Quincey with the ability to represent a moment of deeply personal importance. It is not just the familiar *frisson* of Gothic horror that serves De Quincey's needs. The particularities of the genre's concerns with sexuality, persecution, monastic Catholicism, and Continental depravity provide a narrative within which De Quincey can suitably place the story of his unconquerable addiction: the narrative of an innocent female relentlessly tormented by an unjust—and un-English—authority. In effect, what is at first described as an essentially private moment is finally translated into the arena of the nation. At the end of this passage, addiction is no longer simply a failure of will on the part of the addict; on the contrary, it takes place at the intersection of the powerful, and powerfully social, forces of gender, politics, religion, and nationality. Thus, the rather surprising analogy suggested by the details of the episode—its monastic setting, the baleful presence of the Inquisition, live burial as punishment for a crime that could be sexual, heretical, or both—is that being an Englishman subject to an unconquerable opium addiction is like being the innocent, female, and probably Protestant victim of Catholic religious persecution.

In this passage, the foreign threat of opium addiction takes a shape familiar from Gothic novels of the 1790s: a lurid, irrational, Continental malevolence. Increasingly for De Quincey, though, addiction will be drained of this resonance; in place of the Continent, the East will appear—a far more likely persecutor, if we recall opium's association with the Orient. As the dreams and visions reported at the end of *Confessions* indicate, De Quincey conducts an Orientalization of the Gothic. The most significant instance of this Orientalization occurs in his essays on the Opium Wars with China—essays that constitute, at the same time, a gothicization of the Orient. A similar representation of persecution appears in both Continental and Oriental versions of the tale. As in "Suspiria de Profundis," a tableau of victimization is narrativized and, in the process, translated from a "male" to a "female" genre. Despite such similarity, with this Orientalization De Quincey enters a larger arena and plays, as it were, for higher stakes. From providing a framework for the expression of personal dependence, the Gothic opens up to convey a sense of national peril. Victimization comes to characterize not simply the autobiographical subject, but the English nation itself.

Before turning to the Opium Wars, it will be useful to consider briefly the episode in *Confessions* that immediately precedes the opium dreams: De Quincey's encounter with the Malay, one of a very few moments in the text in which the autobiographer is victor rather than victim. Just before relating his visions he describes being called down from his upstairs study (in Dove Cottage) to meet an unexpected and inexplicable visitor. He descends to find his servant, Barbara Lewthwaite, and a neighborhood child confronting a Malay. Characteristically, the confrontation is first rendered as a tableau, De Quincey himself arranging his subjects and embellishing the details of their appearance:

A more striking picture there could not be imagined, than the beautiful English face of the girl, and its exquisite fairness, together with her erect and independent attitude, contrasted with the sallow and bilious skin of the Malay, enamelled or veneered with mahogany, by marine air, his small, fierce, restless eyes, thin lips, slavish gestures and adorations. Half-hidden by the ferocious-looking Malay, was a little child from a neighboring cottage who had crept in after him, and was now in the act of reverting its head, and gazing upwards at the turban and the fiery eyes beneath it, whilst with one hand he caught at the dress of the young woman for protection. (1822, 91)

Figure 1.   William Mulready, *Train Up a Child in the Way He Should Go; and When He Is Old He Will Not Depart from It.* 1841–53. Oil on panel, 25" × 30". © The Forbes Magazine Collection, New York.

In this account, De Quincey is neither feminized victim nor helpless on-looker. The potential for the victimization of a woman is present—the contrast between Barbara Lewthwaite's "exquisite fairness" and the Malay's "mahogany" skin and "fierce, restless eyes" seems deliberately provocative, and the presence of a English child adds still more tension to an already fraught scene—but De Quincey has this potentiality firmly in hand. His meticulous presentation of the encounter arrests its forward motion and so assures his distance from and control over events. The autobiographer's narration veers into a painterly stop-time, lingering with mingled interest and fear over a scene in which the oceanic distances between England and the Orient have suddenly collapsed.

Some two decades later, the academician William Mulready rendered a tableau remarkably similar to this one as an actual painting. *Train Up a Child in the Way He Should Go; and When He Is Old He Will Not Depart from It* (1841;

repainted 1851, 1853) depicts three very white figures—presumably an English child and two Englishwomen—encountering three lascars on a rural path framed by dark vegetation and towering cliffs (see Figure 1).[26] One of the lascars makes a gesture of entreaty, and the two women encourage the child to place money into his outstretched hand. The title of the painting demands that we read it as a kind of pictorial conduct book for would-be parents: the child receives a lesson in the virtues of charity, the reluctance he feels in risking contact with the lascar only strengthening the effect of the lesson insofar as it is a reluctance that can be overcome. But *Train Up a Child* is particularly charged because of the way in which it approaches—but, as it were, holds in suspension—the myth of a dark man raping a white woman, a myth to which the Gothic was instrumental in giving currency.[27] In accounting for the curious sexualization of this scene, Peter Stallybrass observes that "it is the lascar's hand, in the center of the painting, which breaks the stark division of black from white, male from female, and if it is reaching out to receive the child's gift, it is at the same time turned palm up immediately beneath the breast of the woman on the right."[28]

The threat encoded in *Train Up a Child* is a threat constantly looming but permanently deferred: if the painting implies the before and after of narrative movement, it need not—indeed cannot—depart from the undecidable moment of its present. Like Mulready's painting, De Quincey's account of the appearance of the Malay raises the specter of rape across racial and national boundaries. But autobiography, unlike painting, cannot finally evade the necessity to narrate. The episode proceeds, and De Quincey defuses the horrible possibility of victimization that his tableau suggests by turning to language. With a pretended fluency in eastern tongues, he manages to lord it over both Malay and servant: "I addressed him [the Malay] in some lines from the Iliad. . . . He worshipped me in the most devout manner, and replied in what I suppose was Malay. In this way I saved my reputation with my neighbours: for the Malay had no means of betraying the secret" (1822, 91). The Incommunicable, elsewhere the most unbearable of human afflictions, here provides the opportunity to assert dominance over Malay, servant, and neighbors alike. The inability to explain oneself, earlier compared to lying down helpless before a lion, is surmounted by transforming a babel of mutually unintelligible languages—English, Malay, Homeric Greek—into an occasion for triumph.[29]

Subsequently, however, the triumphant self is refused and reconstituted as the persecuted self. The Malay returns, not as Oriental dupe, but as an endlessly recurring and dizzyingly polymorphous series of Orientalist nightmares: "This Malay . . . fastened afterwards upon my dreams, and brought other Malays with him worse than himself, that 'ran a-muck' at me, and led me into a world of troubles" (1822, 92). We may glimpse in this reversal the strategic value of a Gothic narrative of victimization. By inverting his relation with the Malay so that he is victim rather than persecutor, De Quincey effectively disavows his own power—just as, in the dream recounted in "Suspiria de Profundis," he disavows responsibility for addiction. A similar strategy of disavowal characterizes English accounts of the Opium Wars. In those accounts, military action is required, not to impose the will of England on China by opening its markets by force of arms, but to protect a weak nation from the inevitability of Chinese aggression.

> *I know not whether others share in my feelings on this point; but I have often thought that if I were compelled to forego England, and to live in China, and among Chinese manners and modes of life and scenery, I should go mad.*
>
> DE QUINCEY, *Confessions*

It is a peculiarly sharp irony of history that in 1821, the year in which *Confessions of an English Opium-Eater* appeared in serial form in the *London Magazine,* the rulers of China made their first significant effort to stop the importation of opium into their country. Chinese who sold the drug were arrested and imprisoned or exiled, the export of tea was shut down for some months, and a few British ships were seized temporarily by the Chinese authorities. That the Chinese should have turned immediately to the tea trade reveals that the Chinese addiction was tied to a British one: for many years, China served as a supplier of tea, a commodity that was, by the early nineteenth century, essential to Britain's social well-being. (One participant in the First Opium War refers to tea as "that fragrant herb, become now among us Britons almost a necessary of life."[30]) The large and ever-increasing British demand for tea—which only the Chinese knew how to grow and prepare—occasioned a severe trade imbalance that, because the British produced no goods the Chinese would accept in exchange, Britain was forced to make up in silver.[31]

To alter the situation and put a stop to the flow of silver out of Britain, an officially illegal but in fact state-sanctioned trade in opium was instituted. According to Maurice Collis (who is perhaps too easily convinced of Chinese complicity): "For a very long time the East India Company had sought to find a staple to send to China. But the Chinese had so little use for any of the commodities offered and made their demand for opium so clear that it became inevitable that it would be satisfied."[32] Grown in the poppy fields of British-held Bengal or bought in Turkey, opium was shipped to the South China coast, where it was sold by the chest to Chinese merchants who, in turn, sold it directly to Chinese consumers. Once rare in China, the recreational use of opium spread rapidly and widely—due largely to aggressive marketing by

British and American smugglers, who introduced the drug to more and more remote areas of the country. So successful was this trade that the imbalance between Britain and China was reversed in a relatively brief period. China, once an exporter of tea and an importer of silver, soon found itself exporting silver and importing opium.[33] The effects on Chinese society were disastrous: the growing number of opium addicts disrupted both the workings of the national economy and the effective functioning of the state.[34]

The 1821 attempt by the Chinese to repair such disruption by putting an end to the importation of opium had little effect. In fact, trade in opium seems only to have become more firmly entrenched. As Beeching notes in *The Chinese Opium Wars:* "Chinese harassment continued for two years [after 1821]. . . . The easy-going days were over; but the Chinese addicts were unable to stop their craving for the drug. The trade became more furtive but it increased enormously; by 1835 the number of Chinese opium addicts was estimated at two million."[35] By the late 1830s the problem had grown more serious still, and the Chinese again decided to take action. An imperial statute forbidding the trade in and consumption of opium was issued in 1839.[36] Arrests were made—as in 1821, primarily of Chinese. This time, however, opium was confiscated from British traders. The drug continued to be sold, though, until an order was given by Lin Ze-xu, High Commissioner of Port Affairs, to close Canton entirely to British trade.[37] Lin Ze-xu's action gave the British an excuse to conduct a full-scale war on the Chinese, a war now known as the First Opium War (1839–42). British troops, many of them sepoys, defeated Chinese imperial troops in a series of battles that came to an end in 1842 with the capture of Shanghai and the siege of Nanjing. The Treaty of Nanjing was ratified in 1843; it ceded Hong Kong to Britain and named five ports—Canton, Shanghai, Ningbo, Amoy, and Fuzhou—"treaty ports" in which foreigners would be allowed to live and trade.[38] The issue of opium, the ostensible cause of the war, remained unsettled; it continued to touch off disagreements that would result, in 1856, in yet another Opium War.[39]

De Quincey, describing how his encounter with a destitute Malay lost in England's Lake District gave rise to years of terrifying visions, asserts that this Malay "brought other Malays with him worse than himself, that 'ran a-muck' at me, and led me into a world of troubles" (1822 92). "A-muck," which derives from the Malay adjective "amoq," in English usage frequently appears in the phrase De Quincey employs, "to run a-muck," meaning "to run viciously, mad, frenzied for blood." The *Oxford English Dictionary* cites Andrew Marvell's *The Rehearsal Transprosd* (1672) as the earliest instance of this usage: "Like a raging Indian he runs a mucke (as they cal it there) stabbing every man he meets." Subsequent examples establish that the phrase was standard among British commentators on the East. Indeed, it seems to have been something like an Orientalist cliché.

Nonetheless, that this phrase should appear frequently in accounts of the Opium Wars is suggestive. Arthur Cunynghame, in *The Opium War: Being Recollections of Service in China* (1845), claims to have witnessed a scene in Singapore in which Malays, "maddened by bad fortune [at gambling], losing all command over themselves and their actions, committed the most extravagant excesses, stabbing and maiming all whom chance threw in their way, during which fits of excitement they were described as having 'run-a-muck.'"[40] J. Elliot Bingham, in his *Narrative of the Expedition to China* (1843), opines:

> The Malays, like the Chinese, have a remarkable similarity of feature; in one you behold the face of the whole nation. If excited by jealousy, or other causes, they are most cunning and revengeful, and when 'running a muck,' stab all whom they meet with their kreeses [daggers with ridged, serpentine blades], which are said to be poisoned with the juice of the upas tree.[41]

These comments are made toward the beginning of these two participants' accounts of the First Opium War, separate from their opinions on the war itself. Nevertheless, the comments are striking insofar as they mirror the logic of Britain's excuse for war—that the Chinese empire had itself "run amuck," brutally and rashly destroying British interests, and that it was likely to do so again unless stopped. The fullest development of this logic was undertaken by none other than the English opium-eater, Thomas De Quincey.

Peter Ward Fay, in *The Opium War 1840–1842*, writes of a fever that, in 1842, struck British troops stationed in the south of China: "Among the dead in Hongkong [*sic*] was young Horatio De Quincey. . . . It was as close as his father, England's most celebrated opium eater, would get to the war that bore in a sense his name."[42] De Quincey's second son Horatio did indeed die of fever while stationed near Canton; yet his death was by no means the closest that his father would get to the Opium Wars. On the contrary, De Quincey was an active propagandist for the British cause from the start. As David Masson, the editor of the *Collected Writings*, notes: "China, as known to him by his readings, had always been an object of his special abomination."[43] One of the ways in which he gave vent to this "special abomination" was by devoting an immense amount of time and effort to writing up and disseminating his ideas on the subject of Britain's proper relation to China during the periods leading up to the First and Second Opium Wars. In these writings, the Gothic tropes that in *Confessions* were taken inward and used to represent a life are projected outward and made to serve as an excuse for war—and, finally, as a representation of what it means to be English.[44] The feminized victim of senseless aggression remains, but she is now not De Quincey's sister Elizabeth, nor his London savior Ann, nor even De Quincey himself, but that "mighty mother in Europe," England ("Opium Question," 14:180).

The first of De Quincey's articles on China, "The Opium Question with China in 1840," appeared in *Blackwood's Magazine*.[45] Its author's sentiments as to Britain's proper policy are clear from the outset:

> Very fit it is that so arrogant a people [that is, the Chinese] should be brought to their senses; and notorious it is that in Eastern lands no appeal to the sense of justice will ever be made available which does not speak through their fears. . . . By all means, thump them well: it is your only chance—it is the only logic which penetrates the fog of so conceited a people. ("Opium Question," 175)

It is war that De Quincey wants, and in the event the British government did not disappoint him. This bellicose position—and the estimate of the Chinese that lies behind it—is close to that of those who had most to gain from a war, the opium traders themselves. Two years earlier, in 1838, James Matheson (a trader with Jardine, Matheson & Co., a prosperous opium smuggling concern founded in 1828) had published an anti-Chinese tract entitled *The Present Position and Future Prospects of the China Trade*. Matheson, too, finds a rationale for British aggression in the Chinese character, which he describes as marked by a "marvellous degree of imbecility and avarice, conceit and blasphemy."[46]

Matheson and other opium traders, for reasons of their own, were determined to play down the dangers of war. Typically, they represented the Chinese military as ludicrously inept, as in the following excerpt from an anonymous 1836 essay in *The Chinese Repository:* "What terms can convey an adequate idea of the monstrous burlesque which the imperial navy presents to our astonished gaze? Powerless beyond the power of description to ridicule or portray, yet set forth with all the braggadocio and pretence for which the Chinese are so famous."[47] De Quincey, however, readily admits to the difficulties posed by a Chinese campaign. In fact, the vulnerability of the English and the inviolability of the Chinese obsess him. The very characteristics of China that might be taken as disadvantageous in war, the supposed torpor and barbarism of the "vast callous hulk of the Chinese Empire," provide proof against invasion: "It is defended by its essential non-irritability" ("Opium Question," 176). England, by contrast, is "scattered and exposed": "We are to be reached by a thousand wounds, in thousands of outlying extremities; the very outposts of civilization are held by Englishmen, everywhere maintaining a reserve of reliance upon the mighty mother in Europe" ("Opium Question," 180). This comparison between the two nations, with its suggestion of a hulking evil that endangers the "mother in Europe" by threatening the Englishmen who represent her abroad, maps the Gothic situation of threatened femininity onto the realm of international politics.[48] The invocation of that "mighty mother," England, which is at once a refuge and somehow as "scattered and exposed" as its colonists, recalls the nexus of frailty, family, and opaque but urgent danger so prevalent in *Confessions*.[49] Victimization reappears in "The Opium Question with China in 1840"; it does so, however, not as an event that befalls a narrator or his "sisters" but as the fate of England itself.

Two crucial passages in the essay feature weak England threatened by malicious and powerful China. The first involves abasement and victimized women by way of a meditation on the *kotou*, the ritual act of kneeling and touching the head to the floor in order to show homage. On the first British mission to China, in 1793, Lord Macartney refused to *kotou* before the Emperor, shocking the Chinese but setting a precedent that would be followed in subsequent missions to China from the British Crown.[50] For De Quincey, this refusal is of the utmost significance:

> Some of our anti-national scribblers at home . . . insisted upon it, that our English ambassador ought to have performed the *kotou*. . . . Had Lord Amherst [of the second British mission, 1816] submitted to such a degradation, the next thing would have been a requisition from the English Factory of beautiful English women, according to a fixed description, as annual presents to the Emperor. ("Opium Question," 184)

The leap in logic here is so immense as to be vertiginous: an Englishman abasing himself before a foreign ruler leads immediately ("the next thing") to the exportation of Englishwomen made to order for the Chinese Emperor's delectation. In light of De Quincey's other writings, though, such a leap is also predictable. To show weakness once, to lie down before the lion of the Incommunicable or to allow the Malay to enter into your dreams, is to ensure the playing out of the Gothic plot on the instant.

Even without the *kotou*, atrocities against the defenseless are certain to occur when China is involved. A second passage in the essay in which England stands looking on as China acts the tormentor involves the narration of an incident that took place in 1784. As De Quincey tells it, a British ship at port in China, the *Lady Hughes* (in this context, a name significant in itself), fired a salute that accidentally struck and killed a Chinese. Chinese authorities demanded that the man who had fired the round, an aged Portuguese gunner, be turned over to them for punishment. The British complied, apparently with the intention of securing his release after a short time, but the gunner was hanged before they could get him back ("Opium Question," 187–89).[51] For De Quincey, this incident emblematizes the situation of England victimized by the foreign. Importantly, it also serves as an indication of the threat of contamination posed by the Chinese, an example of "the atrocities which . . . even free-born Britons can commit, and which, under their accursed system of law, the Chinese can exact" ("Opium Question," 189). Just as in *Confessions* the greatest terror of opium resides in its ability to compromise the identity of its user, so in "The Opium Question with China in 1840," the worst aspect of Chinese malevolence is that it will somehow be communicated to Westerners who come into contact with "this wicked nation" (187). What is more, as long as contact with China is maintained there can be no respite from incidents such as that involving the *Lady Hughes:* "The same scenes are eternally impending" (189).[52]

This certainty of the repetition of Chinese outrages is what legitimizes, in advance, the war on China. And, lest the fate of a Portuguese gunner in the eighteenth century seem weak as a demonstration of what might occur should the British fail to "thump" China in 1840, De Quincey quickly transforms this story into one of more awful torment. The recounting of an atrocity committed in the past provides the impetus for prophesying future atrocities:

> And, if some colonial ship freighted with immigrants, or some packet with passengers, should be driven out of her course, and touch at a Chinese port, as sure as we live some horrid record will convulse us all with the intelligence that our brave countrymen, our gentle countrywomen and their innocent children, have been subjected to the torture by this accursed state. ("Opium Question," 193–94)

The case of a single man executed for killing a Chinese metamorphoses into a shipload of men, women, and children tormented by China simply for being English and helpless. The verb tense in the passage, which hovers between future perfect and past perfect, is indicative: these Chinese outrages belong to the future; at the same time, they are so certain that the only appropriate way to describe them is as if they have already happened, as if innocent passengers "have been subjected to the torture."

De Quincey's involvement with China did not end with the ratification of the Treaty of Nanjing in 1843. It flared up again with the advent of renewed hostilities in 1857. In that year he wrote no fewer than three essays on China for James Hogg's *Titan.* As Hogg notes, De Quincey even went to the trouble of collecting the first two of these and reissuing them, together with prefatory material and a postscript, as a pamphlet of 152 pages in length.[53] The third, uncollected essay, "The Chinese Question in 1857," was reprinted in the *Collected Writings.* It repeats—compulsively, almost deliriously—the essay of 1840 in both sentiment and content, differing only in that what was anger has now risen to hysteria: "In the case of China this apostrophe—*The nations hate thee!*—would pass by acclamation, without needing the formality of a vote" (14:349). The *kotou* reappears, and this time the consequences of performing it are even more severe than before: De Quincey goes so far as to assert that the Opium Wars came about because a Russian ambassador to China foolishly agreed to *kotou* before the Emperor early in the eighteenth century (364). The story of the gunner of the *Lady Hughes* is repeated in full—again, as an example of what to expect from the Chinese (366–67).[54] Finally, there is, again, an impending Chinese violation, for the Chinese will assuredly "repeat their atrocious inso- lences as often as opportunities offer" (350).

In the dream-fugue at the end of "The English Mail-Coach," the proclama- tion of English national triumph at Waterloo involves the death of a girl. Earlier sections of the essay provide a local explanation for the necessity of this death, as well as for De Quincey's position as sympathetic but helpless onlooker: the vision combines, in the form of what De Quincey called an "involute," his many coach rides during the Napoleonic Wars with an inci- dent in which a coach on which he was traveling nearly destroyed a carriage carrying a young man and woman. Yet this explanation does little to account for the incessant recurrence of women in danger not only in "The English Mail-Coach" but in De Quincey's writings as a whole. The episode echoes and is echoed by many others: the death of Elizabeth, the loss of Ann, De Quincey's own self-representations as a feminized pariah. In *Confessions,* the result of this attention to victimization is the construction of a self whose most salient characteristic is its openness to threat. Moreover, that threat takes the shape of the foreign: literally, opium; figuratively, in the dream- scape of the visions to which opium gives rise, the East and its corruptions.

If the intent of autobiography is to render visible a distinct self, to repre- sent or construct a subjectivity that will appear unique, De Quinceyan auto- biography achieves this end by continually confronting the possibility of the complete failure of such a project.[55] The "English Opium-Eater" announced in the title of *Confessions* is a being constantly subject to disintegration into some Other because of his use of opium; yet the possibility of such contam- ination is what makes him who he is. The fact that opium is actually imbibed renders this threat particularly visceral: addiction to the drug in this sense amounts to a literal, physical dependence on the foreign. Gothic plotting provides a way to portray that dependence as a narrative of victimization, of a helpless woman persecuted by an invincible enemy.[56]

This narrative functions to represent the autobiographical subject, but it is also transposed into the realm of international relations in order to repre- sent the English nation. In De Quincey's writings on the Opium Wars, England takes the place of the feminized victim and China assumes the role of persecutor. But the emphasis De Quincey places, not just on threat but also on contamination, provides a crucial nuance to an otherwise predictable story. In the Malay dreams at the end of *Confessions,* the consequence of dependence on opium is a polluted, compromised self. In the context of the Opium Wars, an identical pollution threatens the English nation. The agent of this national contamination, though, is not opium but tea—without which, De Quincey writes in "The English in China," "the social life of England would receive a deadly wound."[57] And while drinking tea has been naturalized (or Anglicized) in a way that eating opium has not—witness the absurd redundancy of any *Confessions of an English Tea-Drinker*—the very strength of the connection between England and tea underscores English dependence on China, which for much of the nineteenth century was the primary source of the nation's national beverage. As Brian Inglis notes of the First Opium War, "In a sense, it was really the Tea War."[58]

De Quincey's writings on the Opium Wars embrace rather than deny that dependence, strategically parlaying the contamination and fragility it implies into a definition of English nationality: Englishness amounts to frailty, openness to attack. Such frailty is symbolically constitutive: just as it provides De Quincey with an autobiographical subjectivity, it provides England with a national identity. The workings of this logic explain the necessity of a girl's death beneath the wheels of the coach that bears the news of "*Waterloo and Recovered Christendom!*": the nation, in making itself, must endanger itself— which it can do most convincingly by endangering what is understood to be at once its weakest and its most representative citizen.

One source for this strangely catastrophic construction of self and nation is specific to De Quincey and has to do with his deep conviction of human existence as constituted by pain and suffering. Yet, in the context of imperialist nation-making, such a conviction has strategic value. Nigel Leask has noted that, although apparently innocent, De Quincey's tendency to identify with the victim is "very far from being hostile to imperialism."[59] In the case of England's relation to China, the sense of threat that such an identification enabled worked to generate, by way of response, a war of conquest. The construction of a victimized identity at the national level, that is, provided the most powerful nation in the world with a rationale for aggression based, paradoxically, on a sense of itself as the beleaguered heroine of Gothic romance.[60]

4

Victorian Highs

Detection, Drugs, and Empire

Marty Roth

The war with China has begun, and already several hundred Chinese have been murdered by our cruisers, because the government of China will not allow us to poison its subjects; in which poisoning, it appears, we have obtained a vested right. An expedition is fitting out at Plymouth to "destroy Canton if necessary"; and Pekin also, it appears, if the Emperor "does not do us justice." Was there ever such an atrocious proceeding? It is enough to raise up all Asia to "do justice" on the English, for their centuries of crime, misrule and oppression in the East.

—J. J. DARLING, *Tait's Edinburgh Magazine*, March 1840

Our trouble is that we drink too much tea. I see in this the slow revenge of the Orient, which has diverted the Yellow River down our throats.

—J. B. PRIESTLEY, *Observer*, May 1949

The early history of detective fiction is saturated with narcotic drugs. Edgar Allan Poe was an opium and Wilkie Collins a laudanum addict, and opium circulates through *The Moonstone*. Charles Dickens's *Mystery of Edwin Drood* begins in an East End opium den, and Arthur Conan Doyle's "Man with the Twisted Lip" ends in one. As for other drugs that were soon to become illicit, Count Zaleski, M. P. Shiel's dandified detective, smokes hashish cigarettes: the narrator of "The House of Orven" reports that "the air was heavy with the scented odor of . . . the fumes of the narcotic *cannabis sativa* . . . in which I knew it to be the habit of my friend to assuage himself."[1] And in *The Sign of Four* Sherlock Holmes injects himself with morphine or cocaine three times a day.[2] In an American silent film of 1916 entitled *The Mystery of the Leaping Fish*, even that paragon of athletic health, Douglas Fairbanks, played the "world's greatest scientific detective," a character named "Coke Ennyday" who sticks a needle into some part of his body every thirty seconds.

Conan Doyle's "The Man with the Twisted Lip" is a disjointed tale that seeks to implicate almost all of its characters in addiction. It begins as a different kind of case, a story about a doctor and his patient: a frantic wife pleads with Dr. Watson to find her husband, an opium addict, and Watson finds him where he may well belong, in an opium den in the "furthest east of the city."[3] There he also finds an Asian-looking addict who turns out to be Holmes in disguise, because Holmes is himself looking for a possible third addict, Neville St. Clair, a professional man who was seen by *his* wife apparently threatened by violence at an upper window of this very opium den.

Detectives might have taken drugs to calm or to stimulate their highly wrought and finely tuned nervous systems in what was early recognized as an anxious profession. Holmes "only turned to the drug as a protest against the monotony of existence when cases were scanty and the papers uninteresting."[4] And a female detective of 1917 is confronted by her Watson: "'So you have fallen back on the cola stimulant again, Miss Mack?' She nodded glumly, and perversely slipped into her mouth another of the dark brown berries, on which I have known her to keep up for forty-eight hours without sleep and almost without food."[5] By contrast, they might have done drugs as poets who dreamed the solutions to their mysteries, like Poe's detective C. Auguste Dupin. Prince Zaleski smokes hashish because he is a turn-of-the-century aesthete and decadent—"He lay back on his couch, volumed in a Turkish *beneesh,* and listened to me . . . with woven fingers, and the pale inverted eyes of old anchorites and astrologers"—and the aesthete, we have often been told, is one of the more likely templates for the detective.[6] So the Sherlock Holmes who takes cocaine also reads "old black-letter" volumes, plays Mendelssohn *lieder* on the violin, quotes Goethe and Jean Paul and speaks "on miracle plays, medieval pottery," and "the Buddhism of Ceylon."[7]

Just as early detective fiction is deeply, perhaps constitutively, steeped in drugs, it is also associated with empire, and this connection *is* constitutive. In this fiction, crime is the dark side of conquest and imperial rule returning to pollute the metropolitan homeland. At the very beginning of the genre stands the story of a gigantic ourang-outang taken to Paris from the Indian Archipelago that commits a hideous crime while attempting to imitate its white master shaving. The beast/criminal of Poe's "Murders in the Rue Morgue" penetrates the security of a home and brutally kills a mother and daughter.

The Moonstone is a novel that is both filled with opium and fixated on its connection with treasure from India:

> Here was our quiet English house suddenly invaded by a devilish Indian Diamond. . . . Who ever heard the like of it—in the nineteenth century, mind; in an age of progress, and in a country which rejoices in the blessings of the British constitution?[8]

Collins's novel begins by invoking both the Sepoy Mutiny of 1857 and the presentation to Victoria of the legendary Koh-i-Noor diamond that had been won as booty in the Anglo-Sikh wars of 1848–49. "Imagine then," writes a critic, Ashish Roy, "after this inaugural of formal imperial authority, the provocation of a tale mired in bloodshed for which an English army officer, not a native soldier, is culpable. Imagine, too, the further provocation of linking that culpability to the great matriarch herself, as the final paragraph of Collin's Preface explicitly does."[9]

Invasion from the colonies took a variety of forms in eighteenth- and nineteenth-century British writing, like "the rage for 'Chinoiserie' in fashionable decor, Chinese gardens on the best estates," or "Byron and Southey's Oriental Tales on the bookshelves of those in the know."[10] A sinister form of invasion was the persistent mythology of colonial acquisition as a disease or drug infecting the metropolis. Ezra Jennings, the English opium-eater of *The Moonstone*, is dying of a disease that is implicitly attributed to "the mixture of some foreign race in his English blood."[11] In the mid-nineteenth century, colonial invasion literally took the form of Oriental drugs that disrupted metropolitan life by overstimulating or debilitating it, by causing its citizens either to run amok or to become immobilized. Detective fictions are primary evidence for such anxiety of empire: both *Edwin Drood* and "The Man with the Twisted Lip" are set in the East End of London, a place that, according to Barry Milligan, was configured "as a miniature Orient within the capital of the empire."[12] In his *Tales of Chinatown*, Sax Rohmer writes:

> Yet here [Limehouse] lies a secret quarter, as secret and as strange, in its smaller way, as its parent in China which is called the Purple Forbidden City . . . . there was nothing which could have told the visitor that he had crossed the border line dividing West from East and was now in an Oriental town.[13]

English opium-smokers were even Orientalized by narcotic use; for Dickens's John Jasper, the opium den is charged with "contagion" and an "unclean spirit of imitation."[14] Watson's patient has a "yellow pasty face, drooping lids and pin-point pupils," and Holmes recreates the Orient at the St. Clair house as he

> wandered about the room collecting pillows from his bed, and cushions from the sofa and armchairs. With these he constructed a sort of Eastern divan, upon which he perched himself cross-legged, with an ounce of shag tobacco and a box of matches laid out in front of him. In the dim light of the lamp I saw him sitting there, an old brier pipe between his lips, his eyes fixed vacantly upon the corner of the ceiling, the blue smoke curling up from him.[15]

Drugs in detective fiction are obvious symptoms of this invasion from the colonies, and yet the connection between the drugs and imperial adventure is haphazard.[16] Drug-taking is a Western, not an Eastern phenomenon: the opium in *The Moonstone* is firmly located within the context of Western medicine, and in the Holmes tale Isa Whitney began to smoke opium at college in imitation of Thomas De Quincey. Other stories, however, tell us that drugs and the Orient are intimately connected. Although it is not a detective story, one of Poe's drug tales is crucial to this connection. "A Tale of the Ragged Mountains" features a morphine addict named Augustus Bedloe, a "singularly tall," thin, stooping man of absolutely bloodless complexion and "abnormally large" eyes.[17] As with most middle-class Western addicts in the nineteenth century, his addiction is rooted in practices of medical analgesia: because of extreme suffering from neuralgia, his attending physician, Dr. Templeton, treats him with the morphine, which he swallows "in great quantity" every morning before he goes out alone. The anecdote in the tale occurs on a day when the morphine imbued "all the external world with an intensity of interest" that could be likened to a hallucination (942–43). Bedloe walks into the Ragged Mountains of Virginia and out into Benares, India, at the time of the insurrection of Cheyte Singh in 1780, and he observes the death of a British officer named Oldeb. Soon after, back in Virginia, Bedloe also dies. The miraculous event at the center of the tale is explained as a hallucination (rather than an instance of metempsychosis), induced by the extraordinary mesmeric rapport between Bedloe and Templeton, who had also been Oldeb's close friend and was writing an account of the latter's death in his journal on the morning of the adventure. Such an explanation is structurally debilitating, since it leaves both the drug and the Indian adventure outside the meaning of the tale.

Why India? Partly because the tale operates through a feeble pun: it is set "Upon a warm, misty day, towards the close of November . . . during the strange *interregnum* of the seasons which in America is termed the Indian Summer" (942). For the rest, the great virtue of Poe's borrowing from Thomas Babington Macaulay's essay on Warren Hastings is that it takes us back to a moment in Anglo-Asian relations that grounds the connection between the drug and the colony. The function of drugs in Poe's tale, and in Dickens's *Edwin Drood,* is to take us back to the Orient: *Drood* opens to an opium vision of a clash of cymbals, as the "Sultan goes by to his palace in long procession. Ten thousand scimitars flash in the sunlight, and thrice ten thousand dancing-girls strew flowers. Then, follow white elephants caparisoned in countless gorgeous colors" (1). Even when no specific topography is alluded to, the narcotic dream visions of De Quincey, Théophile Gautier, and others suggest Oriental associations. Samuel Taylor Coleridge, for example, wrote to the Reverend George Coleridge that "Laudanum gave me repose, not sleep; but you, I believe, know how divine that repose is, what a spot of enchantment, a green spot of fountain and flowers and trees in the very heart of a waste of sands."[18] Thomas Burke, the author of East End opium tales, claimed that "As the drug is of Oriental earth, so it works upon brain and eye in Oriental imagery."[19]

Detective fiction, then, begins high on drugs and fully informed by imperial anxiety. By the 1920s, these associations have disappeared. Is there a British crime in the nineteenth century that could be imagined to impose such constraints on a new branch of fiction, so much so that it could even be considered the "crime" of detective fiction? Ashish Roy, remember, reads Collins's preface to *The Moonstone* as a confession of English culpability. If we choose to understand detective fiction as a collective Anglo-Saxon fantasy formed in reaction to some originating event, the Anglo-Chinese Opium War(s) of 1839 to 1860 would be the prime suspect.

After "the great debriefing that has accompanied the dismantling of the British empire," Marek Kohn writes, the opium wars are left as "the only episode in imperial history that is generally seen as unambiguously wicked."[20] At the time, William Gladstone said of them that "a war more unjust in its origins, a war more calculated to cover this country with permanent disgrace, I do not know, and have not read of."[21] In a letter to the American Congress in 1840, Caleb Cushing, the U.S. commissioner to China, described it as a war motivated by "base cupidity," which aimed "to coerce the Chinese by force of arms to submit to be poisoned."[22] The war was fought to protect the British trade in opium, which was grown in India and sold in China, because there was no other way for England to balance its trade payments except by creating a population of addicts and then catering to their desire. "The occasion of this outbreak," Karl Marx wrote in 1853, "has unquestionably been afforded by the English cannon forcing upon China that soporific drug called opium."[23]

England imported enormous amounts of tea from China, for by the nineteenth century tea had become England's drug of choice, relieving the British of the necessity of drinking ale in the morning. "What a curious thing it was," Leigh Hunt wrote, "that all of a sudden the remotest nation of the East, otherwise unknown, and foreign to all our habits, should convey to us a domestic custom which changed the face of our morning refreshments."[24] By the early 1800s, the new drink had become so popular that annual consumption amounted to 12,000,000 pounds.[25] Samuel Johnson confessed that he was a "hardened and shameless Tea-drinker . . . whose kettle has scarcely time to cool, who with Tea amuses the evening, with Tea solaces the Midnight, and with Tea welcomes the morning."[26]

The Chinese, however, had small regard for Western materials or craftsmanship; there was little they wanted to buy in return, as the Emperor Qianlong stated in a letter to King George III:

> The virtue and prestige of the Celestial Dynasty having spread far and wide, the kings of the myriad nations come by land and sea with all sorts of precious things. Consequently there is nothing we lack, as your principal envoy and others have themselves observed. We have never set much store on strange or ingenious objects, nor do we need any more of your country's manufactures.[27]

The English dependence on Chinese products was burlesqued in a letter that Commissioner Lin Tse-Hsu wrote to Queen Victoria during the hostilities: he threatened that "by cutting off the export of tea and rhubarb [the Emperor] . . . could deprive his enemies of their principal source of pleasure and their only relief from constipation."[28] Rhubarb and opium are rhyming commodities, like opium and tea, but, unlike rhubarb, opium slows intestinal action and is one of the principal antidiarrheals in the Western pharmacopia.

The solution was simple, John Keay writes in his history of the East India Company: "Redirect the Indian surplus to finance the China deficit."[29] Medical historians Virginia Berridge and Griffith Edwards put it another way: England had perfected the "technique of growing opium in India and disowning it in China."[30] The opium trade with China was a source of great individual fortunes and generated profits enough to pay a substantial part of the cost of administering England's Indian empire. As Marx wrote in a *New York Tribune* editorial in 1858, "The Indian finances of the British Government have, in fact, been made to depend not only on the opium trade with China, but on the contraband character of that trade."[31] Figures differ as to the profitability of this trade once called "the largest commerce of the time in any single commodity," but in 1838 the value of opium sold in China was estimated as the government of India's third largest source of revenue.[32]

In its conquest of India between 1729 and 1800, Britain acquired vast poppy fields in Bengal. In 1773, Warren Hastings, the governor of Bengal, took over a limited Indian opium trade and expanded it greatly: Hastings actually initiated the Anglo-Chinese opium trade by switching a consignment to Canton when war with the Dutch temporarily closed the market for opium in their East Indian colonies. By the time the company was investigated by the Crown and its monopoly ended in 1833, this operation had become too profitable to be shut down. Thereafter, the opium traffic was run as a British government enterprise, and this included raising and harvesting the crop, preparing the opium, licensing the smuggling operations, and laying out necessary bribes in China.[33]

When the Chinese government tried to enforce its prohibition against opium smuggling, Britain treated this as a provocation and declared war against a militarily enfeebled power. In addition to the human cost of the addiction, the military cost to the Chinese was extremely high: in the Battle of Chapu, for example, the casualties were 1,200 to 1,500 Chinese and 9 British.[34]

The wars were fought over opium, but that fact was rarely mentioned in the attendant discourse of war and diplomacy; the Treaty of Nanking that ended the first Opium War does not even mention the drug.[35] According to Nathan Allen, the real *cause* of all these troubles—the opium trade—was as much as possible kept out of view. . . . Men who had so great interests at stake, whose characters also were implicated, would of course employ the best talents and all possible means that money could command—writers, attorneys, and orators, to make the "worse appear the better cause."[36]

Officially, the war was fought against the kowtow, fought, as Marx phrased it, for "an alleged infringement of the fanciful code of diplomatic etiquette." The demand that free-born Englishmen prostrate themselves to the Emperor of China as a condition of doing trade with him was declared insupportable, a dire violation of the national character. De Quincey declared that if Lord Amherst had made kowtow, "the next thing would have been a requisition from the English Factory of beautiful English women, according to a fixed description, as annual presents to the Emperor."[37]

Lord Amherst refused to kowtow, feeling sure that the Chinese saw "that superiority which Englishmen, wherever they go, cannot conceal."[38] The Opium Wars were supposedly fought to repudiate the Chinese assumption of cultural superiority. The kowtow alibi may have been put in place by the British to obscure the immorality of the opium trade, but it was more a sign of similarity than otherness between the two cultures: it betokened a recognition that China had preempted the Manichean epistemology of the West just as the West was completing its own racist global project. By referring to all Westerners indiscriminately as "barbarians," the Chinese mocked Britain's own linguistic practices: "In various [Chinese] documents the Western 'barbarians' are described as cunning and malicious, impatient and without understanding of values, inconstant, insatiable, avaricious, thinking only of profit and . . . inscrutable."[39]

The images of immigrant Chinese and opium dens in Victorian and Edwardian fiction should have been at least double-edged, since a vocal temperance opposition in England made it clear at the time that the English were contaminating the Chinese, not the other way around. Nevertheless, in a new genre of popular fiction, China invaded England through the East End opium den and proceeded to turn its citizens into addicts. The imperial adventure was inverted, and the Anglo-Chinese opium wars were written in reverse in a corner of London. "This Chinese control of Britain would be anxiety-inducing enough," Barry Milligan writes, "even if it were limited to the marginalized population of the East End":

> But in fact the opium master's influence extends horizontally beyond the East End to more central districts of London and vertically all the way to the uppermost echelons of the empire. Besides attracting "lords and dukes and even princes and kings," one opium master claims to have been visited by no less than the Prince of Wales himself, who allegedly was moved to invite the master and his wife to come directly to the palace to "smokee pipe wi' me."[40]

That opium *went* to China, however, was hardly unknown; it had been written into one of England's master-texts: the second part of *Robinson Crusoe*, where Robinson takes a shipment of opium from the Straits of Malacca to China because it bore "a great Price among the *Chinese*."[41] By the time of Dickens's *Our Mutual Friend*, however, the direction of the traffic had been reversed in the service of ideology, as Bella imagined her Pa "going to China in that handsome three-masted ship, to bring home opium."[42]

Tea and opium were an imperial binary, a trade-off. Both are drugs but one was "civilized" and "mild," the other barbaric and strong. Both were identified with their consumers rather than their producers, so that opium that was British-produced and illicitly sold to China soon became the demonic Chinese product par excellence, and tea, which was Chinese and sold to the English, very soon came to constitute Britishness itself.

Unlike the majority of his countrymen, John Quincy Adams felt that the fuss about opium was a distraction in a civilizing mission against China that the West was bound to carry out one day or other. He was aware of another resonance between opium and tea and between the two Indian empires, the one in the east and the one in the west. In China, chests of opium were dumped into Canton harbor and become the occasion of the first Opium War. In the American colonies, chests of tea were dumped into Boston harbor and become the signal of the American War of Independence.

In the subsequent history of detective fiction, one of the first elements to undergo censorship was the connection between crime and empire. When detective fiction became a genre system in the 1920s, a relatively tight province of writing under official control, rules for writing produced by authors like S. S. Van Dine and authors' organizations like the Detective Club dictated that this link could never again be mentioned: never again might the criminal be a gigantic ourang-outang, nor might three Indians in London dog the steps of the Imperialist plunderers. Well before this "golden age" of detective fiction, however, in the later Holmes tales, Conan Doyle had ruled politics out of order. In "The Bruce-Partington Plans," Holmes asks Watson if there is anything of interest in the papers, but Watson informs us that "by anything of interest, Holmes meant anything of criminal interest. There was the news of a revolution, of a possible war, and of an impending change of Government; but these did not come within the horizon of my companion."[43] But even *The Moonstone* only teased the reader with an imperial solution. According to one recent critic, "to make the point absolutely clear that any political motives in this novel are to be understood as a disguise for something else, the culprit's corpse is discovered in the disguise of a dark-skinned East Indian sailor, only to be unmasked by the police for the [white, Western] philanderer he is."[44]

Drugs were suppressed in the text of detective fiction as they had been in the text of empire. It is fitting that opium should be present in *The*

Moonstone but unconnected to the meaning of the crime. Ashish Roy points out a moment in the novel when Rachel Verinder puts "the Indian diamond in the Indian cabinet, for the purpose of permitting two beautiful native productions to admire each other," but he wisely suggests that the two native productions locked in mutual support are actually the diamond and opium: opium is the only commodity in the imperial traffic that can justify the novel's hyperbole.[45] Opium can carry the weight of both commodities, since it really was the source of fabulous wealth, and Mark Hennelly suggests that the novel's fabulous gem is a screen for opium dreams: "When you looked down into the stone, you looked into a yellow deep that drew your eyes into it so that they saw nothing else. It seemed unfathomable . . . as the heavens themselves."[46]

In *The Moonstone,* Franklin Blake is not only acquitted of the theft of the diamond but also absolved of smoking opium. In "Twisted Lip" the crime that starts out coincidental with opium dens in London is soon detached from them. The two white men in compromising positions, both vaguely accused of opium addiction, are fully exonerated by the story's end. Both are in the opium den on *other* business: one is a private detective impersonating a drug addict in order to pursue an investigation; the other is a professional beggar who finds the den a convenient place to set up shop, while the only "true" opium addict is hustled off the scene before the story fairly begins. This is a tremendous narrative shift in a tale that is otherwise loaded with narcotics and alcohol.

In one set of rules for detective fiction by Ronald Knox, entitled "A Detective Story Decalogue," the fifth commandment reads "No Chinaman must figure in the story." Monsignor Knox (who also wrote detective stories) then told us that he did not know why this should be: "I only offer it as a fact of observation that, if you are turning over the pages of a book and come across some mention of 'the slit-like eyes of Chin Loo,' you had best put it down at once; it is bad."[47] In the reformulated genre, guilt became so subtle and unmarked as to be virtually indistinguishable from innocence. The purpose of the ongoing detective story would be to mystify guilt, to make it exquisitely fine and intricate, hard to detect, painstakingly rarified. But the guilt of smuggling opium and then covering that crime with a declaration of war is not at all hard to detect, except in the actual history of Anglo-Chinese relations. The literary crimes of the detective novel would move as far as possible from crimes of empire and crimes of class.

PART III

Demon Drink

5

The Rhetoric of Addiction

From Victorian Novels to AA

Robyn R. Warhol

The goal of this chapter is to explore the intersections among narration, subjectivity, identity, and addiction to alcohol in canonical mid-Victorian fiction and in the discourse of Alcoholics Anonymous (AA). I'm interested in continuities and discontinuities between nineteenth- and twentieth-century constructions of alcoholism in and through narrative, and in the imbrication of rhetoric and recovery in British and American culture. Given the interdisciplinary nature of this volume, I want to emphasize that I will not be making a traditionally "historical" argument here, in the sense that I will not argue for a cause-and-effect relationship between the models of addiction and recovery to be found in Victorian novels and in AA literature. I am interested instead in identifying the structures of the stories of alcoholism these texts present to the twenty-first-century reader. Furthermore, as a literary critic who focuses on narrative structure, I do not approach the stories of alcoholics in novels or in AA's books as if they were the biographies of "real people": I try to remain actively aware that the "alcoholics" I am writing about are figures created in and by texts. I focus particularly on canonical Victorian novels because the stories they tell have been so widely circulated for the past century and a half, playing a part in shaping cultural attitudes toward addiction. My argument proceeds from the belief that the narrative forms framing alcoholism and recovery in these texts influence contemporary ideas of what addiction is and how it operates. It is no coincidence that my chapter's title echoes Wayne Booth's classic analysis of narrative perspective, *The Rhetoric of Fiction*, because like that venerable literary formalist, I will end up arguing that just about everything—specifically beliefs and values, including and especially our understanding of identity and recovery—depends on (narrative) point of view.

As Helena Michie and I have argued in a recent essay called "Twelve-Step

Teleology: Narratives of Recovery/Recovery as Narrative," the discourse of Alcoholics Anonymous structures "alcoholism" and "recovery." Individual recovering alcoholics come to understand what they call their "disease" by repeatedly reading, listening to, and ultimately telling—and repeatedly retelling—"drunkologues," or first-person accounts of drinking behavior that is construed as "alcoholic."[1] The trajectory of the recovering alcoholic's "AA story" typically follows a master-narrative, roughly corresponding to the actions described in AA's "twelve steps for recovery." The act of telling the drunkologue itself represents the first step—"admitt[ing] we were powerless over alcohol and our lives had become unmanageable"; the happy ending suggested by the recovering person's presence at an AA meeting is framed by the experiences recounted in steps two ("came to believe that a power greater than ourselves could restore us to sanity," that is, received some hope for relief through exposure to the AA program) through twelve. The master narrative operating in AA allows for the two modes of closure that narratologists would call "euphoric"—the happy ending, where in this case the addicted drinker "gets sober," to drink no more—and "dysphoric"—the tragic ending, where the story's protagonist fails to reach the desired goal and ultimately dies.[2]

In AA stories of recovery from alcoholism, the narrative point of view and the mode of closure are closely connected. First-person accounts within AA are always structured as euphoric, because no matter what difficulties the speaking subject may be experiencing in his or her life at the time of speaking, the story reaches closure in the fact that the person is not, at the present moment, drinking, but rather is speaking of his or her recovery at an AA meeting, or writing about it for inclusion in the *Big Book,* or talking about it to a suffering alcoholic during a "twelve-step call."[3] It is unlikely that any AA group would invite someone to speak who had gotten drunk just moments before walking into a meeting, but even if they did, the act of speaking could be understood as the beginning of another iteration of the drunk's sobriety story. In the contrasting mode, AA members hear the dysphoric narratives of alcoholism only at secondhand, as third-person stories circulate in AA communities about alcoholics who "went out" of AA or who "died of this disease." No alcoholic can tell his or her own dysphoric story in the first-person, because if he or she is telling the story in the context of an AA event, there is still hope for euphoric closure, for the happy ending of eventual recovery.

Within both the euphoric and the dysphoric stories of AA, alcoholism is called a disease, but there is a certain degree of rhetorical slippage in the way this term is used. The *Big Book* insists that addiction to alcohol is a condition of the body as well as the spirit and mind, calling it, for instance, "an illness of this sort—and we have come to believe it an illness" (18). The discourse of disease is not consistent, however, even in the *Big Book* itself. In the section of the *Big Book* entitled "The Doctor's Opinion," alcoholism is called an "allergy" afflicting only certain "types" of bodies (xxvi). For "real alcoholics" (30), this condition—whether disease or allergy—has no physical cure, according to the *Big Book:* "We are convinced to a man that alcoholics of our type are in the grip of a progressive illness. Over any considerable period we get worse, never better" (30). According to AA orthodoxy, the disease progresses whether or not the alcoholic "picks up a drink," so that even a long period of sobriety cannot prevent the "real alcoholic's" addiction from becoming increasingly powerful if the alcoholic drinks again (31). Although AA uses a discourse of disease to account for alcoholism, the program does not suggest any medical or therapeutic "cure" or "treatment" for the problem; it offers instead a "spiritual solution." In this sense, AA's discourse does not treat alcoholism *literally* as a disease: disease functions in AA discourse as a rhetorical trope, a metaphor for the alcoholic's condition.[4]

In AA discourse, "being alcoholic" goes beyond being sick or allergic; being alcoholic is an identity, as opposed to a behavior. It is not about what you do or even what you have done, it is about who you are. When a recovering person introduces himself at a meeting, saying, "Hi, I'm Bill and I'm an alcoholic," he is adopting a specific subject position, an identity ascribed to him by AA rhetoric. (Bill might also be, for instance, a father, a brother, a construction worker, a college professor, a homeless person, a gay man, a neo-Nazi, a Chinese American, a Catholic, but in AA the primary marker of his identity is his addiction, modified sometimes—as in "I'm a cross-addicted alcoholic" or "I'm a grateful recovering alcoholic"—but always indicating his "powerlessness over alcohol" as the operative fact of his identity.) To adopt the identity of "alcoholic" within AA rhetoric is to assume the first-person perspective on a story about a drunk who stopped drinking. That identity is reinforced for the individual speaker through the continual retelling of the story. And the retelling is—as Michie and I have argued—what constitutes recovery. The belief that the addicted drinker must never pick up a drink is directly related to the belief that alcoholism is an identity: because of who the alcoholic is, drinking is "not an option," no matter how the drinker might seek to change his or her behavior. So long as the recovering person keeps telling that euphorically structured first-person story of misery and redemption, the recovery remains intact, provided the person does not drink.

Both the euphoric and dysphoric narrative models are present in Victorian novels about alcoholism. Details of the lives and deaths of alcoholics in the novels of Charles Dickens, Elizabeth Gaskell, Charlotte Brontë, Anne Brontë, Emily Brontë, George Eliot, and Anthony Trollope are in many cases consonant with what AA teaches will be the fate of the alcoholic who does or does not recover. (There are some memorable examples of alcoholics in canonical novels from the late nineteenth century by Thomas

Hardy—notably Jude Fawley in *Jude the Obscure* and Michael Henchard in *The Mayor of Casterbridge*—but I will not be discussing them here, as my other examples cluster around midcentury, providing a set of "high-Victorian" models of addiction to alcohol.) The dysphoric story appears most often in these midcentury texts, but I find that the euphoric story, when it does appear, either entirely departs from or uncannily resembles the narrative represented by the Twelve Steps.

The history of the disease model of alcoholism, as recounted by psychiatrists Norman Miller and John Chappel, helps explain this correlation between mid-nineteenth-century novels and AA, founded in 1935. According to Miller and Chappel, physicians held that alcoholism was a disease—characterized by the drinker's inability to control his or her intake of alcohol—as early as the eighteenth century, and "physician-scholars" accepted that view throughout the period of the novels I am citing. "The first inebriate asylum in the world was founded in 1857," in the middle of the period in question, and "in 1870 [a year before the publication of the latest novel I will discuss] a physician group established the American Association for the Cure of Inebriates."[5]

However, the ideology of temperance, which understood excessive drinking as a moral failing, came to dominate mainstream culture through the end of the nineteenth century, culminating in the era of Prohibition, when—according to this account—the disease model of alcoholism all but disappeared from the medical establishment. "When the concept of alcoholism as a disease was dropped by American medicine in response to political pressure during Prohibition, a vacuum was created and . . . replaced by psychoanalysis," which reads alcohol and drug addictions "as symptoms of underlying conflict" in the personality.[6] In the traditional psychoanalytic model, alcoholics "self-medicate" for psychological problems that are the root of their condition.

When the founders of AA revived the idea that alcoholism is a disease, they did so in the context of a culture that insisted that drunkenness was the result of a moral failing or a psychological complex, or both, and that alcoholism is a behavior born of circumstances. The slippage between disease and self in AA discourse, then, reflects the ambiguous status of alcoholism in early-twentieth-century culture. I find that AA's practice of treating alcoholism as an identity and recovery as a process of recounting conversion narratives is already present in Victorian narratives of alcoholism, colored as they are by both the medical account and the temperance account of alcoholism operating in the mid-nineteenth century.

As in AA narratives, whether an alcoholic's story in a canonical Victorian novel ends happily or tragically is directly correlated with the narrative point of view the text takes on the drinker's experience. The protagonists of dysphoric stories—the pathetic minor characters who drink themselves into oblivion or death—are usually granted no subjectivity within the narrative framing of the text. That is, they are described from the point of view of other characters or of a narrator, but they do not give voice to their own condition, either in dialogue or in narrative passages focalized through their perspective. The few characters who are exceptions to this rule do get to tell their own stories within the text, but they die from drinking anyway. These characters occupy dysphoric plots because the characters who hear their stories are not presented as fellow-sufferers. In fictional Victorian plots as in AA practice, the audience for the drunkologue needs to be able to identify with the narrative in order for the speaker to achieve recovery. In the only one of my examples where this occurs, *Janet's Repentance* (1858) by George Eliot, the resemblance between Janet's process of recovery and the Twelve Steps is striking.

Dysphoric stories about alcoholics in Victorian novels follow a trajectory that closely parallels the AA master-narrative of those alcoholics who do not recover. My examples in this category include Sir Roger Scatcherd and his son Louis in Trollope's *Dr. Thorne* (1858); Esther, John Barton's sister-in-law, in Gaskell's *Mary Barton* (1848); Raffles in George Eliot's *Middlemarch* (1871–72); Hindley Earnshaw in Emily Brontë's *Wuthering Heights* (1847); Arthur Huntingdon in Anne Brontë's *The Tenant of Wildfell Hall* (1848); "Mr. Dolls," Jenny Wren's father, in Dickens's *Our Mutual Friend* (1864–65); Mrs. Stephen Blackpool in Dickens's *Hard Times* (1854); and Mr. Dempster, Janet's husband, in George Eliot's *Janet's Repentance*. Each of these characters embodies the story of the alcoholic who cannot or will not stop drinking. Each of them is supposed to have begun with a high tolerance for alcohol, and each progresses in his or her drinking to the point of physical debility and death. For a few, the motive for drinking anticipates the psychoanalytic concept of "self-medication" (Esther drinks to numb the pain of having been seduced and abandoned, now that she is a penniless prostitute alienated and isolated from her family; Hindley's drinking escalates with his despair over Heathcliff's mounting efforts to wrest away his family legacy). For most of these characters, though, the motivation to drink excessively is obscure, as indeed, it is in AA's *Big Book*. In these stories, drunks are not drunks because of what has happened or is happening to them, but because of who they are.

In some of the Victorian plots, drinking increases despite outward successes in life. Sir Roger, for instance, is a phenomenally productive engineer who has ascended from a working-class background to national prominence and great wealth; Arthur is a pampered member of the leisure class whose material desires have never been thwarted; Raffles is an opportunist who could blackmail Bulstrode indefinitely in order to support himself, but whose uncontrollable addiction to alcohol interferes with his scheme; and Mr. Dempster is a powerful small-town lawyer whose drunken driving eventually kills him. As Eliot's narrator remarks of Dempster: "You do not suppose Dempster had any motive for drinking beyond the craving for drink; the presence of brandy was the only necessary condition."[7] In other stories, where poverty or disappointment might seem to provide circumstantial explanations for excessive drinking—as in the cases of Stephen Blackpool's wife and Jenny Wren's father—other persons sharing the same circumstances (Steven Blackpool and Jenny Wren themselves) do not succumb to excessive drink. The fact that there are no clear reasons why characters would continue drinking—even when their doctors (including Lydgate in *Middlemarch;* the physicians consulted in *Tenant of Wildfell Hall;* and Dr. Thorne himself, as well as his professional rivals, in *Dr. Thorne*) tell them that alcohol has become, for them, a fatal poison—shows a consensus among Victorian novelists that alcoholism is to be presented not so much as a matter of circumstances as an issue of moral character, the Victorian equivalent of what postmodern usage calls "identity." The alcoholics in these dysphoric stories cannot control their behavior, the narratives suggest, because of who they are.

Nor can they recover because the narrative frameworks they function within do not permit it. Most of the drunks who die in Victorian novels are never in a narrative position to tell their own stories from their own point of view. Hindley Earnshaw's binges, for example, are narrated at two removes, as Lockwood reports what Nelly Dean tells him about the Earnshaw family history. Arthur Huntingdon's drinking and demise are similarly narrated in journals written by his wife, Helen, which are transcribed in letters by the novel's narrator, Gilbert Markham.[8] In heterodiegetically narrated novels (with "omniscient" narrators and shifting focalization that travels from one character's consciousness to another's throughout the text) the hopeless alcoholic is seldom granted a subject position; much more often he or she is objectified by the text. The most striking examples of this are in the Dickens novels, where the drunks are the objects of ridicule and scorn (like Jenny Wren's father, whose own daughter treats him as a wayward child, and who is the source of much merriment among minor male characters) or of fear and loathing (like Mrs. Stephen Blackpool, whose spouse lives in dread of her return to their home). The novels' narrative structure grants the drunken characters no subjectivity, no speaking position from which to tell the story of their addiction.

The objectification of the alcoholic in these dysphoric plots is most vividly illustrated by Dickens's narrative habit of referring to the hopeless drunk not as "he" or "she," but as "it." This practice doubly objectifies the drunken characters by recounting their stories from a third-person perspective while assigning to them the impersonal pronoun appropriate to objects that have no subjectivity. The narrator of *Hard Times,* for example, focalizes through Stephen Blackpool the scene of encountering his drunken wife at home:

He stumbled against something. As he recoiled, looking down at it, it raised itself up into the form of a woman in a sitting attitude. . . . Such a woman! A disabled, drunken creature, barely able to preserve her sitting posture by steadying herself with one begrimed hand on the floor, while the other was so purposeless in trying to push away her tangled hair from her face, that it only blinded her the more with the dirt upon it. A creature so foul to look at, in her tatters, stains and splashes, but so much fouler than that in her moral infamy, that it was a shameful thing even to see her.[9]

Note the rhetorical positioning of the passage: Mrs. Blackpool enters the scene as an object, "something," an "it" that is revealed to be "a woman," but that more personal term quickly gives way to the word "creature," repeated twice. Throughout the passage the narrator never once says "she," never assigning a subject position to the drunken woman. Her hand has some agency ("trying to push away her tangled hair" [*Hard Times*, 52]), but the only pronouns referring to the woman herself are "it" and possessive or objective uses of "her." The narrator says—presumably because Stephen feels—"it was a shameful thing even to see her" (*Hard Times*, 52), but here and throughout the novel, the text never allows for any perspective on her besides that of the voyeur: there is no glimpse of her story from her point of view.

The narrative treatment of Jenny Wren's father in *Our Mutual Friend* is more extensive and much more comic in tone, but it maintains the pattern of objectifying the hopeless drunk in telling his dysphoric story. When Jenny Wren confronts her "bad old boy" for the first time in the novel, the narrator assigns neither gender nor personhood to the father:

The shaking figure, unnerved and disjointed from head to foot, put out its two hands a little way, as making overtures of peace and reconciliation. Abject tears stood in its eyes, and stained the blotched red of its cheeks. The swollen lead-coloured under lip trembled with a shameful whine. . . . The very breathing of the figure was contemptible, as it laboured and rattled in that operation, like a blundering clock.[10]

As in *Hard Times*, the narrator presents the inebriated alcoholic as a revolting spectacle, an object placed on view by the narrative perspective. In a subsequent scene, the narrator sarcastically remarks of Jenny's father that "in his worse than swinish state (for swine at least fatten on their guzzling, and make themselves good to eat), he was a pretty object for any eyes" (*Mutual*, 595). Later in the same scene, the narrator insists on the spectacularization of this "object" by framing him in the narrative point of view of Eugene Wrayburn, who is indulging in a bit of *flânerie* on a London street. Eugene was "lounging on again, when a most unexpected object caught his eyes. No less an object than Jenny Wren's bad boy trying to make up his mind to cross the road. A more ridiculous and feeble spectacle than this tottering wretch making unsteady sallies into the roadway . . . the streets could not have shown" (*Mutual,* 597). The drunk is an object—ridiculous, feeble, tottering, unsteady—placed on view by the text's narrative perspective.

What Dickens does with these two drunken characters is only a more extreme version of what Victorian novels in general seem to do with the figure at the center of a dysphoric narrative of alcoholism. Mrs. Blackpool is an object for Stephen's view, Jenny's father is an object for Eugene, and both become objects for the reader. The pattern holds for the other dysphoric drunks in these texts, not just those—like Hindley Earnshaw and Arthur Huntingdon—whose stories are told in other characters' voices. In *Middlemarch,* George Eliot's narrator departs from her usual practice of granting at least a momentary subjectivity to every recurring character in her novel by presenting the drunken Raffles from the perspectives of Bulstrode and also of Dr. Lydgate, but never from his own point of view.

In Trollope's *Dr. Thorne* and Gaskell's *Mary Barton,* the drunken characters' thoughts are only fleetingly rendered by the omniscient narrators, though they do get the opportunity to tell their own life stories to relatively sympathetic listeners within the text. Still—like Hindley, Arthur, Raffles, Mrs. Blackpool (presumably), Jenny's father, and Dempster—they die from drinking. In Victorian fiction, as in AA discourse, a subjective speaking position for the alcoholic is not quite enough to ensure that the story will be about recovery. Evidently, though, without that first-person perspective on the drunkologue, there is no hope for the alcoholic: in this respect, the dysphoric narrative in AA and the dysphoric narrative of alcoholism in Victorian fiction are in accord.

Turning to Victorian plots that do not end in the drinker's demise, we find stories of addiction to alcohol in Victorian novels that do not correspond with AA master-narratives. These narratives are the traces of cultural assumptions about alcoholism as a moral failing or as a behavior, rather than an identity, assumptions that compete with AA's conflicted model of alcoholism as both an identity and an incurable disease. One of these competing notions is the idea that a good marriage and a happy home life can save a man from drinking himself to death. Victorian fictions, like eighteenth-century novels, retain the figure of the reformed rake whose youthful alcoholic binges give way to responsible behavior after marriage, like Lord Chiltern in Trollope's *Phineas Finn* (1869) and in *Phineas Redux* (1874). Often, though, the idea that a happy family life would save the alcoholic is presented only hypothetically, as if the texts were anticipating AA's assertion that such "cures" for alcoholism are mythological, at best. For example, Trollope's narrator says of Louis Scatcherd, Sir Roger's alcoholic son who is also killing himself with drink, "To do him justice it must be admitted that he would not have been incapable of a decent career had he stumbled upon some girl who could have loved him before he stumbled upon his maraschino bottle. Such might have been the case with many a lost rake."[11] "If Janet had been a mother," Eliot's narrator assures us, "she might have been saved from much sin, and therefore from much of her sorrow" (*Janet's*, 334). The very same novels contain evidence to refute this hypothesis, however: Louis's mother, Lady Scatcherd, is presented entirely sympathetically as the best wife Sir Roger could have had, and yet she is unable to influence her husband's drinking; and though Janet's drunkenness is attributable to the lack of love in her life, her husband's is not, because both his wife and his live-in mother have adored him. If alcoholism is a matter of circumstances for Chiltern, Louis Scatcherd, and Janet, it is not for Sir Roger Scatcherd and Dempster: the identity model of alcoholism and the behavior model exist side-by-side in these texts.

The alcoholic whose daily drinking never leads to a tragic end is a figure who is absent from AA's master narrative but present in Victorian fiction in, for example, the character of Grace Poole, Bertha Mason's caretaker in Charlotte Brontë's *Jane Eyre* (1847). Grace's habitual drinking of porter leads Jane to accept the suggestion that Grace is the one who is emitting Bertha's nighttime howls and cackles, though Jane does find Grace's stolid appearance puzzling, given her habit. Anne Brontë's *Tenant of Wildfell Hall* presents another model of alcoholism that AA orthodoxy would not endorse, by suggesting that alcoholic drinking is a learned behavior that can be stopped through something like aversion therapy. Helen Huntingdon shocks her new neighbors by explaining to them that she has taught her little boy to loathe alcoholic drink by adding an emetic to it and forcing it on him until he gets sick. She does not explain why, but the novel eventually reveals that she wanted to spare her son from his father's alcoholic fate. In that same novel, Lord Lowborough becomes what AA would call a "white-knuckle" or "dry" drunk, resisting his craving for alcohol in order to be a good father to his children. Lord Lowborough's marriage to a faithless woman is bad enough to lead to legal separation, and his bearing—especially after he stops drinking—is always grim. Still, he manages to stay "dry" despite concerted and even malicious temptations from his former drinking buddies, in a way that AA's master-narrative would present as highly unlikely. For Lord Lowborough, personal willpower is enough to achieve long-term sobriety; he is the opposite of "powerless over alcohol," whose sobriety is a personal triumph of human will over human moral failure—though it is certainly not figured as a source of any joy or satisfaction to him.

Of course, AA discourse maintains that neither domestic bliss, nor aversion, nor willpower can conquer alcoholism. The only solution, within the AA master-narrative, is a spiritual program based on the Twelve Steps, and the "promises" associated in the *Big Book* with that solution point the recovering alcoholic toward a "new freedom and a new happiness" (*Big Book*, 83) that Anne Brontë's dry drunks never achieve. In *Janet's Repentance*, by con-

trast to *The Tenant of Wildfell Hall,* George Eliot provides a euphoric narrative of recovery that closely parallels this AA model of recovery. Thrown out
of the house in the middle of the night by her drunken, abusive husband,
Janet resolves in desperation to turn for help to Mr. Tryan, the evangelical
minister whose career she has heretofore done her best to undermine. She
"reaches out for help," as AA would have it, and the seemingly saintly Mr.
Tryan responds just as a recovering alcoholic on a "Twelve-Step call" would
do, by telling Janet his own story. Mr. Tryan's vice is not drinking per se, but
in his youth he had seduced a young woman who eventually committed suicide to escape the life of prostitution her fall brought on. He tells Janet this
story, and tells her how he had confessed the episode to someone else, who
"made it clear to me that the only preparation for coming to Christ and par-
taking of his salvation was that very sense of guilt and helplessness that was
weighing me down" (*Janet's,* 361). To translate this into AA terminology, he
had to "hit a bottom" and "admit his powerlessness" before he could
recover. Janet's primary fear is that she will drink again, but Tryan recommends, in effect, that she take AA's first three steps:

> Your evil habits, you feel, are too strong for you; you are unable to wrestle with
> them; you know beforehand you shall fall. But when once we feel our help-
> lessness in that way, and go to the Saviour, desiring to be freed from the power
> as well as the punishment of sin, we are no longer left to our own strength. . . .
> As soon as we submit ourselves to his will . . . it is as if the walls had fallen down
> that shut us out from God, and we are fed with his spirit, which gives us new
> strength. (*Janet's,* 361)

Here are the roots of the Twelve-Step program expressed in a fictional representation of evangelical Christianity: if Janet can admit she is powerless
over her "evil habits" (Step One), "come to believe that a power greater
than [herself] can restore her to sanity" (Step Two), and "turn her will and
her life over to God" (Step Three), she can follow Tryan's example and
move toward recovery. Steps Four and Five are paralleled by Tryan's confessions, first to his friend and now, again, to Janet, as well as the drunkologue that Janet tells him in response. The reconstruction of character represented by Steps Six through Ten occurs in Tryan's change of life, from
youthful reprobate to self-denying minister. He recommends Step Eleven
("praying only for the knowledge of [God]'s will for us and the power to
carry that out") when he asks Janet to "pray with me," "Not my will, but
Thine be done" (*Janet's,* 363). Step Twelve—"having had a spiritual awakening as a result of these steps, we carried this message to alcoholics and
practiced these principles in all our affairs"—is clearly illustrated in Tryan's
ministry to Janet.

Following Tryan's example, Janet, too, has a spiritual awakening. Having
been tempted once again to drink, and having confessed the temptation to

Tryan (who functions, here as elsewhere, as if he were her AA "sponsor"),
Janet walks out across a starlit meadow and has an epiphany:

> The temptation which had so lately made her shudder before the possibilities
> of the future, was now a source of confidence; or had she not been delivered
> from it? Had not rescue come in the extremity of danger? Yes; Infinite Love
> was caring for her. She felt like a little child whose hand is firmly grasped by
> its father, as its frail limbs make their way over the rough ground; if it should
> stumble, the father will not let it go.
>   That walk in the dewy starlight remained for ever in Janet's memory as one
> of those baptismal epochs, when the soul, dipped in the sacred waters of joy
> and peace, rises from them with new energies, with more unalterable long-
> ings. (*Janet's*, 398)

Janet's story is, of course, a conversion narrative, grounded in Christian tradition. In Eliot's version of that narrative, however, it is the human connection Janet feels to Mr. Tryan that makes her conversion possible. Eliot's
famous humanism, then, is a precursor to the agnosticism that AA orthodoxy can accommodate. What the founders of AA did, in effect, was to
remove the specifically Christian references from a conversion narrative like
Tryan's or Janet's to create the master-narrative of recovery contained in the
Twelve Steps.

Centrally important both to Eliot's version of this euphoric plot and to
AA's version is the idea that the suffering alcoholic needs to tell her own
story, from her own perspective, not just to God but to "another human
being" (as Step Five puts it) who can identify with that story. Esther, in *Mary
Barton*, tells her story to the entirely upright Jem Wilson; Sir Roger, in *Dr.
Thorne*, tells his to the nearly faultless eponymous hero. Although Esther's
and Sir Roger's narratives open up a space in those novels for a sympathetic
readerly response—in a way that Dickens's objectification of drunks, for
instance, does not—they nevertheless do not result in the characters' eventual recoveries. In Victorian fiction, as in AA, a first-person perspective on
the experience of addiction is crucial to recovery, but it can only work when
there is a second person inside the narrative frame who can hear the story,
identify with it, and affirm it. In this sense, AA's discourse can be read as a
revival—or maybe even a survival—of the Victorian emphasis on communitarian values, living on in the fragmented-alienated-individualist modern
and postmodern periods through the practice of those who have found
relief in the telling and retelling of their recovery stories.

Whether there is any hope for an alcoholic in a Victorian novel is a matter, then, of narrative point of view, of the opportunities afforded to the
drunk not just by the plot but also by the narrative structure of the text.
When the drunk is granted subjectivity, the possibility for the audience's
sympathy opens up; when that subjectivity is received by a kindred con-

sciousness like Mr. Tryan's, his consciousness becomes a model for the text's ideal reader. In this respect, AA's emphasis on specifically situated first-person narrative is already present in these representative texts from dominant culture in the previous century.

One might object that the two forms of discourse are fundamentally different, in that novels make no pretense of referring to material persons' individual lives, while AA stories are conventionally intended and understood as individual people's sincere representations of "what we used to be like, what happened, and what we are like now" (*Big Book,* 58). My point is not that "real" recovering alcoholics are as fictive as characters in novels, nor that fictitious Victorian characters are somehow subject to the same social and psychological processes as real people. I am suggesting instead that the ideas about alcoholism that shape the recovery and the identity of the contemporary real-world alcoholic are created and circulated through narratives that have had currency in our culture for at least 150 years. Victorian novels and AA do have one important thing in common: both are driven by storytelling. And stories are always shaped by their internal momentum toward closure. The teleology of narration requires that the selection of details in any given narrative add up to the resolution of those details that constitutes the story's ending. Victorian novels shape their accounts of bodily experience—of alcoholism among the myriad other kinds of experience they describe—to fit the exigencies of narrative discourse; they hurtle toward closure, and—eventually, in a matter of four hundred or eight hundred or thousands of pages—they come to an end, even though their closure (as D. A. Miller, Marianna Torgovnick, and others have noted) is ambivalent, contingent, and conflicted.[12]

AA narratives are different in at least two important ways: their closure cannot afford to be ambivalent, contingent, or conflicted, because the individual subject's sobriety (and AA figures that as a life-or-death matter) depends on the story's euphoric end, and the closure they deploy exists only at the moment of the story's enunciation. The narrating subject walks away from the act of narration and into the next chapter of his or her life. AA orthodoxy insists that even the longest standing members are only a drink away from their next drunk, and that no one is immune from the danger of slipping, no matter how often (or how effectively) he or she has told the recovery story with the euphoric ending. The recovering alcoholic has to "keep coming back," to hear and retell the story over again. Recovery in AA can be seen as a triumph of the discursive over the bodily: the recovering alcoholic keeps telling the story and, in doing so, finds a way not to swallow another alcoholic drink. The structure of the AA program itself seems to mirror the Victorian novel's acknowledgment of the monumental power of narrative, while evading the earlier form's inevitable need to come to an end.

6

Firewater Legacy

Alcohol and Native American Identity in the Fiction of James Fenimore Cooper

Nicholas O. Warner

Alcohol's threat to Native American life has been a persistent theme in American cultural history, from the earliest days of colonization to the present. It appears in such forms as Benjamin Franklin's "specious little equation in providential mathematics: Rum + Savage = o" (as D. H. Lawrence so mordantly put it), as well as in the many Native American portrayals of liquor as an extension of white exploitation.[1] And the theme plays a central role in the depiction of Native American racial identity in the work of a profoundly influential purveyor of both myths and realities about Native Americans: James Fenimore Cooper. My purpose here is to demonstrate the importance of drinking in Cooper's portrayal of Native Americans and to examine alcohol's destructive effects in one major Cooper text, *The Pioneers*. In doing so, I hope to clarify the ways that Cooper's fiction mediates between "pity" for the Native American, on the one hand, and "censure," on the other—these being the dual sides of an attitude that, in the words of Roy Harvey Pearce, has dominated "the American obsession with the problem of the civilized vs. the savage."[2]

By the time Cooper began writing novels in the early 1820s, two dominant discourses of Native American drinking had already taken shape. In one, drink served merely as a catalyst to unleash the supposedly innate depravity and moral weakness of the "savage." In the other, alcohol appeared as a sinister tool in the ruthlessly systematic extermination of a rich indigenous culture. Ironically, both of these discourses took root in the same phenomenon: the seemingly unstoppable persistence of alcohol abuse among Native Americans. Once introduced, alcohol appeared to act on tribal culture as a poison does on the body, spreading unchecked throughout the system. The result was a legacy of firewater that burned through entire tribes and over entire generations. To Native Americans and their supporters, that legacy spoke (as it still speaks) of the dishonor of whites irresponsibly or maliciously plying Native Americans with liquor and of the tragedy of tribal cultures destroyed by the multiple weapons of munitions, disease, and alcohol. Many colonizers, however, were all too eager to see in the same firewater legacy testimony to Native American inferiority and to the inevitable triumph of white culture over red—that is, to the rightness of manifest destiny.

The discourse of Native American drinking as a mark of racial inferiority appeared early in the history of Native American-European contact, as in the sixteenth-century explorer Henry Hawks's comment that tribal peoples "are soone drunke, and given to much beastlinesse, and void of all goodnesse."[3] But the second, more sympathetic discourse also emerged early. Already in 1685, an Abnakis chief complained that his people were being deliberately made drunk by French and British traders—a view supported by the fact that, as Craig MacAndrew and Robert Edgerton point out in their important study, *Drunken Comportment* (1969): "The literature on the fur trade abounds with instances in which every conceivable form of deceit and coercion was employed in forcing liquor upon the Indians" in order to render them more tractable in trade negotiations.[4] In the early nineteenth century, the Pequot writer, missionary, and tribal rights activist, William Apess, continued a long-standing tradition of Native American protest against the liquor trade when he sardonically invited his readers to "review again [the Pilgrims'] weapons to civilize the nations of this soil. What were they? Rum and powder and ball, together with . . . the smallpox and every other disease imaginable."[5] In our own time, the Acoma Pueblo author, Simon Ortiz, writes in similar terms of the campaign to dominate Native Americans: "Whiskey was only one way, and guns another."[6] But one of the pithiest and most touching expressions of white responsibility for the evils of Native American intoxication appears in the address, made in 1805, by the Seneca chief Red Jacket: "We took pity on white men . . . gave them corn and meat; they gave us poison [rum] in return."[7]

Native Americans were not alone in condemning European promotion of heavy tribal drinking. In fact, one commonly finds white authors, such as Increase Mather in 1673, inveighing against not only drunkards but also those who lead others to drink, such as colonists who "have sold intoxicating Liquors to these poor Indians, whose Land we Possess, and have made them Drunk therewith."[8] Similarly, in 1779, Alexander Hewatt, after listing the various trials imposed on Native Americans by European newcomers to their land, asserted that "the introduction of spirituous liquors" proved more destructive to tribal culture than dispossession, smallpox, or even war.[9] In the following century, Margaret Fuller attacked white liquor dealers for their hypocrisy in plying Indians with copious amounts of liquor on weekdays, only to kneel down together with them in prayer on Sunday.[10]

At times, however, the distinctions between these two main discourses could blur, resulting in a particularly insidious variety of racism—a kind of "it's not their fault that they are red" mentality that often employed native drunkenness as a convenient scapegoat and rationalization for white displacement of the Native American. A typical articulation of this attitude is that of Peter Chester, the colonial governor of West Florida, who in 1774 wrote, "It is often bad enough with white people when they are [drunk], therefore what can be expected from Indians who are void of sense and reason, born in savage ignorance and brought up in the same way, but the most barbarous and inhuman murders and cruelties?"[11] "What can be expected?" Governor Clark asks. Embedded in the rhetorical question itself is a presumption of Native Americans' inherent inferiority and of the inevitability of their decline. This sense of the Native American as a being fated to alcoholic self-destruction (the firewater myth) appears also in Benjamin Franklin's comment on rum's Providence-guided effect on indigenous tribes:

> And, indeed, if it be the design of Providence to extirpate these savages in order to make room for the cultivators of the earth, it seems not improbable that rum may be the appointed means. It has already annihilated all the tribes who formerly inhabited the seacoast.[12]

Although Franklin seems to have felt genuine indignation over white persecution of peaceful Native Americans, his comment on tribal drinking in the previous paragraph typifies the notion of the unavoidable decline of the Native American. Phrases such as "design of Providence" and "appointed means" resonate with the message of divinely sanctioned inevitability, while alcohol alone, in the Franklin passage, is the active agent in tribal annihilation—not a word about westward expansion, war, or white men's shrewd dealing for land. "It"—meaning alcohol—and not anything or anyone else, is responsible for having "annihilated" the Native American.

The comments reviewed here show that the Native American could simultaneously be portrayed as a victim to be pitied and as a victimizer whose own worst enemy was himself. Native Americans, helpless before the onslaught of drink, became solely responsible for their own demise. Such a view provided white expansionists with a conscience-soothing explanation for the destruction of native culture. It also gave them a sense of racially grounded moral superiority over the Native American, as demonstrated by native peoples' susceptibility to drink. Above all, it absolved whites for the extermination of tribal culture precisely because, so the argument ran, that culture's decline was the ineluctable result of the Native American's own nature. Thus the "drunken Indian" gave white imperialism the perfect formula for conquest without guilt.

Variations on all of these perspectives inform Cooper's fiction. In general, Cooper blends considerable sympathy with criticism in his view of

Native American drinking problems. But his work also reveals a tension between this view and more hostile perspectives on Native Americans and their drinking. It is often in the ambiguous struggle to resolve or at least to articulate that tension that Cooper's treatment of Native Americans and drink gains its greatest interest.

As with many of his white drinkers, Cooper occasionally depicts the drinking done by Native Americans as a source of befuddlement, stupor, and rather labored comedy. In *The Pathfinder,* for instance, liquor both incites and disables the savagery of the braves who have captured Mabel Dunham. Drunk, they try to set fire to the blockhouse with Mabel in it, but before they get very far, they become incapacitated by rum. The clever and kind Native American woman, June, tells Mabel of a similar incident from the past, in which June's mother, captured by an enemy tribe, unceremoniously tomahawked her drunken captors before making her own escape. And in one of his last novels, *The Oak-Openings,* Cooper attempts to wring some humor from a description of Indians duped by the novel's hero into thinking that they have discovered a magical whiskey-flowing spring. Much more substantive, however, is the representation of Native American drinking in *The Pioneers,* first published in 1823.

Two scenes in this novel are particularly important to Cooper's delineation of Native American drinking. The first takes place at the Bold Dragoon tavern, where we see Chingachgook, also called John Mohegan or Indian John, through the eyes of the narrator and of Natty Bumppo. The second scene, the famous one of the turkey-shoot, occurs two chapters later. In it, the reader perceives Chingachgook's situation partly through the eyes of others, such as the idealistic, young Oliver Effingham, but also through Chingachgook's own perspective, as he describes his situation and the role of liquor in bringing it about.

The very structure of the Bold Dragoon scene ties in with the whole question of race and addiction. The scene features a Native American (Chingachgook) in a tavern—that is, in a European-owned, European-invented institution. This particular Native American, moreover, finds himself surrounded by whites, with whom he sits, drinking, on the European holiday of Christmas Eve. The result is a situation and cast of characters that provide a kind of laboratory setting in which to explore the relationship of the Indian drunkard to the society that introduced him to "firewater" in the first place and, thus, to the addiction that destroys him. With its quaint dialogue and good-humored, if condescending, authorial descriptions of colonial drinking habits, the first half of the Bold Dragoon scene, which takes place in chapter 13, seems to be no more than a pleasant but minor dash of local color in Cooper's narrative. But in chapter 14, when Chingachgook enters the tavern with his friend Natty Bumppo, the juxtapositions of cheerful bluster about drink with Chingachgook's sodden inebriety quickly endow the scene with a darkly ironic tinge. Just before Chingachgook (Indian John) arrives, the landlord of the tavern commends him as one "enlisted in the cause of Christianity, and civilized."[13] But his praise cannot help but seem ironic in light of the obvious personal devastation that Chingachgook's exposure to civilization has wrought. From the moment he enters the door, Chingachgook is not just exposed to alcohol but immersed in an atmosphere of drink, not through malice but through the insensitivity to his addiction shown by the people gathered at the Bold Dragoon. Although unintended, the results of their mindless pushing of drink onto Chingachgook are as negative as those of the most manipulative white trader. As soon as Chingachgook appears, the landlady cries, "Here, John, is a mug of cider lac'd with whisky. An Indian will drink cider, though he niver be athirst" (158). Similarly, the bombastic Richard Jones, that paragon of imperceptiveness whom Cooper uses for ironic purposes throughout the novel, presses drink on Chingachgook saying, "Here, John; drink, man, drink." Completely oblivious to Chingachgook's condition, Richard Jones persists in pressing drink on Leather-stocking as well, holding out two "mugs of foaming flip," or punch (164).

In the previous chapter (chapter 13), the atmosphere in the Bold Dragoon resembles something out of the famously robust drinking scenes of Franz Hals. But with the introduction of Chingachgook and Leather-stocking, Cooper deftly modulates the tavern scene into a sympathetic yet unsentimental rendering of the pathos and indignity of Chingachgook's condition, as shown in the following passage:

> He [Chingachgook] shook his head, throwing his hair back from his countenance, and exposed eyes, that were glaring with an expression of wild resentment. But the man was not himself. His hand seemed to make a fruitless effort to release his tomahawk, which was confined by its handle to his belt, while his eyes gradually became vacant. Richard at that instant thrusting a mug before him, his features changed to the grin of idiocy, and seizing the vessel with both hands, he sunk backward on the bench, and drunk until satiated, when he made an effort to lay aside the mug, with the helplessness of total inebriety.
>
> "Shed not blood!" exclaimed the hunter, as he watched the countenance of the Indian in its moment of ferocity—"but he is drunk, and can do no harm. This is the way with all the savages; give them liquor, and they make dogs of themselves." (166) [Natty here speaks, we learn, in Chingachgook's language, so that the whites will not understand him.]

In this brief passage, Cooper indirectly expresses a remarkable number of white stereotypes and assumptions about Native American drinking. We encounter native violence (the fumbling for the tomahawk); native untrustworthiness (even Natty Bumppo, Chingachgook's closest friend, fears that he may "shed blood" amid the friendly group in the tavern); native weakness of character (first in accepting the drink and then in succumbing to it with "helplessness"); and native degradation to a subhuman level ("they make dogs of themselves") (166). But added to these issues is yet another theme that contrasts with the common antebellum assumption that natives alone are to blame for native addiction. That theme is white complicity in the degradation of tribal peoples, as exemplified by the behavior of the landlord, landlady, and above all by Richard Jones. But in this particular scene the complicity stems not from malice but from a moral obtuseness that prevents Chingachgook's white companions from recognizing the damage that their own actions produce. Further complicating the scene is Natty's use of the Delaware language to address Chingachgook—his offensive cliché about drunken Indians making dogs of themselves seems to be addressed half to Chingachgook and half to himself, but in any case is obviously not intended for the whites at the tavern. Thus any insult to Chingachgook remains essentially a private matter between himself and Natty. As for the assembled whites, they either ignore Chingachgook's state or make light of it, as Richard Jones does: after Cooper's somber description of Chingachgook, and Natty's disturbing comments, Jones jovially exclaims, "Well, old John is soon sowed up," and gives orders for him to be put up for the night in the barn (166). And the chapter ends with the unmistakably ironic touch of Jones blithely singing into the night, "Come let us be jolly,/And cast away folly" (168).

The Bold Dragoon scene conveys Cooper's ambivalence about Native American drinking, as clichés of drunken savagery chafe against a subtext that implicates Europeans in the process that turned Chingachgook, the expert hunter, warrior, and leader of his people, into a drunken hanger-on in the village of Templeton. If left undeveloped, the scene would amount to little more than a somewhat confused amalgam of pity and censure of the native American; Cooper here seems torn between two opposing forces: the firewater myth of inevitable Indian degradation, and his own sense of the ways that social convention and cultural expectations can blind even the best-intentioned of persons—to say nothing of such moral myopes as Richard Jones—to the realities of alcoholic addiction. As Cooper shows, unexamined assumptions about social drinking and hospitality can actually contribute to the drunkard's addiction—all in the name of good cheer. But in the turkey-shoot scene that follows in chapter 16, Cooper rises to the challenge offered by the complexity of Chingachgook's drunkenness. Here Cooper goes beyond both the stereotype of the drunken Indian, and the "sentimental indulgence"[14] that some find in his portrayal of Chingachgook.[15] Rather, he invests Chingachgook's personal addiction with tragic dignity and with broader meaning as he connects that addiction to the fragmentation of Native American racial identity and, by extension, of an entire way of life. The result is an expansion of the tavern scene's motifs into an intense, thematically sophisticated vision of that fatal triad: Native Americans, whites, and liquor. And that expansion occurs primarily in the passage where Chingachgook himself comments on the debilitating effects of the white man's firewater:

> "Beast! is John a beast?" replied the Indian, slowly; 'yes; you say no lie, child of the Fire-eater! John is a beast. The smokes were once few in these hills. The deer would lick the hand of a white man, and the birds rest on his head. They were strangers to him. My fathers came from the shores of the salt lake. They fled before rum. They came to their grandfather, and they lived in peace; or when they did raise the hatchet, it was to strike it into the brain of a Mingo. They gathered around the council-fire, and what they said was done. Then John was the man. But warriors and traders with light eyes followed them. One brought the long knife, and one brought rum. They were more than the pines of the mountains; and they broke up the councils, and took the lands. The evil spirit was in their jugs, and they let him loose.—Yes, yes—you say no lie, Young Eagle. John is a Christian beast." (185)

At the core of this statement's irony is, of course, the yoking together of the terms "Christian" and "beast." For all of his own unquestionably Christian perspective, Cooper links the spread of Christianity to the European destruction of tribal life. Chingachgook's irony must, to a degree, be Cooper's, as he acknowledges that the advance of Christian civilization entailed the destruction of a way of life that the novelist found at once alien and profoundly admirable. Indeed, in chapter 7 of *The Pioneers*, Cooper tellingly corrects the word "Europeans" to "Christians" in the sentence that begins, "Before the Europeans, or, to use a more significant term, the Christians, dispossessed the original owners of the soil" (83). Chingachgook's bitter lament about his enervating addiction is, in one sense, but an extension of an idea raised earlier in the text by the narrator himself.

The dispossession of the Native American described in *The Pioneers* is inseparable from the abuse of alcohol. Similarly, in Cooper's later novel, *The Last of the Mohicans*, a younger Chingachgook than we see in *The Pioneers* suggestively describes alcohol as an instrument of both spiritual and material dispossession: "The Dutch landed, and gave my people the fire-water; they drank until the heavens and the earth seemed to meet, and they foolishly thought they had found the Great Spirit. Then they parted with their land."[16] Exemplifying the personal results of such dispossession is the title character of one of Cooper's less-widely known novels, *Wyandotté*. More overtly than any other Cooper character, red or white, Wyandotté reveals an identity split between his alcoholic and nonalcoholic selves. And each self attaches to a different name. "Saucy Nick" is the semi-Europeanized hanger-on who scrounges for drink and gets ignominiously whipped by his white master. "Wyandotté" is the original name of the man's more traditionally tribal self, characterized by courage, fierce independence, and pride. This side of Wyandotté reasserts itself at various points in the novel, most notably at the end when, despite his having committed a murder, Wyandotté reappears with regained sobriety and dignity.

In *The Pioneers,* as in the later novels *The Last of the Mohicans* and *Wyandotté,* Cooper raises important questions about addiction and race that he does not fully pursue. In *Wyandotté,* the theme of split identity never develops beyond the level of vague, if intriguing, implication. In *The Last of the Mochicans,* Chingachgook's comments on drink and the Great Spirit suggest Cooper's possible awareness of the way that alcohol use among inexperienced Indian drinkers could produce a deceptive parallel to the altered states of consciousness promoted among many Native American religions.[17] Yet, perhaps because of his profoundly rational, Enlightenment mind-set, Cooper never followed up on the possibilities for a more probing analysis of the Native American response to alcohol on the level of mystical or visionary experience. And, despite the sophistication and complexity of perspective in *The Pioneers,* Cooper does not explore the full implications of Chingachgook's indictments of white culture—not surprisingly, perhaps, since those implications could lead only to the repudiation of an ideology that was much too close to that of Cooper himself.

Cooper never resolved the problem of Native American intoxication, just as he was never able to reconcile white dominance in North America with his own awareness of, and guilt over, the destruction of native life resulting from that dominance. But if Cooper's work fails to overcome the contradictions I have described here, it does show his willingness to engage those contradictions and to include them as part of his vision of America. For all of its unresolved ambiguities, the discourse of Native American addiction in Cooper functioned partly to challenge the hypocrisy and moral complacency of westward expansionism and partly to support Oliver Effingham's condemnation, in *The Pioneers,* of the "cupidity that has destroyed such a race" (185). It also enabled Cooper to find imaginative means of dealing with the painful realization that the decline of Native American cultures was not, after all, inevitable.

PART IV

Pleasures, Repressions, Resistances

7

Smoking, Addiction, and the Making of Time

Helen Keane

In anti-smoking discourse the smoker often appears as a squanderer of the precious and scarce resources of time. Not only does the purchase and consumption of the drug take up time in the smoker's daily routine, but also the smoker's attachment to its dubious pleasures is steadily subtracting time from the future. The rate of loss has been quite precisely calculated—about 5½ minutes of life per cigarette, according to one source.[1] No wonder troubled smokers think of their habit as "an insidious slow form of suicide."[2] Each cigarette consumes energy and income and brings illness and death one step closer. Images of smokers as prisoners of time, unable to break free from the chains of their past actions, appear most vividly in texts that understand smoking in terms of a powerful physical addiction to nicotine. In this model, nicotine addiction is an alien and malign force that takes over the life of its victims, compelling them to continue no matter how strong their desire to stop. Moreover, for the addict, smoking no longer produces pleasure; all that is achieved is normal functioning and the avoidance of withdrawal symptoms.

This chapter looks at some of the tensions present in these understandings of smoking as addictive disorder, focusing particularly on the issues of time and pleasure. Even in texts devoted to the dangers and despair of nicotine addiction, the multifaceted and autoerotic pleasures of smoking keep emerging, polluting the apparent purity and transparency of the anti-smoking case. One common response to this tension is to emphasize the serious future consequences of smoking. But once the pleasures of cigarettes are taken as seriously as their dangers, the relationship between smoking and time becomes more complex than the rhetoric of future risk can admit. Not only is confining the meaning of smoking to the pathology of addiction not possible, but also the move to reduce smoking to these terms has a quite different effect from the one intended. It stretches and weakens the boundaries of the category of addiction, blurring distinctions between health and pathology, order and disorder, production and destruction, and present and future, in the process advertising the attractions of addictive desire itself.

The influence of Richard Klein's work (1993) on the philosophical and cultural significance of cigarettes will be apparent in this discussion, although the popular texts studied are a long distance from the major literary, philosophical, and visual works that are his sources. Whereas Klein's main thesis is that the sublime beauty of cigarettes has been forgotten and repressed in an era of puritanical healthism, my argument is more that the virtues of cigarettes and the appeal of addiction cannot be excluded, even from the discourse of nicotine addiction. In addition, readers of Klein will recognize the themes of the temporal productivity of smoking, the alluring repetition and brevity of the act, and its ability to accomplish "a little revolution in time."[3] I develop these themes in a different direction by juxtaposing them with the economies of time and risk that operate in health promotion and anti-smoking discourse.

The chapter begins with an examination of nicotine as an addictive drug, then moves on to consider the figure of the nicotine addict and her relationship with smoking, as constructed in a self-help recovery guide and an autobiographical text.[4] The next section shifts the focus to mainstream anti-smoking texts and guides and the deployment of "risk" in their case against cigarettes. In both contexts, the smoker is regarded as an individual trapped in a negative relationship to time and alienated from genuine pleasure, but these textual constructions are unstable. The final part of the discussion exploits this instability and the tensions identified earlier to present a different picture of the smoker.

NICOTINE ADDICTION

In 1988 the U.S. Surgeon General's report on the health consequences of smoking was devoted to an extended discussion of nicotine addiction. The report concluded that cigarettes are addictive, that nicotine is the drug in tobacco that causes addiction, and that the processes that determine tobacco addiction are similar to those that determine heroin and cocaine addiction.[5] It termed tobacco use "a disorder which can be remedied through medical attention" (i) and wrote of the achievement and maintenance of "tobacco abstinence" (9).

The pharmacological/medical approach of the report has become widespread in popular literature on smoking, particularly in how-to-quit guides. According to one recent text, smokers who cannot quit are "enslaved not by cigarettes but by a single chemical, $C_{10}H_{14}N_2$, or nicotine."[6] Another claims that "if you take people who are smokers and withhold cigarettes from them but give them syringes containing nicotine, they will inject nicotine into their veins, exactly like heroin addicts."[7] The language of drug addiction is also routinely adopted in smokers' self-presentations. Actor Mel Gibson, referring to his twenty-six-year smoking career in a magazine interview ("His right hand plays with a cigarette, despite the fact that only months ago he was celebrating kicking the habit"), is reported as saying that nicotine is harder to get out of the system than heroin.[8] Nicotine replacement therapies are the technological counterpart of these views.

Whatever the scientific validity of nicotine's particular pharmacology, reducing the meaning of smoking to "enslavement to a chemical" and insisting on its identity as a drug addiction are discursive events that produce the smoker as a pathological subject. The smoker's problem is transformed from a (bad) habit into an addictive disease, and his disordered inner being becomes the proper object of rehabilitative self-discipline. In addition, contemporary discourses of addiction have a disturbing tendency to deny the heterogeneity of human existence: they invoke a totalizing, ready-made narrative to explain the experiences and actions of all addicted subjects, and they install a teleological and universalistic morality in which the attainment and maintenance of health and normality are the principal values.[9]

At first glance, the construction of "the smoker" from the template of "the heroin addict" would seem to further the status of smokers as weak and immoral deviants. But to its adherents, the discourse of smoking as addiction is both scientific and humane, an alternative to old-fashioned moralizing about bad habits and lack of self-discipline.[10] It argues that overcoming dependence on "the most addictive substance known to humankind" is much more than a matter of willpower, and that smokers should not be blamed for their addictive disorder.[11] In this context, the smoker is often presented as an innocent victim of evil and rapacious tobacco companies. All smokers are regarded as passive, whether first- or secondhand inhalers, while the tobacco industry fills the role of active agent of disease and death. One of the conditions of this benevolence is, however, the embracing of an identity based on pathology. The discourse of nicotine addiction suggests that smokers are fundamentally different from non-smokers at a physiological level. Their bodies not only tolerate but also require a poison to function. Twin studies have supported the existence of "smoking genes" that control susceptibility to nicotine addiction, thereby suggesting that the smoker/addict identity is encoded at the deepest and most immutable level of personal identity, that is, on the DNA.[12] According to smoking cessation expert Renée Bittoun, there is mounting evidence that individual reaction to nicotine and even difficulty in quitting may be inherited (*Stop Smoking*, 6).

Viewing smoking as a symptom of affliction, rather than a cultural practice or individual lifestyle choice, transforms the political landscape of tobacco use. Arguments based on rights and freedom are disarmed in the face of biology and the absence of choice it implies.[13] For example, Bittoun suggests that children may become addicted to nicotine before they can speak, from inhaling parents' smoke. She also argues that passive smoking is a crucial issue for former smokers, because they can be so sensitized to nicotine that inhaling secondhand smoke triggers "a neurological reaction" (*Stop Smoking*, 98–99). Pleasure and enjoyment are also largely excluded from the picture, except in the disembodied form of "psychoactive euphoriant effects" in the brain. Smoking is seen as an irrational behavior that serves no useful purpose and can only be explained in terms of pathology. If smokers are not suffering from a disorder, then why do they continue a dangerous habit that they do not really enjoy?

However, the move to refigure smokers as powerless victims of an addictive drug does not remove the debate from the realm of ethical and moral judgment. Rather, it widens the scope of normalization and imbues it with the authority and familiar appeal of medical discourse. True, the discourse of nicotine addiction constructs addicted smokers as sick, not bad, but it assumes that the only way to live a meaningful, productive, and happy life is to adopt a healthy nonsmoking lifestyle, a lifestyle that consists of much more than abstinence from nicotine.

The ethical dimensions of addiction discourse are made obvious in the theories of Nicotine (formerly Smokers') Anonymous (NicA).[14] A Twelve-Step program based on Alcoholics Anonymous, NicA combines a notion of physical addiction with an explicit moral stance. For NicA, smoking is a physical, emotional, and spiritual disease with "deep-seated origins and symptoms that pervade every aspect of the addict's waking and sleeping life."[15] In the words of the "first step," addicts are powerless over the drug and their lives become unmanageable. What is required is not merely cessation but recovery, involving a process of "thorough moral housecleaning."[16] The smoker-nicotine relationship is much more than a physical dependency in this model; "smoker" becomes a subjectivity defined by reliance on a drug and marked by a deep and pervasive emotional impairment.[17] *Recovery from Smoking*, a Twelve-Step guide to quitting, devotes fifty-two pages to the process of emotional recovery, more than twice as many as it uses to discuss the physical problems faced by quitters.[18] In this text, the nicotine addict's smoking habit is the exterior sign of a deep inner anguish, which the smoker attempts to mask and control with the compulsive use of cigarettes. Beneath their generally competent and rational demeanors smokers are intensely lonely, controlled by fear (ranging from the fear of gaining weight to the fear of abandonment), suffused with shame and, most tragically, emotionally numb (*Recovery*, 45–76). They have used the powerful effects of nicotine and the rituals of smoking to hide their feelings, not only from others but also from themselves, and to successfully recover they must embark on a long and painful journey of emotional reeducation, learning to "identify, accept, and express feelings of shame, fear, sadness, loneliness, grief, depression, and anger" (*Recovery*, 46).

A smoker, then, becomes a subject requiring self-improvement, and *Recovery from Smoking* offers a series of exercises to help the reader on the path to healthy living. The tasks for the recovery of emotional well-being are varied: completing charts, answering questions, and making lists on topics such as "feelings," "boundaries," and "intimacy;" recalling childhood memories of loneliness and parental substance use; repeating affirmations such as "I can play and have fun without being self-destructive" (*Recovery*, 90) and "Accepting my sadness heals my pain and helps it pass" (*Recovery*, 66); and visualizing and drawing pictures of different emotions. Together, they provide training in a regularized discipline of self-examination, self-interpretation, and self-expression, through which an accessible, orderly, and balanced inner self is produced.

PORTRAIT OF THE SMOKER AS A DRUG ADDICT

An engrossing and affecting portrait of one smoker/addict subject is presented in *Smoker: Self-Portrait of a Nicotine Addict,* by Ellen Walker, an eloquent champion of the NicA model. Walker's story has many of the elements of classic addiction narratives: obsession with the drug, secrecy and shame, failed attempts to quit, and despair and self-hatred. But her account, nevertheless, undermines as well as supports the case for the pathological power of nicotine and the aberrancy of its devotees. The very fact that she is still an active nicotine addict at the time of writing the book distinguishes her addiction from the more flamboyant and dramatic addictions, which only allow their stories to be told once they have been conquered.

Walker presents her personal story as representative of the stories of millions of other smokers whose lives are delineated by the most insidious of addictive desires. A long-term smoker who watched her father die of lung cancer, she is desperate but unable to give up. She presents herself as suffering from an incurable disease, forced to continue smoking by an addiction to a powerful drug that controls her life. She insists that, just like other drugs nicotine becomes the center of the addict's existence, leading to reprehensible behavior, abdication of responsibility, and a pervasive "spiritual bankruptcy."[19] Adopting a familiar addict identity she states, "As with other addictions, a drug often dictates where I go, which people I associate with, even where I will work" (*Smoker*, 13–14).

But the stubborn ordinariness of smoking and smokers undermines her attempts to inhabit the junkie persona. As Walker herself states, most smokers' lives appear relatively orderly, autonomous, and productive. To prove this is an illusion, she relates the low points of her own smoking career: drying out old butts from the rubbish with a hairdryer, refusing to go on church trips with her children because they entail two smoke-free hours, spending her honeymoon sneaking cigarettes in the bathroom, and risking her life smoking outside in a snowstorm. Her confessions are touching because of the strength of her self-directed frustration and shame, but as a portrait of the degradation of addiction the effect is less than dramatic. The fact that she finds these incidents so horrifying and alienating emphasizes, rather than casts doubts on, her general probity and sense of responsibility.

Since a steady supply of high-quality nicotine can still be relatively easily maintained, smokers are not generally desperate junkies controlled by an unmanageable, compulsive desire—at least until they attempt to stop. When she writes about her own longest period of abstinence, Walker unintentionally but eloquently suggests that smokers only become addicts when they quit. After a week without cigarettes she is "a useless lump" (*Smoker,* 51). She gains 40 pounds, her blood pressure rises, she develops a stiff neck, a painful rash, and aching joints, and she becomes a depressed recluse unable to concentrate, work, sleep, or stop crying. After eight months of torment, she starts smoking again. She ironically notes that having recommenced her unhealthy habit, she becomes healthier and more optimistic every day. All her symptoms gradually disappear and she is able to resume her normal busy life.

The dichotomies of addiction and normality, and disease and health, central to disease models of addiction, are unstable in the case of smoking, despite the specters of cancer, emphysema, and heart disease. Part of the reason why the disease and disorder of addiction remain remote is that for Walker, like many quitters, the serious consequences of smoking are yet to be. They exist as abstract possibilities, while the distress of giving up is corporeal and immediate. Doing the healthy thing makes her unhealthy. Nicotine is the *pharmakon* in her narrative, both poison and medicine. It is killing her but can also cure her.

The very existence of *Smoker* is testimony to the peculiar status of smoking among drug addictions. The book's publisher is the Hazelden Foundation, a major provider of drug rehabilitation services, whose publishing mission is to provide literature and material to inspire and assist readers in their own Twelve-Step recovery programs. In view of this aim, its policy is to publish books by people who have successfully recovered from the addiction they are writing about, *Smoker* being the first exception to this policy.[20] According to editor Sid Farrar, the prevalence of nicotine use among members of the recovery community who are otherwise abstinent, and the damage it causes, makes smoking a unique case that is worthy of such an exception.[21] What he does not mention is that the acceptability of a still-smoking smoker writing about her addiction also depends on the incongruity between smokers and other drug addicts. Despite their inability to control their drug use, smokers are regarded as capable of rational thinking and realistic assessment of their situation. In marked contrast to an active alcoholic locked in denial and self-delusion, Walker has insight into her addictive disease and can describe it clearly and honestly. The text argues that smoking is an addiction as destructive as all others, but the fact that the book exists suggests otherwise.

Another unacknowledged paradox is that the "uniquely cunning" drug that Walker is addicted to is not what is endangering her health.[22] Nicotine, in itself, is not generally regarded as particularly harmful, and has been observed to have beneficial effects on the brain.[23] The harmful substances, in medical terms, are the tar and carbon monoxide in cigarette smoke.[24] But this distinction, between addictive agent and source of harm, cannot be made in a discourse that constructs dependence and physical harm as interlinked elements of the one overarching disorder. The NicA philosophy supported by Walker argues that the evil effects of smoking and the tyranny of addiction cannot be separated, because the disease of addiction is, in itself, the source of physical and psychological harm.

The current popularity of nicotine replacement devices as aids to smoking cessation brings the double identity of the drug to the fore. Good nicotine in the form of (ever more potent) gum, patches, and nasal spray is being celebrated as a breakthrough treatment for attachment to bad nicotine.[25] Ironically, nicotine as cure may, at least in the short term, cause more distress to the user than nicotine as poison: nausea, vomiting, dizziness, sore mouth and throat, rashes, and insomnia are possible side effects of treatment. Another danger is excessively accurate mimicry, causing the good to blur into the bad. Addiction to nicotine gum can occur after long-term use, with some users experiencing symptoms "very similar to those associated with cigarette withdrawal."[26]

The final irony is that, while Walker insists that smokers are "junkies," the authority and appeal of her story depend on the fact that she is a "normal," law-abiding, middle-class citizen. Identifying with her struggles is easy for the "average reader" because they represent the mundane but heroic efforts of a woman to do her best by her husband and children, her work, her friends, and her community. Walker does not deserve the indignities of addiction because she is otherwise so respectable and competent.

Despite Walker's best efforts, smoking fits awkwardly into the Twelve-Step disease model of addiction. Given the tensions and paradoxes already discussed, it is not surprising that the pleasures of cigarettes emerge as clearly, if not more clearly, from her text than the costs. She confesses that smoking "gives me a peace that I've found no place else" (*Smoker,* 19), and that "nicotine does everything asked of it. It works" (*Smoker,* 18). Later, she adds that the drug becomes a god to smokers because "it never fails. It is always there"

(*Smoker,* 108). These tributes are powerful and resonant in their conciseness. No wonder smoking cessation guides talk about quitting as mourning the loss of a loved one and warn neophyte former smokers about the possibility of vivid smoking dreams (*Stop Smoking,* 73–74).

It is not only such narratives as Walker's that evoke smoking's virtues as supremely reliable and inimitably versatile. Much mainstream anti-smoking material contains clinical, but no less enticing, portrayals of the unique qualities of nicotine and the efficiency of the cigarette as drug delivery device. We are told that the drug is both calming and stimulating (*Stop Smoking,* 12), and that the nicotine from a cigarette can reach the brain in seven seconds, faster than if it were injected.[27] Dedicated smokers can deliver up to four hundred hits of nicotine to their brains a day, and far from becoming intoxicated, their mental efficiency is increased.[28]

What is more, smokers learn to maintain a constant level of nicotine in their blood. They are sensitive to tiny variations in dose, and if given milder cigarettes will inhale more deeply to achieve their preferred concentration. Anti-smoking texts portray this as an entirely unfortunate reaction, reducing the potential benefits of low-tar brands. For them, the finely tuned and specialized corporeality of the smoker is a corruption of the body's natural state of organic and self-contained integrity. But the inhaling and exhaling of the smoker's body, its connection with the atmosphere through the medium of smoke, also brings to mind the radically different understanding of embodiment constructed by Deleuze and Guattari. In *A Thousand Plateaus,* they theorize bodies as inorganic and untotalizable assemblages, formed through the making of provisional linkages between heterogeneous objects. No ontological or hierarchical distinctions are made between animate and inanimate bodies, biological, social, or textual bodies.[29] Appropriating Spinoza, Deleuze and Guattari define bodies by their specific capacities or "affects," by what they can do, the sensations they can experience and the range of their potential interactions with other bodies.[30] From this view, the smoker's connection with the cigarette and her responses to nicotine appear as increases in the range of the body's powers, that is, the body's capacity to affect and be affected. In addition to the delicate manipulation of drug levels are the sensory and aesthetic stimulations of smoke in the airways, object in the mouth, and movement of the hand. The actions and reactions of smoking can be read as a testimony to the adaptability and sensitivity of a body that can actively produce and experience pleasure through all sorts of connections, flows, and intensities, including regulated flows of toxins.

Of course, the recognition that cigarettes are not only useful, but contain a "darkly beautiful, inevitably painful pleasure" has been convincingly expressed elsewhere, most recently, and comprehensively, in the work of Richard Klein (*Cigarettes,* 2). But locating the pleasures of smoking in unequivocally anti-smoking texts has a sly appeal of its own. It is not surprising that, as Klein notes, anti-smoking warnings can incite the practice they hope to discourage (*Cigarettes*, 1, 89, 189).

SMOKING AND FUTURE RISK

In the broad field of contemporary anti-smoking literature, Walker's autobiographical narrative and Hoffman's Twelve-Step guide are unusual in their emphasis on psychic and spiritual damage. As smoking does not have the obviously life-disrupting and socially harmful consequences of other addictions, most texts give a dominant role to physical health in their production of tobacco use as a major social issue. But for most smokers the seriously deleterious medical consequences of their habit lie in the future, while its rewards are experienced in the present. Hence anti-smoking material highlights links between the remembered past, present behavior, and the anticipated future, constructing a unidirectional and linear notion of time. Through its deployment of the notion of risk, anti-smoking discourse tends to negate the gratifications of the present in favor of the dangers of the future.

In the plane of two-dimensional time, a "smooth flowing continuum in which everything in the universe proceeds at an equal rate," the smoker is produced as at best a time waster, at worst a perverse and self-destructive time destroyer.[31] The idea that addiction is a form of disordered temporality appears in many different locations. For example, sociologist Norman Denzin, drawing on Heideggerian categories, calls alcoholism a disease of time. The alcoholic is living with an altered and inauthentic temporal consciousness, out of sync with and alienated from "normal time." He is fearful of the future and the past, but trapped within them, unable to live in the now of the present. In contrast, normal time grounds us in the present and is not threatening or anxiety producing, but is part of our ongoing presence in the world, allowing us to work toward achievable goals.[32] In Walker's text being an addict means failing to live up to the challenge of passing time. She sees herself as stuck in a "perpetual teenagedom," slave to an impulsive decision made thirty years ago by a naive and lonely college student (*Smoker*, 64). Relying on a drug to solve her problems has meant missing her chance to learn how to be an adult. Her addiction holds her present hostage to her past and is destroying her future.

Mainstream public health literature is less metaphorical in its use of temporal explanations. It depends explicitly on the truth of the connection between smoking and future ill health, aiming to make the probable and the possible real enough to motivate behavior change. While accepting that nicotine addiction is a central aspect of smoking, this literature downplays its power, placing faith in the ability of education and awareness to provide the resolve needed to quit. Accurate information about risk is the key weapon against addiction in the approach of mainstream public health literature, exemplified in the Australian book, *SmokeScreen: A Guide to the Personal Risks and Global Effects of the Cigarette Habit.*[33] Much of the highly detailed (and rather tortuous) information this book provides is conveyed in the form of statistical links between smoking, disease, and premature death. In the preface, author Barry Ford, sets out the book's field of inquiry:

> To really understand the dangers of smoking, people need information that will provide explicit answers to questions like: What are the chances that it *will* happen to me? What are the odds of a smoker developing lung cancer, some other form of cancer, emphysema, heart disease, or one of the other diseases that can be caused by smoking? What is the overall probability of one's death being caused by smoking, and for those who are killed by smoking, how many years prematurely do they die, on average? (*SmokeScreen*, xi)

After reviewing the research, the text suggests that people who die as a result of their smoking are likely to do so fifteen to twenty years before their time (*SmokeScreen*, 210). Overall, U.S. smokers suffer a life-loss of about eight years (*SmokeScreen*, 132). More precisely, according to one study cited, men aged around thirty lost 4.6 years of life expectancy if they smoked up to ten cigarettes a day; 5.5 years for ten to twenty cigarettes; 6.2 years for twenty to forty; and 8.3 for more than forty (*SmokeScreen*, 131). In terms of specific diseases, *SmokeScreen* estimates that, on average, long-term smokers face a 1 in 6 chance of dying of lung cancer, a 1 in 8 chance of dying of heart disease, and a 1 in 19 chance of dying from emphysema (*SmokeScreen*, 122).

"Real understanding," then, depends on accepting isolated and precise probabilities as accurate reflections of reality and on seeing one's future as an individually held commodity that one either judiciously protects or recklessly gambles away.[34] But this represents a particular view of the world, not a transparent window on the real. While not denying the reality of the dangers, I want to point out that the argument is not as straightforward as antismoking texts suggest.

Mary Douglas has observed that the contemporary concept of risk has departed from an earlier neutral meaning in which high risk described a probability of great gain or great loss. Stripped of its connections with positive outcomes, and with the element of chance de-emphasized, "*risk* now means danger; *high risk* means a lot of danger."[35] In health promotion texts like *SmokeScreen,* the valorization of specific risk calculations into "the truth" brings the future smoothly into existence in the present, imbuing it with a solidity that masks the uncertainty and inaccessibility that are its necessary attributes. The very unpredictability of the future is translated into a series of solely negative outcomes. In fact, in the world of *SmokeScreen,* the practice of smoking is reduced to its potentially most undesirable outcomes; namely, various premature, painful, and protracted forms of death. The enhance-ments of existence that can come with smoking are dismissed as illusory and excluded from the calculations of risk. How could they be included? The benefits of such things as solitary peace, self-sufficiency, style, concentration, camaraderie, and rebellion cannot be quantified. Moreover, in the dis-course of "health risk" there are no willing gamblers, lucky or unlucky, there are only pitiable or foolish victims. It is assumed that making choices about risk can and should be done "objectively," but this ignores the diversity of values and commitments people draw on, and refer to, when assessing risks in daily life.

Also obscured is the extent to which our individual futures are not sepa-rate channels that we can steer independently in any direction, but are more like threads in a woven fabric, the pattern of which is determined by social forces and the relations of power in which we are all embedded. Our decisions alone do not control our futures, and our decisions themselves are not made in an abstract space of pure choice. The irony is that it is only the future's supposed openness that makes it possible for people's actions to influence it, but they must assume the yet-to-be can be known in order to choose their actions rationally.

Reference to risk inevitably has political dimensions, the concept brings with it questions of responsibility and blame. Douglas notes that the con-temporary language of risk works as "a common forensic vocabulary with which to hold persons accountable."[36] For smoking, the attribution of blame is complex. The logic of addiction does not cancel out the belief in individ-ual responsibility for health, central to health promotion discourse. As an addict the smoker is not to blame for her current dependence on cigarettes, and the role of tobacco companies as predatory risk-mongers is acknowl-edged. But, by contrast, for texts like *SmokeScreen* to make sense, individuals must be presumed to have control over their "lifestyle" choices and, hence, their health.

Again this tension is resolved through contrasting the unalterable neces-sity that is the present with the possibilities of the future. The implication is that the forces of culture and addiction that currently imprison and deceive the smoker will somehow weaken their grip or disappear in times to come, allowing her to free herself from dependency. Anti-smoking texts can thereby maintain an optimistic tone despite their grim message. Armed with the truth, smokers can ensure that their future is different from their pre-sent; they are reassured that giving up is highly effective in reducing the risks and that the body has an "astounding repair capacity." After four smoke-free months there are no remnants of the four thousand chemicals in smoke left in the body.[37] And after ten to fifteen years, risk of premature death returns to near that of people who have never smoked (*SmokeScreen*, 204).

However, the smoking body's potential for recovery is only half the story.

The notion of future risk simultaneously produces the smoker's body as always already diseased and unhealthy. According to *SmokeScreen,* for one long-term smoker out of two the addiction will prove fatal (123–27). There is no way of knowing who will be struck down and who will be spared, therefore all smokers must presume they will be among the former. In addition, the statistical construction of smokers as people who die eight years younger than nonsmokers, produces all smokers as already suffering a loss of life. As Nelkin and Lindee have observed in another context, "possible future states, calculated by statistical methods, are often defined as equivalent to current status."[38] The smoker who takes comfort in her present health and fitness is living in ignorance of the true identity of her body that lies in its future deterioration.

Sociologist of science Helga Nowotny's work is useful in thinking about the production and deployment of future risk in these texts. She argues that in contemporary Western life the future is disappearing and being replaced by what she calls the "extended present."[39] We believe we can, and should, determine the future in our activities in the present through technological innovation, planning, and solving of impending problems. This allows us to imagine a better future, but also means the problems that could formerly be deferred into the future reach into the present. And as the future is worked out in the present, the limitations of the utopian dream become apparent. Thus there is a tension between the desire for the yet-to-be conceived to remain inconceivable, and the desire to control and know the repercussions in advance.

Nowotny's focus is on technology, but her ideas can be applied fruitfully to the way the boundaries among the past, present, and future are made porous in anti-smoking and health-promotion texts. The culturally endorsed and heavily promoted habit of thinking in terms of health risks means our present behavior is seen as determining the quantity and quality of our individual futures. This knowledge both opens up possibilities and closes them down. We know we can look forward to a longer and happier future by giving up smoking, and by exercising and eating well, but every day as we fail to do these things, fulfillment of the promise becomes less likely. In making the choices we make today, we have to consider our responsibility to our future selves, just as we can berate our past selves for choices that have had negative outcomes. Seemingly small and trivial acts, such as the impulsive trying out of cigarettes as a teenager, are refigured into "deadly choices," to quote the title of a popular book.[40] The distinction between the disordered temporality of addiction and the natural, unthreatening passage of normal time is hard to maintain. It is not only the addicted who are unable to live in the present. They may be controlled by their pasts, but joining the ranks of the healthy brings control by, and obsession with, the simultaneous knowability and unknowability of the future.

In both the discourses of addiction and of future risk there are strains and gaps through which alternative understandings of smoking can be glimpsed. If the attractions of cigarettes are taken seriously and thought of in relation to temporality, it becomes possible to construct a different relationship between smoking and time, one from which the smoker emerges as an active and skillful producer of time and pleasure. Moreover, this not only refigures smoking, it also brings out positive attributes of addiction itself. The concluding section sketches out these possibilities.

TEMPORALITY AND ADDICTION

The pleasure of smoking is connected to temporal effects, the small ritual marking the passage of time as well as taking up time. Indeed, cigarettes can be argued to make time. To quote Klein:

> The moment of taking a cigarette allows one to open a parenthesis in the time of ordinary experience, a space and a time of heightened attention that give rise to a feeling of transcendence. (*Cigarettes,* 16)

This image is translated into a matter of everyday survival by the young, white, working-class mothers studied by British sociologist Hilary Graham. Cigarettes enabled them to bring structure and order to otherwise chaotic working days. In addition, the assertively self-directed activity of smoking represented making and taking space and time for themselves. In lives dominated by the demands of others, the availability of such a resource made the difference between coping and losing control.[41] A consideration of temporality adds to understandings of sexual difference and smoking, beyond the boundaries of Graham's specific study. The vulnerability of women to the lure of cigarettes and the difficulty with which they quit have been discussed and lamented by many. In feminist accounts like Bobbie Jacobson's, women's dependence on cigarettes reflects their subordinate status. They smoke to deal with the frustration of always having to be "nice," with the stress of their multiple roles, and because they have few other opportunities to exert control. Another often-cited factor in women's smoking is fear of weight gain, described as coming "close to paranoia" (*Stop Smoking,* 80). Interpreting this as a symptom of patriarchal oppression, Jacobson states that "being thin is one of the few sources of self-esteem society allows us."[42] In contrast to the dependent and oppressed female smoker central to these interpretations is the popular representation of a new breed of hard-drinking, heavy-smoking career women, adopting "masculine" habits in their quest for power and success.[43]

These explanations, whatever their veracity, construct women as motivated by lack, while leaving the male smoker unmarked and unproblematized. Women use cigarettes as substitutes for power, self-esteem, self-confidence, freedom, or love. Men, by comparison, are smoking purists, they smoke for smoking's sake. But if smokers are viewed as manipulators of time and space, it is possible to imagine typically male needs filled by the practice. In the Wayne Wang/Paul Auster movie *Smoke*, smoking is an enabler of male intimacy. Protected by a haze of smoke, the male characters share secrets and stories, console each other, give advice, and cement friendships. Perhaps the location of smoking somewhere between activity and idleness brings about a space that is open enough to allow self-exposure and emotional connection, without being so gapingly and threateningly empty to inhibit the cautious unfurling of masculine forms of responsivity.

The important, if obvious, point is that the nature of the time and space created by cigarettes is not universal, but depends on the context and the identity of the smoker. In contrast to the male characters of *Smoke*, Ellen Walker, the self-described nicotine addict, calls cigarette smoke a "tangible wall" that she uses to distance herself from others, both physically and emotionally (*Smoker*, 105).

By bringing together the themes of addiction and time, it is possible to argue that the temporal qualities of smoking are as central to its addictiveness as the pharmacology of nicotine. Like the novel reader, the lone smoker can remove herself, at least partially, from common social time, shielded behind a curtain of smoke as she indulges in a solitary pleasure. Nowotny observes that in the West making more time is the supreme principle of human activities (*Time*, 97). Time is understood to be in short supply, and the wish for "more time" is common and heartfelt. Usually the longing for is not merely for more, but for a different kind of time. People want "time for themselves," beyond the socially organized and solidified mappings of work and leisure.[44]

Smoking can be seen as an efficient method of acting on the "longing for an [autonomous] moment" (*Time*, 132). One remains in touch, but a contemplative distance is placed between the doer and the deed, mediated by the actions of smoking. Smoking is not considered doing anything, but neither is it doing nothing (*Cigarettes*, 35). A smoker quoted by Walker states that having a cigarette generates a sense of accomplishment, "even if I'm doing nothing else—I feel as though I'm getting something done, as though I'm busy" (*Smoker*, 48).

The temporal otherness of the cigarette depends in part on circularity and repetition. The sameness of each act suggests a recursive and reversible time, a soothing contrast to the steady marching on of linear time towards death. Klein observes:

> Every single cigarette numerically implies all the other cigarettes, exactly alike, that the smoker consumes in series; each cigarette immediately calls forth its inevitable successor and rejoins the preceding one in a chain of smoking more fervently forged than that of any other form of tobacco. (*Cigarettes*, 26)

In the context of this discussion the chain is more like a wheel. Each cig-arette makes a link with past and future cigarettes, but not necessarily its immediately preceding and succeeding neighbors. The connection is between repeated moments that recall and foreshadow each other: the morning coffee cigarette, the waiting for the train cigarette, the cigarette after sex, the last cigarette of the day. On the wheel of smoking, the sense of accomplishment engendered by smoking results from the inciting of desire as well as its fulfillment. This makes addiction not the terrible cost of smok-ing, but rather an intrinsic part of its pleasure, ensuring as it does the pre-dictable return of desire. Anti-smoking texts promote the tendency of each cigarette to be a disappointment as a reason for quitting (*SmokeScreen*, 178), but their ability to deliver an unsatisfied promise of fulfillment has also been celebrated as part of cigarettes' perfection.[45] What ultimately emerges is the addictiveness of desire itself, in Barthes's words, "it is my desire I desire, and the loved being is no more than its tool."[46] After all, it is addiction that guar-antees a potentially endless repetition of pleasure.

Smoking, by creating another time outside of ordinary duration, a time that is neither busy nor idle, is like other technologies that are valued for their temporal alterity: listening to music, swimming, meditating, rebirthing, and s/m rituals to name a few. Rather than simply destroying time in the future, smoking also creates a different time in the present, where the need for it is felt most forcefully. The addictiveness of cigarettes, an aesthetic as much as chemical property, is part of this power, and this power is an ele-ment in their addictiveness.

The smoker who quits is trading one form of extra time with another. The inclusive ideal of health celebrated in the discourse of health promo-tion obscures this exchange by collapsing together avoidance of future dis-ease with the adoption of self-enhancing and fulfilling practices. The use of "health" to encompass almost all that is worthwhile and valuable ignores the fact that the desire for a long and disease-free life can, and often does, con-flict with practices that make us feel like we are doing more than merely existing.[47] In her self-portrait Walker presents her inability to quit despite the risks as testimony to the strength of her addiction. But it could also be read as a product of the tension between living in the present and protect-ing and improving one's future. Striking the balance is perhaps a question of taste, rather than truth.

An Intoxicated Screen

Reflections on Film and Drugs

Maurizio Viano

Dedicated to the memory of Pierre Bourdieu.

A time to rend, and a time to sew, a time to keep silence, and a time to speak; a time to love, and a time to hate; a time for war, and a time for peace. What gain has the worker from his toil?
—ECCLESIASTES III, 7–9

INSTRUCTIONS ON HOW TO USE

There is a drug war out there that, like all wars, has its deaths and innocent victims, atrocities, and destruction. There has been a war for some time, "America's longest war" some call it, and I am for peace. Ironically, however, in order to ensure peace I have to fight, because if I do not fight I will not contribute to the creation of a counterforce capable of opposing those who want to keep us in a state of war. Thus my writing, here, is also a form of fighting: I will fight by writing about film and drugs in a certain way.

What follows is a mixture of information and provocation, scholarship and militancy, film history and theory. I have taken many liberties with academic discourse. In fact, if you have never felt dissatisfied with academic writing and reading, if you have never dreamed of a greater usefulness for our profession and labor, if you have never wished that academic writings could become more like the media and effectively negotiate the images and representations of reality, if you have never felt pangs of Sartrean nausea at the thought of the ghetto we inhabit, then this essay is not for you. If, on the contrary, you have had such feelings, and you would like to probe and grope with me in search of a use-value for our labor, then be patient with my writing: it is searching for a route to flee the academic citadel. In graduate school and the years before tenure, my writing was forced into an addiction to academic rules, and addictions are hard to break. As argued by several theorists on the Left (for example, Eagleton), academic writing may be constitutionally unable to be the vector of a struggle, precisely because of the rules governing its style.[1] A flight from academic style is thus also a sort of fight.

This chapter is about the representation of drugs in the cinema: "the intoxicated screen" (to be defined later). I write about the cinematic screen (although the television and computer screens are just as precious as sources of information) because cinema is my academic specialty and is the oldest of the public screens. I am intrigued by the fact that, chronologically speaking, the inception of the "drug problem" roughly coincides with the birth of cinema, and I am convinced that an investigation of the latter can yield a better, archaeological understanding of the former. To be sure, in the late nineteenth and in the first half of the twentieth century, motion pictures did not have as fundamental a role in shaping the public perception of drugs and addicts as the press did, but things have changed in the course of time. In addition, the movies' impact on the public sphere was/is magnified by cinema's capacity to create the by now (in)famous "impression of reality." And the more or less endemic presence of drugs in the film world, though not quite as determinant as in music, no doubt enhances cinema's unique role in the creation of the signs "drugs" and "addict."

This chapter has two sections. In the first, I attempt a historical reconstruction of the field under scrutiny. In the second, I formulate some theoretical reflections from the borders of the intoxicated screen. To anticipate my thesis in its unoriginal simplicity: the lack of realism and compassion that undergirds the war effort is largely a question of representation, or, to put it in a no longer fashionable "semiospeech," a question of signs: it is what drugs and addicts signify to the majority of people that creates the context for "Zero Tolerance." The representation of drugs in various films has intersected sociohistorical reality in ways that imperiously demand our attention. At once "reflecting" and fabricating reality, these films have occasionally expressed dissent, but, for the most part, have been responsible— together with the other media—for the uncanny consensus that keeps the war churning. Indeed, this thesis is not much compared with what we will find along the way, the questions I shall be forced to ask, the answers you will be pushed to envision. As in most cases, getting there is what counts: exploring and exposing the tangents that make this topic not only fascinating but also imperative.

"Imperiously" . . . "uncanny" . . . "imperative": to legitimize the sense of emergency of this beginning, I will alternate the chapter's two main sections with three communiqués. Conceived as some kind of unpleasant tours of the war zones (this is after all a wartime essay), these communiqués aim to drag into the picture a few harsh realities. Fragments of a reformer's discourse, they will convey some of the facts and arguments that circulate in antiprohibitionist circles and are surprisingly ignored by most of us. In the context of my essay, the information relayed by these communiqués will be like complementary food for thought. Or, better, since both the FDA and I believe that food and drugs should be ruled by the same epistemology, these communiqués are like drugs for thought: they will hopefully provoke an ideal humoral state in the reader.

COMMUNIQUÉ N. 1

As happens in several other states, California's legislature does not allow needle exchange programs. There are, however, loopholes. In San Francisco and Los Angeles, for example, the city health officials periodically declare a state of emergency and are thus able to distribute sterile syringes. Elsewhere in the state, activists run semiclandestine programs with the unofficial tolerance of the police. On occasion, however, (as recently happened in Santa Cruz) these activists get busted, only to be later released (meanwhile taxpayers' money and court time have been wasted) and return to the streets to face more harassment. Now, they get busted because they are giving addicts clean syringes so that AIDS will not spread. Let me repeat that, to let the enormity of this reality resonate through to the end of this essay. People get arrested because they give addicts clean syringes so that AIDS will not spread. How can one take seriously politicians who fret about AIDS and health care, while letting the United States be *the only* Western country in which clean syringes are not available (and are thus sold on the black market). How many lives could be saved if we made the sale of syringes without prescription legal overnight? You don't know? Neither do I, but I am sure it's many—even one would be many. Clearly, something is wrong. What kind of images of drug addicts have the American people been fed over the decades, for them to acquiesce in a policy that is tantamount to saying, "These people should die anyway, so let AIDS take them?" And if someone who does not use drugs gets infected, too bad for her/him. What was s/he doing with drug users anyway?

THE INTOXICATED SCREEN

With the general and provocative title "intoxicated screen" I intend to delineate and set aside, demarcate and designate, an area of cinematography that, I hope, will become a frequent topic of investigation in the near future. I have, in other words, the ambition of earmarking a body of films and authors, thus creating something that has the self-legitimizing authority of a genre or a style. Just as we have political cinema, black cinema, film noir, and so on, I suggest that we have a "Cinema of Intoxication and Addiction" (hereafter referred to as C.I.A.—a playful reminder of the dark side of American politics so often linked with the maintenance of the drug problem). I think that we, academics in film studies, can make our small contribution (whatever its slant) to this most pressing sociocultural problem by bringing to the surface the layers of images that have sedimented in the collective imagination.

Naturally, an investigation of the C.I.A. should include the screen representation of legal drugs, alcohol and cigarettes, food and love addictions, and, ultimately, obsessive behaviors of all kinds. The global picture would thus acquire monumentally vast proportions. Here, I restrict myself to the "intoxicated screen": films that somehow intersect the problematic imaging of substances that are currently illegal and, though different in history, effects, and chemical compositions, are, perhaps irresponsibly, grouped under the umbrella term "drugs." It would be interesting to start with a semantic de(con)struction of the term drugs, but I do not have enough space. I encourage readers to complement what follows with a Derridean reflection on the ambiguity of the term "drugs," an ambiguity all the more relevant since sweeping legal and cultural decisions are made as if we knew for sure what drugs are and do.

To analyze the intoxicated screen does not mean stopping at the verification of the drugs' presence in a film, but rather using such presence as a point of departure for an investigation of cultural, *pharmako*-aesthetic, and political reflections. From a taxonomic point of view, the field under examination begins with the literal, that is with films that have drugs in them. This category in turn should be further divided on the basis of whether a film portrays drugs as its main topic (for example, *Trainspotting*) or in the background (for example, *Pulp Fiction*). Then there are those (films made by) directors who have made a point of reminding critics and the media that they took drugs: Jean Cocteau is the best example of such a subcategory. Finally, there are those individual films of which everyone in the field knows that drugs were somehow involved. The most blatant example that comes to mind is Scorsese's *Taxi Driver*. According to its producer, Julia Phillips, everyone on the set was doing cocaine—especially its director and main actor—and references to "dope" appear in Scorsese's interviews about this film. In fact, several of the Italian American director's films wait to be analyzed from the standpoint of intoxication and addiction, his use of "drug music" (most notably the Rolling Stones), and the presence of narrative paradigms that are typical of the C.I.A. (for example, the problematic expression and containment of a bodily excess that, in Scorsese's films, is usually personified by Robert De Niro and is given a spiritual dimension by a gnosticlike reversal of values).

The most useful taxonomy, however, is perhaps the historical, one that interrogates films as cultural documents produced in a specific time and place. The history of the intoxicated screen has already been exhaustively and painstakingly documented by Michael Starks's *Cocaine Fiends and Reefer Madness*, a 1982 book that lists virtually every film having any reference to psychoactive drugs. Written in the late 1970s, Stark's book is framed within the optimism of a decade that regarded drug prohibition and censorship as moribund. Needless to say, he was in for a surprise, as the drug war intensified, the "drug scene" changed dramatically, and so did its cinematic representation. Be that as it may, Starks's book is invaluable and cannot be ignored, but constitutes a mere starting point. A closer look at the constellations of films that he hastily identifies, an update of the film production since the late 1970s, and, above all, a theoretical reformulation (Stark shuns theory contemptuously) are sorely needed. Since I wish, here, to emphasize the synergistic relationship among drugs, cinema, history, and prohibition/war, I introduce the demarcation proposed by Albert Gross and Steven Duke. Respectively a journalist and a Yale law professor, Gross and Duke cowrote *America's Longest War,* a book that can be viewed as the first symptom of a "serious" counteroffensive after the Reagan/Bush administrations effectively closed the debate and escalated the war.

Under the title of "Lessons from the Past," chapter 5 of their remarkable book provides its readers with a sketchy but dense overview of drug prohibition. Arguing that "most Americans operate as though drug prohibition were an immutable law"—when, in fact, we have had it for a little more than eighty years—the authors thus propose the following demarcation: the pre-Prohibition epoch (the dawn of history to 1914); the pre-cold-war period (1914 to 1945); the Pax Luciano (1945 to 1964); the Age of Aquarius (1964 to 1978); and the Age of Narco Glitz (1978 to the present).[2]

It should be noted that Gross and Duke themselves pay an indirect tribute to cinema's hegemonic influence by entitling two of this chapter's subsections after two famous films, respectively, *Reefer Madness* (the section that reconstructs the emergence of the 1937 cannabis prohibition) and *The French Connection* (the section that explains how the Italian Mafia "entered into an arrangement with Corsican syndicates in Marseilles"). Moreover, in describing the Age of Aquarius period, the authors suggest that "among intellectuals and artists, a favorable attitude toward drugs was pronounced, and the consequence was an upsurge in pro-drug propaganda" (*America's Longest War,* 100). The list of "artists" who developed "a favorable attitude" would certainly include filmmakers and actors, just as "the pro-drug propaganda" would include numerous films. Finally, "Narco Glitz" cannot but refer to the glorification of antidrug police units and operations that has infested our large and small screens. As they put it, since "the late 1970s, the topic of drug smuggling and interdiction has been a staple of low-brow motion-picture and television entertainment and a sure ratings-getter for the nightly news and documentaries" (*America's Longest War,* 101). If I were to outline a historical demarcation with cinema in mind, I would perhaps distinguish only four periods and introduce, of course, the Hays Code as one of the turning points. The overall result, however, would be strikingly in synch with that of Gross and Duke: Pre-Code (from dawn of cinema to 1920s); the Code (1920s to 1950s); the Great Illusion (1960s to late 1970s); and Wartime Cinema (1980s to the present).

I will now proceed to sketch a brief history of the intoxicated screen. Assuming the reader's greater familiarity with the last two periods, I give the former two a little more attention. Alternating fragments of film history with fragments of history proper, I hope to identify some of the most problematic areas while providing the reader with a sense of what can be achieved by an investigation of the C.I.A.

The representation of drugs was one of the first objectives that early filmmakers pursued with cinema in its prelinguistic infancy. Entitled *Chinese Opium Den*, the first-known kinetograph was made in the mid-1890s, lasted half a minute, and could be watched by dropping a coin in one of the newly installed kinetoscopes. The representation of drugs is thus coextensive with the history of cinema. It is likely that the visions supposedly afforded by the drug experience well suited the intention of Meliés-like filmmakers desirous to test cinema's potential for visionary images. (Meliés is regarded as the numinous forefather of special effects and fantasy, at the opposite pole of the Lumière brothers' realistic impulse.) It was not until 1912 that a major cautionary film was made, inspired by the recent vicissitudes of Coca Cola—in the wake of the 1906 Pure Food Act, the soon-to-be-giant corporation had been accused of misbranding its product and denying the presence of cocaine in it. Made by no less than D. W. Griffiths, *For His Son* narrated the story of a young man who becomes the hopeless victim of an addiction provoked by a soft drink containing cocaine. The first in a series of films depicting drugs along lines similar to those of the temperance-inspired films (the alcohol prohibition movement was gaining momentum), *For His Son* was rapidly followed by such "drug scare" films as *Slaves of Morphine, The Drug Terror,* and *The Drug Traffic.* In addition to suggesting their box office appeal, the sheer number of drug films made between 1912 and 1914 constitutes the first example of Hollywood's "collaboration" with Washington, for these were the years in which momentous sociohistorical changes were taking place.

In 1912, the Foster Bill, the first federal attempt at legislating the commerce, sale, and use of opiates and cocaine was defeated in Congress. But two years later, in 1914, Congress passed the Harrison Act, commonly regarded as the beginning of drug prohibition. In fact, the act's wording was ambiguous and doctors retained the power of freely prescribing drugs and thus maintaining their addict patients. It was not until 1919 that the Supreme Court made two historic decisions (*Doremus v. United States; Webb v. United States*) that gave more power to the federal government and prohibited the maintenance of addiction by doctors and clinics.[3] Drug addicts found themselves in the impossible situation of needing an illegal substance and were thus turned into criminals. Meanwhile, attracted by the prospect of large profits, the underworld stepped in, or, if it was already in (narcotics were already restricted in many states even before the Harrison Act), it increased its involvement with drugs. As the drug world was being pushed underground, the profile of the drug-taking population changed definitively, crowning a trend at work since the beginning of the century. Middle-class women, doctors, and nurses, all in all respectable, if "weak," people, had been the typical nineteenth-century drug addicts.[4] With time, however, users became increasingly younger, lower class, and were often associated with ethnic minorities, undoubtedly one of the main reasons for which prohibitionist measures were taken.[5]

Meanwhile cinema seemed preoccupied with glamorizing the danger that drugs represented for innocent women (these were also the years of the white-slave hysteria) and the representation of drugs was not in synch with these sociohistorical shifts. According to Kevin Brownlow, the author of the most authoritative study of the C.I.A. in the silent era, most of the major films of the time continued depicting middle- and upper-middle-class addicts (for example, *The Dividend,* 1916). Although their descent into a narcotic hell was often shown as caused by either unscrupulous doctors or fiendish friends, compassion for their plight was becoming rare (especially after the "Red Scare" linked drugs with subversion), soon to be replaced by disgust, contempt, and fear. A lot more research, however, is needed to illuminate the field of forces at play in these first years of prohibition, monitor the progression from compassion to contempt, and achieve a better understanding of the relationship among class, historical changes, and cinema. One should also keep in mind that the film world was, in reality and in popular imagination, infested with forbidden powders and therefore part of the very problem that antinarcotic laws wanted to fix. Quite a few drug scandals involving actors and actresses took the public opinion by storm.[6] Concomitantly, there were also films that took the topic of drugs lightly, and ironically, with an eye perhaps on the massive drug use within the Hollywood community. In addition to the so-called coke comedies, an extant, if silly, gem of the period is *The Mystery of the Leaping Fish,* in which a Sherlock Holmes-wannabee injects cocaine gleefully in a way that would be unthinkable in the 1980s, and perhaps even today.

Then, as happened with the representation of alcohol and sex, violence, and other bad habits, the Hays Code set in. At first, drugs could appear only in morality plays (*Human Wreckage* [1923], inspired by the death of star Wallace Reid); then they all but disappeared from the screen. *The Pace that Kills* (1928) was the last "intoxicated" film. For almost three decades, cinema broke its relationship with reality. Only a few hints at drugs surfaced here and there, the most famous of which was to be found in Charlie Chaplin's *Modern Times* (in jail, the tramp unknowingly administers himself an elephant dose of some unknown powder and acquires a superhuman courage that allows him to squash a prison riot). The 1930s, however, saw the production of a handful of unsubtly titled exploitation films on marijuana, a substance left out of the Harrison Act: *Assassin of Youth* (1935); *Tell Your Children*, better known with its later title *Reefer Madness* (1936); and *Marijuana: Weed with Roots in Hell* (1937). Bearing in mind that the Marijuana Tax Act, the bill that initiated hemp/cannabis prohibition, was voted by Congress in 1937, these films constitute an invaluable source of information on hegemonic representation.[7]

Reefer Madness, for example, harbored a series of discursive and representational gestures (images, dialogues, an appeal to parental concern, editing associations) that are still the staple of antidrug films today. More important, it was one of those priceless faux pas, made by hegemonic representation, a piece of unadulterated ideology that showed just how ignorant the decision-makers were (misrepresentation, in the media as in the government, is often not a matter of conspiracy, but of plain, old ignorance). *Reefer Madness* constituted perhaps the most telling example of the synchronicity existing between Washington and large sections of the press and the cinematographic establishment. What actually happened exemplifies Gramsci's notion of hegemonic block at work and deserves mentioning, however briefly, here. Harry Aslinger, the first federal drug czar and the most viciously repressive and intolerant fighter of the drug war's initial stages, wanted to make sure that the marijuana bill would pass smoothly in Washington. The Hearst papers, which had vested interest against hemp as a cash crop and had been rallying against it for more than twenty years, intensified their attacks against marijuana's violence-inducing properties.[8] And cinema made Anslinger and Hearst a gift in the form of a short film that unhesitatingly depicted cannabis as worse than cocaine and heroin.

According to official figures, drug addiction reached a historical low in the period of WWII. It is more likely, however, that the social researchers' attention was aimed elsewhere and overlooked the trends in drug use, at least for drugs like cannabis. Consumption of opiates may indeed have gone down since America depended on foreign countries for its supply. The postwar period is called the "Pax Luciano" by Gross and Duke, in reference to the ease with which heroin reached the United States under the aegis of Mafia boss Salvatore Luciano, aka Lucky Luciano. Virtually nobody outside the field of drug studies knows that it was the American government that indirectly facilitated the massive comeback of heroin after the war; similarly, many people ignore that heroin became a drug used predominantly by African Americans because the Mafia decided that it should be sold only in their neighborhoods.[9] One should credit mainstream cinema for depicting, albeit with a twenty-five- to thirty-year delay, this complex situation in two films, both made in the early 1970s (the most "enlightened" period with respect to the representation of drugs): *Lucky Luciano* (1971) and *The Godfather* (1972).

An Italian film by Francesco Rosi, *Lucky Luciano* showed how the boss, who had been tracked down, convicted, and jailed by the FBI in the late 1930s, was mysteriously released after the war on account of his collaboration from inside his golden prison—Luciano had used his clout to get the Sicilian Mafia to cooperate with the Allies during their invasion of Sicily. Exiled from the United States, Luciano set up shop in Italy, buying heroin from the Turin-based pharmaceutical company Schiapparelli and sending it to the United States via Marseilles. Rosi's film, which American audiences were never able to see in the director's cut version, contains one scene in which U.S. officials blame Italians for allowing legally manufactured heroin to slip into Luciano's hands, while Italians blame Americans for reinstating numerous mafiosi into power in Sicily in return of services rendered during the war (*America's Longest War,* 99–100).

Made by the Italian American director Francis Ford Coppola, *The Godfather* followed the 1969 novel by Mario Puzo to the letter and thus contained, tucked away in the folds of its epic grandeur, the priceless sequence of the godfather's acceptance of the drug trade. During the top bosses' meeting in a New York high-rise, the don from Detroit lays out the strategy with which the old-guard mafiosi defused the guilt, if any, associated with the drug trade: "In my city I would try to keep the traffic to the dark people, the colored. They are the best customers, the least troublesome, and they are animals anyway." Interestingly, it was yet another film made in this period, *The French Connection* (1973) that depicted Luciano's successors, the Marseilles gang. What this Hollywood, mainstream film forgot to mention was that the French and Corsican mafias had up until then operated with the implicit blessing of the American government because, as in Sicily during the war, the mafia provided help, this time against the communist unions (*America's Longest War,* 99–100). *The French Connection* incidentally, is a good example of how in cop films, a large subgenre of the intoxicated screen, the evil of drugs is taken for granted: the spectacle of violent police activities, in which the law is broken repeatedly by the enforcers themselves, are offered to spectators without any explanation because, in fact, none is needed. The evil of drugs is supposedly so self-evident that Popeye Doyle's brutality against derelict users in Harlem needed no softening, no explanation, in the same way that John Wayne's ruthless killing of Native Americans in the 1940s and 1950s could go unquestioned: Bloodthirsty savages were the Indians, hopeless and dangerous psychopaths are the addicts, no questions asked.

Returning to the postwar period, we should notice that alcohol, after being equally cast out of the screen by the Hays Code, made its powerful comeback with a string of "social problem" classics (from *Lost Weekend* [1945] to *Days of Wine and Roses* [1954]), films in which the Alcoholics

Anonymous model replaced the Victorian. Alcoholism was no longer a matter of immoral and fiendlike behavior, but a disease. Tellingly, no such permanent conquest has been made in mainstream drug films.

In the 1950s, drugs too began resurfacing in the mainstream cinema with Otto Preminger's courageous *The Man with a Golden Arm* (1954). Although its hopelessly Hollywoodesque treatment all but destroyed Nelson Algren's novel, this film humanized a heroin addict and opened the way to more accurate, though less commercially successful, efforts (for example, Shirley Clarke's *The Connection* [1960]). Orson Welles's haunting tale of madness and corruption on the Mexican border also was made in the 1950s. Although a great film, indeed one of his best, *A Touch of Evil* (1958) may, in fact, have irresponsibly contributed to the public perception of cannabis as a menacing weed from hell, for it showed a group of Mexican youths under the influence of a smoked product threatening the hero's wife with rape. Not only did the film reinforce the lie that associated cannabis with violence (as *Reefer Madness* and Anslinger's "scientific" arguments had done twenty years before), but, most importantly, it continued the racist association of the drug with Mexicans.

The racist and xenophobic aspect of the drug war, and of the intoxicated screen, is perhaps the area that most needs exploration and exposure. It is as if the evil of drugs could not be accepted as American and thus had to be portrayed as foreign or black. Just as opium use was associated with the Chinese, cocaine became the subject of hysterical fears in the South because of the superhuman powers it allegedly bestowed on "negroes." Needless to say, the threat of sexual assault and miscegenation always lurked behind the scenes. Finally, cannabis hemp was associated with "lazy" Mexicans laborers (and, of course, with black musicians, as happened with heroin). Think of the subtle ideological effects achieved by the introduction of the word "marijuana" into the English language. By hammering a slang Mexican word into the heads of Americans in the 1930s (when, as we have seen, the American public at large found out about it), Anslinger and the media at once forced a subliminal association of the "drug" with Mexicans and severed any connection with hemp, a plant that had been a prized cash crop for more than two centuries. This fantasy of drugs as a virus coming from outside to corrupt an otherwise healthy body seems to be a universal ideological practice. During World War I, France blamed Germany, whose pharmaceutical companies were unrivaled in the production and dissemination of cocaine and morphine/heroin, for corrupting the French youth and army. Today the United States blames Colombia and Mexico (again), just like India, for example, blames Pakistan for the flow of "brown sugar" in its cities.

Cinematography is of extreme help in this case, allowing a close examination of the iconography of traffickers, dealers, and other evil influences. Let me bring to your attention, at this point, the one film that Michael

Starks, in his frighteningly accurate list of films-with-drugs around the world, overlooked: *Open City,* one of the most important films in the history of cinema. Made by Roberto Rossellini in 1945 and regarded as the harbinger of the revolution in filmmaking that went by the name of neorealism, this Italian film narrated the last days of the Nazi occupation of Rome. Italians, even the Fascists, were portrayed as a basically good people destroyed by a foreign pathogen agent called German Nazi. Associated with homosexuality, the latter also used drugs to corrupt a hapless Italian girl and make her collaborate with their nefarious plans.

Open City set up a rigid good/evil binary opposition that contained a revealing pharmacological dimension: whereas drugs are evil and used by the Germans to corrupt the Italians, wine, which Italy copiously produces, consumes, and resists considering a drug, is depicted as having the redeeming quality of inducing truth: *in vino veritas.* One night, a drunken Nazi officer launches himself into a tirade against the German army, saying the truth about himself and his country. The following day, sobered up, he reverts to being a ruthless assassin by killing a priest whom an Italian firing squad had refused to shoot. Indeed, the analysis of *Open City,* a film everyone in film studies and in Italy knows, from the standpoint of drugs is but one example of the work that needs to be done: looking into the crevices and folds of films that are not about drugs and have been watched by millions of people.

The period that Gross and Duke call the "Age of Aquarius"—"The Great Illusion" in my demarcation—is characterized by the dissolution of the Hays Code and by the exponential growth of the number of films depicting drugs, more or less prominently. Rather than flooding readers with titles (we are entering the territory that most readers' knowledge and memory can cover), I prefer to make a few points that bear relevance to my investigation.

- Drugs like cannabis acquired a political status (Abbie Hoffman's "Every time I smoke a joint is a revolutionary act"), and it was not uncommon for films to portray its use in very different terms than before (for example, *Easy Rider* [1969]).

- LSD and the psychedelic movement entered the scene, engendering not only films about it (for example, *The Trip* [1967]) but a whole aesthetics that spilled over into many films that have nothing to do with drugs.

- Drug-abuse films multiplied and became a vast subgenre with political, cultural, and (non)aesthetic traits.

- Cocaine acquired a new cult status that differentiated it from heroin. Whereas the latter saw its image as the devil incarnate solidified (typically, the big dealers of the cop films of this period are heroin dealers) cocaine's image softened (for example, *Superfly* [1972] by African

American director Gordon Parks, contains a quickly edited sequence in which the powder emerges as something desirable).

· Drugs became a staple of exploitation films, in concoctions of sex, drugs, and violence. And "blaxploitation" all too eagerly filled the screen with users and pushers (for example, *The Disco Godfather* [1979])

· Closely related with the rise of subgenre films about drug abuse was the phenomenon of avant-garde and underground filmmakers (for example, Kenneth Anger and Jordan Belson) whose drug, and/or drugged films often are "personal, honest, free, and unpredictable to a degree rarely attained in the commercial cinema."[10]

· Last but not least, drug use began to appear in many films as a background activity of characters of all races, creed, and social status, an activity among others, thereby prompting the conclusion that drugs were being somehow assimilated by our culture.

On the sociocultural front, we could, for brevity's sake, summarize the turmoil of these two decades with five names/symbols:

· *Timothy Leary* (the puncturing of the American Dream through the "turn on, tune in, drop out" mythology and "the politics of ecstasy");

· *William Burroughs* (a different sort of puncturing the American Dream, "the algebra of need" instead of psychedelic illumination, heroin instead of LSD);

· *Vietnam* (main catalyst in the formation of a countercultural ethos, it brought to national attention the unsettling news of American soldiers hooked on Golden Triangle "smack," the first time in which the government truly worried about heroin addicts);

· *Richard Nixon* (the president who declared the War on Drugs and used it as a political weapon); and

· *Jimmy Carter* (the ultimate symbol of an epoch of mistakes, distractions, the ultimate failure to evaluate the conservative backlash that was waiting just around the corner).

The "Great Illusion," the dream of harnessing (some) drugs on a collective change of consciousness, faded, as violence and all sorts of contradictions began to surface. Hippie mythologies shattered. Drug use reached epidemic proportions, or, to put it more cynically, it reached the white, suburban communities, because certain drugs had been present in the black areas for a long time without stirring the "epidemic" panic. And just when Western culture needed a more honest and unbiased dialogue, a neither-pro-nor-against assessment of drugs, the debate was cut off, and the cinematic screen became intoxicated with the intolerance that marked the Reagan/Bush period: enter "Wartime Cinema."

If we exclude a few independent productions of the early 1980s (for example, *Liquid Sky* [1982]), the cinematic depiction of drugs deteriorated. Narco Glitz made its entrance, with its endless celebration of the police and its transformation of the drug world into a criminal underworld. The films made in this period tended to associate drugs with death, violence, and a whole range of socially dysfunctional behavior. Old stereotypes were reproposed again, with the seeming acquiescence of a public that had grown tired of drugs and regarded them as a thing of the 1960s. Few mainstream films in the entire decade can be said to have avoided the traps of the period, as did Joseph Ruben's *True Believer* (1985), in which an efficient lawyer is shown smoking cannabis as a choice that does not impair his functioning.

Consider *Clean and Sober,* 1988, one of the decade's "best" C.I.A. films. It set total sobriety as the only possible goal, regarded alcohol on the same level as cocaine (whose status had plummeted), and proposed the Narcotics/Alcoholics Anonymous disease model as the only way out: one is *born* an addict and doomed to either say forever no or perish, in a sort of biochemical replay of Calvinism. It also made a woman die in a car accident soon after (which is to say *because*) she had snorted a pinch of cocaine. Most important, *Clean and Sober* marked a return to the uncanny synchronicity between Hollywood and Washington. First, it focused on a yuppie coke user, Darryl Poynter, when, in March of the same year, Ed Meese, sensitive to charges that the War on Drugs was turning into a war on blacks and the poor, "sent a memo to all of his U.S. attorneys encouraging selective prosecution of middle and upper class users."[11] Second, in one scene, the father of a girl who had died a coke-related death in Darryl's condo posts on the latter's door a sheet accusing him of murder. This shot was virtually a cinematic translation of an image used by Nancy Reagan that same year: during a White House drug conference, she claimed that "the casual user may think when he takes a line of cocaine or smokes a joint in the privacy of his nice condo . . . that he's somehow not bothering anyone." In fact, Reagan continued, "There is a trail of death and destruction that leads directly to your door" and "if you are a casual drug user you are an accomplice to murder."[12]

By the early 1990s, however, there was a slow upsurge of drug films and a concomitant intensification of sequences with drugs in all sort of movies. Something was changing. To be sure, Narco Glitz continued—and continues. But next to the justifiably angry depictions of drugs-as-symptoms-of-inner-city-decay by some black filmmakers (Spike Lee, Bill Duke, Mario Van Peebles), a different type of film hit the screen with drug representations unthinkable in the previous decade. This new wave was initiated by Gus Van Sant's *Drugstore Cowboy,* which portrayed the adventures of four junkies in the 1970s in an ironic, nonjudgmental manner and contained an understandably famous sequence with underground cult figure William Burroughs. Playing Father Murphy, a defrocked priest of old age, Burroughs hit the nail on the head when he said, with his screeching baritone voice:

> Narcotics have been systematically scapegoated and demonized. The idea that anyone can use drugs and escape a horrible fate is anathema to these idiots. I predict in the near future rightwingers will use drug hysteria as a pretext to set up an international police apparatus.

In the context of this "new wave," Abel Ferrara's drug tetralogy (*King of New York, Dangerous Game, Bad Lieutenant,* and *The Addiction*) bears scrutiny, as do many small productions such as Perry Farrell's *The Gift* and Tupac Shakur's last film, *Gridlock'd,* the nationwide success of the youth film *Dazed and Confused,* and the Australian documentary *The Hemp Revolution,* which extols the virtues of the hemp movement. One cannot help the impression that someone, somewhere, is fighting back, that the blanket pulled over the screen by the drug warriors has been lifted in spite of the Clinton administration's insistence on the war efforts. We still have to see a film that shows the horrors of the drug war from the other side. We still have to see films that incorporate the reformers' struggle toward a Harm Reduction policy.[13] In other words, we still have to see films that somehow point in the direction of a drugpeace, films that can be called postwar in their representation and conceptual framework. But such films are perhaps impossible under the present epistemological regime.

COMMUNIQUÉ N. 2

Take a trip to the Pacific Northwest, drive through the redwood forests and enjoy the magic of the sunbeams dashing through the trees—those cones and shards of light that are employed by the movies to suggest a visitation by the gods. Especially if you live in the crowded East, or in the flat Midwest, you will find it hard to resist the charm of these densely forested area. Regardless of your political beliefs and environmental awareness, you will not be able to ignore the sight of the many trucks that carry from three to five huge trunks on their trailers: Yes, deforestation is on its way. Personally, I felt pangs of sadness and anger; you might feel something else, but you will agree with me that it is not a comforting sight. Each truck reminds you of some tall standing redwood trees that have been felled. It is not hard to imagine a future in which entire areas, once cathedrals of green light and auburn beauty, will be transformed into bald, stump-ridden, sad-looking slopes. For what? Why are we destroying so many trees? Well, lumber has many uses. In North America, for instance, houses and public buildings go natural and use up a lot of wood. Furniture is another important sector in which wood is employed to get that organic feeling. Lumber has so many uses. But a significant portion of these trees are cut to provide us with the wood pulp that feeds the ravenous hunger of our copying machines and newspapers, magazines and junk mail, the overload of paper that we take for granted in this age of consumption of plenty.

Let me ask a few questions. Are we sure that there are no other sources for paper? Do we know the history of the paper industry? What if there were an alternative way to make paper, what if our technology exerted its amazing skills to perfect the methods of paper making from other sources? Wouldn't that be a dream? Wouldn't that make your drive through the redwoods more pleasant, less guilt-ridden? Wouldn't you be less ashamed to belong to the race of warriors that not only subjugated the world into one "new world order" but also disfigured the planet in preoccupying ways?

You can imagine how I felt when I discovered a 1916 U.S. Department of Agriculture bulletin that reported that one acre of hemp in annual rotation during a twenty-year period would produce as much pulp for paper as 4.1 acres of trees being cut down over the same period.[14] Unfortunately, the bulletin explained, this alternative method could not be implemented until the invention of decorticating and harvesting machinery allowed for its economical utilization. But in February 1938, the journals *Popular Mechanics* and *Mechanical Engineering* both proudly announced that the decorticating technology was finally available and predicted a bonanza for hemp farmers. The problem was that only a few months before the Marijuana Tax Act had been passed, and Anslinger's agents were getting ready to travel to the forty-eight states to uproot the ubiquitous weed. According to some, it was not a mere coincidence. Once again the synchronicity of events was so astounding that it deserves one more paragraph.

When mechanical hemp fiber-stripping machines and machines to conserve hemp's high-cellulose pulp finally became state-of-the-art, available, and affordable in the mid-1930s, the enormous timber acreage and business of the Hearst Paper Manufacturing Division, Kimberly Clark (USA)[a], St. Regis[a]—and virtually all other timber, paper, and large newspaper holding companies—stood to lose billions of dollars.[15] Moreover, Lammot Du Pont, the chief munitions maker for the U.S. federal government, patented, in 1937 (!), the synthetic fiber nylon and a polluting, wood-pulp paper sulfide process. Needless to say, he had all the interest in effacing the competition that hemp, one of the easiest and most environment-friendly plants to grow, was about to pose. And, Du Pont's chief financial backer was no less than Andrew Mellon of the Mellon Bank of Pittsburgh who, in his role as Hoover's secretary of the treasury, appointed as head of the newly established Federal Bureau of Narcotics and Dangerous Drugs, his future nephew-in-law: Harry Anslinger!

What other economic interests were/are at stake in the suppression of the information on what used to be the one of the most coveted crops in the

United States? Hard to say, but one thing is certain: the possibility of using hemp to slow deforestation (and perhaps even replace fibers whose making requires polluting chemicals) is left unexplored because hemp has been regarded /discarded as a drug. Clearly, something is wrong, and it is imperative that we understand what intoxicating representations of hemp have been provided to get the American people to accept such illogical behavior

THE F(L)IGHT OF THEORY

And they were amazed and wondered, saying, "Are not all these who are speaking Galileans? How come, then, that each of us hears in his own native language? Parthians and Medes and Elamites and residents of Mesopotamia, Judea and Cappadocia, Pontus and Asia, Phrygia and Pamphilia, Egypt and the parts of Libya belonging to Cirene, and visitors from Rome, both Judeans and proselytes, Cretans and Arabians, we hear them talking about mighty works of God in our own tongues." And all were amazed and perplexed, saying to one another, "What does this mean?" But others mocking said, "They are filled with new wine."

Acts of the Apostles, II 9–13

During a call-in radio program on a local Boston station, shortly before the 1993 gay march on/in Washington, the host expressed his disagreement with a caller who supported the march by exclaiming: "But . . . homosexuality is a private matter, you don't go around doing marches. What's gonna be next? Are we gonna have a heroin addicts' march?" In his delirious wish that both gays and junkies do their thing without throwing their scandalous presence into the public's face, the radio host actually fueled an idea that I had been entertaining for a while, namely that the fate of drug users and sexual minorities had something in common. My work on the Italian homosexual filmmaker Pier Paolo Pasolini had alerted me to the fact that in a repressive, Catholic, sociohistorical context, homosexuals can live (are likely to live) their sexual preference as a transgressive act. Inscribed in the homosexuals' subject position is the potential, if not the likelihood, that they experience themselves as guilty users of forbidden pleasures. Furthermore, homosexuality has often been linked with drug use by homophobic representations equating same-sex relationships with vice and decadence. In the last fifteen years, the AIDS crisis and the specter of death have continuously associated intravenous drug users and homosexuals. And, if we turn our gaze to the hidden, revelatory power of language, we cannot help noticing that "straight" designates both being not gay and not under the influence of drugs. [16]

Shortly thereafter I chanced upon the brilliant writings of Eve Kosofsky Sedgwick, whom I shall quote at length to reintroduce a breath of academic air in my essay. Writing about addiction, Sedgwick suggests that, as happened with homosexuality, "under the taxonomic pressure of the newly ramified and pervasive medical-juridical authority of the late nineteenth century, and in the context of changing imperial and class relations, what had been a question of acts crystallized into a question of identity." [17] The addict and the homosexual were thus born at the same time and out of similar discursive impulses.

> The two new taxonomies of the addict and the homosexual condense many of the same issues for late-nineteenth-century culture: the old antisodomitic opposition between something called nature and that which is *contra naturam* blends with a treacherous apparent seamlessness into a new opposition between substances that are *natural* (for example, "food") and those that are *artificial* (for example, "drugs"); and hence into the characteristic twentieth-century way of problematizing almost everything of will, dividing desires themselves between the natural, called "needs," and the artificial, called "addictions."
>
> Furthermore, from being the *subject* of her own perceptual manipulations or indeed experimentations, [the addict] is installed as the proper *object* of compulsory institutional disciplines, legal and medical, that, without actually being able to "help" her, nonetheless presume to know her better than she can know herself—and indeed offer everyone in her culture who is not herself the opportunity of enjoying the same flattering presumption. [18]

I suggest that many films of the intoxicated screen have done just that: they have offered to millions of spectators the flattering presumption of knowing more about addiction than addicts themselves. By the same token, spectators have also been offered the equally flattering exemption from having to heed the addicts' voices. For, unlike what happens in all other cognitive domains, the discourse on drugs is regulated by this funny dynamic: experience makes one's voice suspect, and only those furthest removed from any experience with either drugs or drug users are entitled to legitimacy.

In *Epistemology of the Closet,* Sedgwick confronts and explores the leading metaphor that has regulated the lives and discourse of homosexuals: the closet. She argues that the closet, and the binary oppositions that it intersects, are central to an understanding of twentieth-century culture. Her argument that the silence of not coming out has a performative value and therefore is not really a silence is particularly convincing. She also defends the gay specificity of the metaphor, wishing to distance it from the recent sociolinguistic trends that cause the expressions "being in/coming out of the closet" to be appropriated by the nongay. I would argue that, in the case of drug addicts, we can pretty much adopt the notion of closet without worrying too much: drug addicts *are* (perhaps) the last minority to be forced, legally, morally, and culturally, into the closet, without really having the option of coming out.

Not that they would necessarily want to. Many users would probably be wary of the inevitable identity attribution that accompanies the gesture of coming out, the de facto "I am out therefore I am" (an addict) that would ensue from their courageous self-positioning. Nor am I sure that our culture, fragmented as it is by identity politics, needs more identities, more "I am this and that, and you can't understand me." Or maybe it does. Undoubtedly, it is a thorny question, made thornier by the seemingly insurmountable stigma that brands drug addiction and prevents those who do not use drugs from taking interest in the addicts' scandalous plight as modern scapegoats.[19] Some argue that the stigma will not be defused and defeated until respectable addicts acquire visibility, until the drug warriors are forced to face the existence of thousands of productive users. Some others feel that the whole notion of addiction needs overhauling, along the lines of Stanton Peele's work that, in many ways echoes Sedgwick's, albeit in a totally different framework and language. A psychiatrist devoted to research on addiction, Peele argues that the concept of addiction as it stands reifies people and substances, is *pharmako*-centric, and creates a cultural horizon that makes it nearly impossible to expect and pursue a break from addiction. Both Sedgwick and Peele seek to dodge the strictures of a binary system in favor of the multiplicity of paths and of identities.

However fascinated by this whole question, I must return to my cinematic concerns and verify the usefulness of the connection established between homosexuality and drug use/addiction. If drug users are a closeted minority, an analysis of the cinematic representation of drug use is then bound to turn into an examination of another "celluloid closet," to use the felicitous expression coined by Vito Russo to define the films that have depicted homosexuality. To be sure, the drug celluloid closet is different (we have seen how drugs surfaced in films from the beginning), but it is a closet nonetheless. Although no generalizations can be made about the enormous number of films depicting drugs, I propose to look at them as various manifestations of a celluloid closet of sorts.

Unlike what happened in the representation of homosexuality, there have been no periods of invisibility in the drug celluloid closet—except during the years of the Hays Code. Quite the contrary, drugs have tended to be seen so much and in such a light that they have been worse than if invisible. Their hypervisibility has made spectators feel that they have seen all that can be seen, and thus need no new vision(s). Too much visibility has bred invisibility. Moreover, in the dim, distorted light of the closet, a whole series of narrative (for example, a Jekyll and Hyde dialectic) and iconographic (for example, the xenophobic and racist images of the bad guys) gestures has coalesced and crystallized. To a certain degree, some stereotyping is inevitable in any genre, but the frequency of intoxication and addiction representations in a celluloid closet mode has turned stereotyping into stigmatizing. The cultural stagnation due to the permanence of a prohibitionist context, the unwillingness of hegemonic representation to be truly democratic and heed subaltern representations, and the quasi-religious framework typical of any discourse that thrives on words such as "fiends" and "demons," have stifled, when not suppressed, the possibility for celluloid users and addicts to change over time. They (users and addicts) are often portrayed now as they were ninety years ago, as if history stood still.

The drug celluloid closet does not reward the researcher with a sense of teleology. The story of the homosexual celluloid closet as outlined by Vito Russo presents some kind of linearity, from silence and the mask to misrepresentation to gay cinema. Indeed, if we consider the emergence of a queer cinema, or even mainstream concessions like *Philadelphia* (Demme, 1994), one cannot help feeling that there is some progress at work. Compared with its homosexual counterpart, the history of the drug celluloid closet is far less linear and more schizophrenic. No doubt this is a reflection of a historical reality, that is, of the way things turned out after the 1960s popular struggles. Whereas gays' rights successfully resisted the conservative backlash of the 1980s, the drug users' rights, which were never actually established, and were only selectively granted to *some* users (middle class, white) in *some* places and for *some* drugs, have disappeared pretty much everywhere. In the United States, drugs have had the doubtful honor of bearing the cross of the official scapegoat, formerly the privilege of communism. The pipe and needle have replaced the hammer and sickle. Thus, at a time when the gay celluloid closet started opening up, the representation of drugs saw the repressive tendencies of the closet radicalized by the escalation of the War on Drugs and thus entered the wartime phase that continues to this day. Because of the war, users and addicts are not the only ones to suffocate in the closet. The latter's long shadow has enshrouded even those (filmmakers/critics/producers of knowledge) who might want to represent drugs and addicts as other than demons.

All cultural production (including, therefore, cinema and writing about it) is straitjacketed by what I call a "wartime epistemology," where by epistemology I intend the often unconscious and theoretical grounds for knowledge and signification. A wartime epistemology only tolerates an either/or regime of signification and brings the binary tendencies of our culture to a rigid extreme. Out of all the possible questions that the knowing subject can ask of the object, wartime epistemology foregrounds only those that aim to verify the object's relationship to the war effort. Can this be a weapon? Is this an enemy? When Chief Darryl Gates of the Los Angeles Police Department remarked that drug users should be taken out and shot (!) because they are like traitors undermining their country at war, he was operating under a wartime epistemology. By repeatedly asking the same question and bringing out only one side of the object, the knowledge thus produced conjures up the idea of a stable universe. (Self-)questioning becomes a weakness. Deprived of their multiplicity and ambiguities, objects are perceived as fixed, values as absolute, and knowledge as objective. But the postmodern condition has convinced most of us, at last, that objectivity is impossible and that knowledge and representation, far from being disembodied activities, must somehow flaunt their subjective dimension. Everything we see and think is partially colored by who we are. Only those discourses and representations count that take this into account and inform their recipients about the subject's relationship with the object. The blossoming of autobiographically tinted theory in the last few years of the millennium can be traced to the theorists' realization that they have to let their readers know "where they come from." As the boundaries between mind and body fade out, what I incorporate, what I put in my body, acquires great discursive importance. Vegans are but the most visible symptoms of the growing awareness that dietetic identity matters. In sum, knowledge proceeds from a "bodymind" that is positioned racially, sexually, economically, and *dietetically/pharmacologically*.

In the case of illegal drugs, however, what kind of knowledge and representations can one produce, if one cannot bring the necessary subjective dimension to the topic (lest s/he be singled out as a war enemy)? An embarrassment in the eyes of posterity, wartime epistemology forces both the knowledge and the representation of drugs into a false position, at odds with the requirements of the postmodern epistemology that otherwise regulates all the other cognitive domains today. People have neither the ease to experiment with drugs, nor the freedom of creating a public sphere that might enhance their understanding of their experimentations. As a matter of fact, there can be no public sphere on the topic, no social architecture designed to host and facilitate a collective conversation on the issue's myriad ramifications. Merely raising the topic with any attitude other than condemnation is itself bound to create problems. Talking/writing about drugs, in academia, as well as in any other situation where a job, a career, a reputation, are at stake, is no easy task. And although the world of cinema lives in relative autonomy and is seemingly unaffected by "drug scandals," filmic representation does, in the last instance, depend on the dominant, wartime epistemology: *both* those who make films and those who talk/write about them are locked in a closet of sorts by wartime epistemology.

If producers of cinematic knowledge and representations are restricted in their movements by the wartime epistemology, on the other end of the spectrum, consumers of images are given representations that at best distort, at worst fabricate, a *false* reality. Let me pause here and direct your attention to the irony of a wartime celluloid closet that so distorts reality and vision as to become itself intoxicating (when not poisonous). Differently put, the wartime celluloid closet brings about those very effects against which the War on Drugs is fought. It may be worth noting, in passing, that cinematic representation is already in and of itself "intoxicating." Indeed, a fascinating subtext of the C.I.A. would consist of the investigation of those aspects that make film a drug of sorts:

- Cinema is a purveyor of visions—so much so that many films use (d) the drug theme as an excuse to explore the visionary potential of cinematography;

- Cinema is a form of escape, just like drugs are said to be;

- Films take their spectators on a trip, a voyage of the body and the mind, in the shadowy area of what I would call, borrowing the term from a recently formed branch of medicine, "the psychosomatic";

- Television, which Pasolini regarded as an "audio-visual technique" similar to cinematography, is in all seriousness spoken of as addictive; and

- Finally, if intoxication, as defined by Avital Ronell, "names a method of mental labor that is responsible for making phantoms appear," cinema, indeed, does make phantoms appear, phantoms that are larger than life.[20]

With their "narcotic" potential intensified by the wartime/closet epistemology, films about drugs have acted like the worst of psychoactive substances, instantly addictive and highly intoxicating. In the dim, distorted light of the closet, the C.I.A. has caused certain phantoms to appear time after time, thereby setting the notorious "truth-by-repetition" phenomenon in motion: show an image often enough, and it will be taken for real, the norm, the truth. It is for this reason that I decided to call this investigation of the C.I.A. the "intoxicated screen"—because in addition to representing intoxication, many films also produce it. I know of people who changed their image of drugs considerably after witnessing some users' ritual administration of dangerous drugs such as heroin. They were astonished by the extent to which the users' behavior was a far cry from the image they previously held—an image that had largely, if not solely, been formed on the basis of movies. Mainstream cinema has intoxicated millions of spectators, people whose only visual exposure to actual addicts and drug use/abuse consists of a string of celluloid villains and heroes.

You may have been wondering all along if things are as bleak as I portray them. After all, you remember seeing some honest films, and there were/are directors out of the drug closet. Film history does contain a substantial body of films that lie outside the mainstream and have portrayed drug use differently. Differently? That is the question. I would argue that most of the "different" films (and I do not mean those that irresponsibly exploit(ed) the glamour of drug use, but those that attempt "a certain realism") are still produced within and influenced by the wartime/closet epistemology; they are, in short, films that depict drugs as something transgressive. Many of these films reinforce the romantic myth about drugs, which may actually be the second worst thing after prohibition. The romanticization of drugs is made of the same cloth as their condemnation—both are problematic, and both are the by-products of the phantoms of the closet.

It is hard to imagine what the discourse on drugs would be like if it had not been subjected to the dialectic of transgression, and my anger is aimed precisely at those institutions that keep such a dialectic in place and thus delay our culture's apprenticeship in the use of drugs. Western culture has found a way of dealing with alcohol that, though not perfect, does not threaten the fabric of our societies. Most people know how to drink wine; we have dealt with it for millennia. Our ability to deal with alcohol is not something innate, nor is it some benign characteristic of the substance itself. We learned.

MacAndrew and Edgerton's 1969 pathbreaking study, *Drunken Comportment,* shows that "over the course of socialization, people learn about drunkenness what their society knows about drunkenness; and accepting and acting upon, the understandings thus imparted to them, they become the living confirmation of their society's teachings."[21] Drunkenness is thus partly learned. Several studies of drugged comportment have reached similar conclusions. Already in 1947 A. Lindesmith signaled the existence of powerful cognitive elements in heroin addiction.[22] Howard Becker's 1963 classic on deviant behavior, *The Outsiders,* suggested that pot smoking is no mere biochemical reaction to the plant's active principles, but a moment in which historically situated subjects act out what they know about and expect from the administration of the drug.[23] Most influential of all, however, is the work of the late Harvard psychiatry professor N. E. Zinberg who has encapsulated drug intoxication's cultural and cognitive components in the memorable "set and setting" formula, where "set" refers to the psychological, personal situation of the individual and "setting" to the context in which the experience takes place.[24]

If intoxication and addiction depend in part on what the individual has learned about them, what are the sources of such learning? In the essay "On Alcohol and the Mystique of Media Effects," Andrew Tudor has tried to define the extent to which the media (films) have represented and influenced the reality of alcohol consumption. Suggesting that learning about drunkenness is a complex process, Tudor argues that "our images of drunkenness have more than one source, but it is surely inevitable that the media play an important part in this process of collective articulation."[25] The exact same argument could be made about drugs, with the important difference that drugs are a recent acquisition in Western culture, and cinema has played a larger role in their cultural articulation than it has with alcohol. We must be able to envisage a postwar knowledge about drugs, together with a postwar cinema (what would a postwar cinema look like?), which might facilitate their incorporation in our culture. No prohibition will ever eradicate *cannabis indica, papaver somniferum* and *erythroxylon coca* from the earth. Only a slow incorporation, a careful digestion might work. But, when forced underground, digestion becomes all too easily indigestion. I am reminded here of a wonderful short film that Pier Paolo Pasolini made in 1962, *La Ricotta*. The film's protagonist is a disenfranchised outsider plagued by chronic hunger who works as an extra in a biblical film shot on the outskirts of Rome. Throughout the entire film, he tries to procure some food for himself, while the people around him ignore his needs and tease his frantic movements. When, at last, he gets to eat, he does so in the seclusion of an underground cave, far from everybody's eyes. Having thus unreasonably stuffed himself, he dies on the cross where he plays the bit role of the repentant thief next to Christ. Pasolini's cinematic parable images a theory of the risks involved in transgressive desire and consumption—and I mention it here to strengthen my claim that an investigation of the homosexual celluloid closet may indeed offer insights into its drug counterpart.

Perhaps we should go back to a pretransgressive period, when drug taking was not subjected to the good/evil binary. But is going back ever possible? Or we should perhaps revisit, with a postcolonial eye, those non-Western cultures (and, when possible, their cinematographies) that have a far longer history of coping with drug use, the Andeans who have for centuries chewed coca leaves or the Indians who have used hemp cannabis for millennia. A heartwarming, cinematographic example comes from the making of Satyajit Ray's masterpiece *Pather Panchali* (1956). The character of Indir Thakrun, the old toothless woman whose performance gave the film much of its timeless, touching beauty, was played by Chunibala Devi, an eighty-year-old retired actress who, apart from a small salary, demanded and obtained that she be provided with her daily dose of opium. Ray recounts the episode without any implication that Chunibala was immoral or sick. She just had that habit, much like you, reader, may have the habit of using caffeine to get going in the morning. But it is enough to see the damage we have done in these very countries, first exporting transgressive myths and new ways of drug administration, and then forcing a drug war agenda on their governments, to lose the hope that even they can go back to pretransgressive days. Satyajit Ray's last film, *The Visitor* (1992), depicts an old man who returns to India after a life spent in the developed West. Critical of India's Westernization, he recounts the horror of a world in which "there are millions of young people injecting poison in their blood."

So, dear reader, things are bad. And the drug war makes them worse. I did not come this far in the chapter to suggest a solution. As I announced in the preface, my thesis was merely a call to arms, an invitation to start working on the C.I.A. Films, insofar as they are produced within a cultural framework, reflect and represent their culture's reality. They also shape reality, fabricate consensus, inspire dissent. Either way, this complex, mutually defining relationship between cinema and reality needs thorough exploration and exposure. The C.I.A. is anxiously waiting (y)our contribution.

COMMUNIQUÉ N. 3

It has been calculated that the number of people in the United States who are currently either incarcerated, on parole, on probation, or under some form of court supervision approximates 5.2 percent. Five point two percent! The United States is currently the Western country with the highest number of people in jail per capita (you knew that). Needless to say, drug offenses make up almost 50 percent of the prisoners, and a staggering proportion of these belongs to the category of nonviolent drug offenders, or victimless crimes. Recently—and I could come up with dozens of similar examples— a Vermont man was arrested for growing six marijuana plants. The man was given a suspended sentence by the state court, but under U.S. federal law, his family lost the 49-acre farm. The forfeiture of property for drug violations has become a lucrative business, and so has prison building.

The Web informs me that Will Foster, a medical marijuana user suffering from rheumatoid arthritis, was recently sentenced by the state of Oklahoma to ninety-three (yes, you read well, ninety-three) years of prison for growing the forbidden medicine in a 5-foot-square room in his basement. He is currently being held in a Texas jail and, since his sentencing on February 27, 1997, has been denied access not only to his medication of choice but also to medicine prescribed to him by his family doctor, Voltarin and Napersyn, both anti-inflammatory medications, and Vicodin, a pain medication. Meg Foster, his wife, says that her husband's legs are swollen, discolored, and extremely painful and that her pleas that he be properly medicated have gone totally unheeded.

Clearly, once again, something is wrong. It is necessary to investigate what kind of images have been imprinted on the retinas and minds not only of the American people in general, but of the many professors in film studies who celebrate strategies of subversion in filmmaking, defend minorities, and give voice to the subaltern, but hardly ever say a word about what is happening to the victims of the War on Drugs, right here, right now. I want to understand why the discourse on drugs and the war against them is not on the liberal intellectuals' agenda. And yet drugs are quintessentially interdisciplinary and multicultural, the two buzzwords in academia these days. Drugs have enormous global (neocolonial), racial, and class ramifications. Is it fear? Is it puritanism? Is it the tacit assumption that Foster and the man in Vermont deserve their fate? Ninety-three years: Did a rapist ever get that much time? Many of you, academics and others, feel exempted from having to take an interest in the drug war since you do not do drugs (any longer). Well, it does not matter. One of the first things to throw out is the aura of suspicion surrounding the topic. You don't have to be a drug user to take an interest in the victims of the drug war, or in the Cinema of Intoxication and Addiction, just like you do not need to be black, or gay, or a woman, when you fight against the discrimination and oppression of these groups. So, once more, the C.I.A. needs YOU.

PART V

Trauma, Media, Cyberspace

9

Welcome to the Pharmacy

Addiction, Transcendence, and Virtual Reality

Ann Weinstone

It has become a truism to say that virtual reality (VR) is addictive. Case, the protagonist of William Gibson's *Neuromancer,* dreams of connection to the net like a junkie jonesing for a fix. In Jeff Noon's novel *Vurt,* you get to cyberspace by tickling the back of your throat with addictive, government-produced feathers. Verity of Kathleen Ann Goonan's *Queen City Jazz* sports nanotechnology implants that compel her to enter virtual worlds into which she sinks with feelings of deep bliss. As in *Vurt,* in Pat Cadigan's *Synners,* everything's an addiction: cyberspace, people, rock and roll.

But let's move away from fiction. Graphic cyberartist Nicole Stenger, a self-professed Neoplatonist, writes: "What if the passage to a new level of humanity actually meant abolishing indeed the natural one, or at least some part of it? . . . Will it not require immense effort to recover from this enhancement of the senses, from this habit of perfection?"[1] Michael Benedikt, editor of *Cyberspace: First Steps,* deems VR "a new and *irresistible* development in the elaboration of human culture and business under the sign of technology."[2] Ad copy in a May 1995 issue of *Wired* for "Origin," a VR game, reads, "You must die to learn how to live. . . . Death is not an option. It's an addiction." And an article in *The New York Times* titled "The Lure and Addiction of Life on Line" displays a graphic of a bespectacled male, tapping away at a computer located inside of a panopticon-sized rendering of a globe to which the avid user is happily chained.[3] From advertisements to scholarly texts, it is difficult to find any writing about VR that does not engage in and rely on the rhetorics of addiction. William Gibson dubbed cyberspace a "consensual hallucination." That was 1984. In 1996, critic Robert Markley rechristened VR "a consensual cliché."[4] Surely, the "addictiveness" of cyberspace contributes to the sense of tired familiarity. My questions are these: Why does cyberspace have to be addictive? What work is addiction doing in discourses of virtual reality?

I'm concerned here with the production of what might be called "hyper-real transcendence." Jean Baudrillard, in his influential schema "three orders of simulacra," identifies a first, "natural" order in which "a transcendent world, a radically different universe, is portrayed . . . in contrast to the continent of the real." Second-order simulacra are additive and productive; they enhance the real. Science fiction belongs to this order. Third-order simulated simulacra collapse the distance between the model and the original, the space across which transcendence has traditionally been produced. Baudrillard writes that the aim of simulation simulacra is "maximum operationality, hyperreality, total control. . . . Models no longer constitute an imaginary domain with reference to the real; they are, themselves, an apprehension of the real, and thus leave no room for any fictional extrapolation—they are immanent, and therefore leave no room for any kind of transcendentalism."[5]

I propose that a third-order, hyper-real, transcendence has survived the collapse of the distance between the model and the original. This transcendence relies on rhetorics of disembodiment, immortality, and extrahuman reproductive and generative powers within virtual spaces. Such spaces include scholarly and technical essays about VR or cyberspace, science fiction, advertisements for VR games, VR game narratives, and other advertising copy that borrows from current discourses of virtuality. Although "virtual reality" is clearly a locus for fantasies about transcendence of the body, it is my purpose here to show exactly how these fantasies rely on rhetorics of addiction, and how, within the context of a general "transcendentalizing" of the concept of code, they attest to the advent of an expanded notion of writing that no longer does the antiauthoritarian work of deconstruction but constitutes a refigured zone of uninterrupted presence.

In *Of Grammatology*, Derrida wrote that "scientific language challenges intrinsically and with increasing profundity the ideal of phonetic writing and all its implicit metaphysics."[6] Derrida published this inaugural section of his landmark work in 1965 during a time when cybernetic concepts and rhetoric were disseminating through diverse fields such as psychology, anthropology, literary studies, and molecular biology. The cybernetic urge, he wrote, is to "oust all metaphysical concepts," those such as soul, life, and memory. "[Cybernetics] must conserve the notion of writing . . . until its own historico-metaphysical character is also exposed." Even at this early date, Derrida intuits that the yet-to-be-fathomed historico-metaphysical character of cybernetics involves a "movement of inflation . . . which has also taken over the word 'writing,' and that not fortuitously." This inflation is a saying of "writing" to designate everything from action to experience to the unconscious, to the pictographic, the ideographic, and indeed, "all that gives rise to inscription in general" (*Grammatology*, 9). Despite holding out a certain hope for "scientific" or nonphonetic language, he ends the section by saying that "this nonfortuitous conjunction of cybernetics and the 'human sciences' of writing leads to a more profound reversal" (*Grammatology*, 10). This "reversal," hinted at by Derrida, can only mean the usurpation by nonphonetic language, by code, of the metaphysical import and effectivity formerly ascribed to voice and logos. I want to consider this "reversal," this apotheosis of code that, occasioned by the inflation of the domain of writing, has become a total world coding. In doing so, I will consider how the metaphysical character of cybernetics is revealed at the nexus of addiction and transcendence, and how, even in the writings of some progressive theorists, the maintenance of rhetorics of addiction conserves a certain metaphysical impulse.

In the Western tradition, transcendence commences with the penetration of the self by a supraenlivened Other, whether that other be a king, a god, nature, the voice of logos, the law, or an abstracted version of vitality itself. My initial point will be that following the established Western logocentric tradition, rhetorical relationships of addiction between VR users and VR narratives are the "software" with which hyper-real transcendence is produced and sustained. In other words, VR demands, as the price of transcendence, that the user become of the medium, of the other, through a relationship of compulsion, penetration, repetition, and bodily subsumption. Following this, I argue that the transcendental teleology of logocentrism achieves reproduction in VR discourses in part because the attribution "life" is shifting from the realm of the biological (DNA) and natural language to the postvital and code. Code is coming to function as the transcendental, unifying, and ideal substance of life—for the nonreferential, the unmediated—while at the same time, it retains attributes, or the trace if you will, of writing, replacing the body with a less mortal letter. To ingest, to become code, thus becomes the possibility condition for what I see as the conservative, Platonic notions of transcendence at play in narratives of VR.

RHETORICAL SOFTWARE: WHAT'S INCLUDED IN THIS PROGRAM

In *On Beyond Living: Rhetorical Transformations of the Life Sciences,* Richard Doyle develops the notion of rhetorical software. Viewing language as rhetorical software de-emphasizes language as a site of meaning and representation, and foregrounds instead the activity or force of language. Doyle writes:

> Rhetorics work more on the model of contagion than communication or representation; they pass through fields and agents as intertextual forces that recast knowledges and their knowers while sometimes remaining in the realm of the unthought. . . . There can be no easy distinction between writing and its "objects"; both are elements of an interface. The relations that make up this interface are maps of power.[7]

The urge for the author of a project such as this to define "virtual reality" takes on an imperative cast when the ubiquity and fluidity of usage is taken into account. But it is precisely this ubiquity, this transferability, this anything-goes mutability that marks the extreme rhetoricity of the term, that marks it as a fast-moving cultural force or agent. Consider that if VR can be located, it consists of animated games, some rudimentary VR "environments," the rare commercial VR arcade, unwieldy data gloves and visors, military and medical simulation programs, and an international communications network, the Internet, that is still primarily text-based. To this list I would add the essays, advertisements, fictions, and other narratives that are actively and forcefully participating in the production of VR. The heterogeneous contents of *Cyberspace: First Steps* attest to the presumption that natural language, code, and hardware are all reagents of VR. Here, fiction, cultural critique, anthropology, and essays about VR architecture and design are all recognized co-constructors. Rather than attempting to define VR, my modus operandi will be to include whatever is said to be included, in other words, to let the rhetorical software spin out its instructions, to see where it goes, what it produces.

Building on Doyle's notion of rhetorical contagion, or interfaces that produce maps of power, I want to follow two contagious or contiguous rhetorics that exemplify the Western tradition of linking addiction to transcendence and comprise crucial subprograms of the rhetorical softwares of VR that are producing transcendence out of addiction. I will start with William Burroughs's first novel, *Junky*, published in 1953. The influence of Burroughs's cut-up method of writing, particularly his novel *Naked Lunch*, on William Gibson's originary articulation of the cyberpunk mise-en-scène has been widely discussed.[8] Fronted and backed by notes from a sobered author warning against the physical and spiritual poverty caused by addiction, *Naked Lunch* serves largely as a cautionary tale. In *Junky*, however, no such cautions are in evidence. Here Burroughs explicitly maps, and to an extent valorizes, connections between addiction and transcendence.

Moving backward, I read discursive connections between transcendence and addiction in light of the professed idealism, or citational Platonism, of much of the constitutive rhetoric of VR. Discussions of cyberspace often make reference to Platonic idealism. Michael Benedikt speaks of a "mental geography" (*Cyberspace*, 3) that has existed for every culture. He relates cyberspace to ideas of a transcendent, heavenly city and to ancient Greek deductive geometry, which relied on idealized geometric forms to exemplify the nature of perfect reasoning (*Cyberspace*, 19). Michael Heim, author of *The Metaphysics of Virtual Reality*, terms cyberspace "Platonism as a working product." "The computer," he says, "recycles ancient Platonism by injecting the ideal content of cognition with empirical specifics. . . . The computer clothes the details of empirical experience so they seem to share the ideality of the stable knowledge of the Forms."[9] I reread the Platonism evident in VR discourses through the lens of Burroughs's take on addiction and Derrida's exegesis on Plato's pairing of "writing" with the *pharmakon,* with writing-as-drug, with unlife, and the simulacrum. My point will be that the production of transcendence via addiction is mapped here in the classic text of addiction and the classic text of logocentrism; VR discourses reproduce relationships of transcendence to addiction in exactly these well-established terms. Addiction, as a relationship of repetitious exchange and bodily subsumption by the drug, code, allows one to produce simulacra effects of disembodiment, life extension, and suprahuman powers, exactly the danger that writing poses to logocentric notions of presence, authority, and authorship. Yet because code is coming to signify transcendental, ideal life, this replacement of the biological by code in a phantasmatic space figured as an ideal "brain" allows the user to engage in rhetorics of the production of unmediated consciousness, the transcendence of representation, a virtual walk out of Plato's cave.

DEATH IS NOT AN OPTION (IT'S AN ADDICTION)

One of the most compelling and brilliant challenges any contemporary writer has raised against the absurd jurisdiction of death.

The Washington Post, as quoted on the back cover of *Junky* by William Burroughs

I confess I know something about heroin, about junk. I've never been a user, but my family members, friends, and lovers have. Long before I read *Junky,* I heard what I would term "junk myths," urban lore about the transcendence-producing powers of junk.

- Junk Myth #1: Junk makes you live longer. Junk time is slower than real time.

    Burroughs: "When you stop growing you start dying. An addict never stops growing. . . . Most addicts look younger than they are."[10]
    "I'm forty-one now. I feel about twenty-five or so. Look it too. Living in Vurt really slows down the rate of change."[11]

- Junk Myth #2: Junk endows the user with special powers. Junk is magic.

    Burroughs: "I do want usable knowledge of telepathy." (*Junky,* 152)
    Stenger: "Communicating at the speed of light on the computer networks induces euphoria, boosts intuition." ("Mind," 57)

- Junk Myth #3: Junk replaces human cells by turning them into junk.

> Burroughs: "I think the use of junk causes permanent cellular alteration."
> (*Junky*, 117)
> "There never seems to be enough time when your brain is being eaten
> by a cyber-virus. . . . Hardwire your neurons. Critics are calling Burn:Cycle
> 'a totally synthesized, fully transcendental, bio-controlled, electronic
> rush.'"[12]

This is junk rhetoric. It's also commodity rhetoric. Spend a lot of time
using our product (junk), trade your brain cells for cybervirus (junk/code),
and get a "transcendental" rush. In *Junky*, what gets traded in is the sensual,
affective body and its pains. What it gets traded for is transcendence. Not the
transcendence of the high—Burroughs spends little time reflecting on the
sensation of being doped up—but a transcendence brought about by being
an addict: immortality, extrahuman powers, reembodiment. Burroughs
writes, "A man might die simply because he has to stay in his own body. . . .
Junk is an inoculation of death" (*Junky*, 97, 127).

Burroughs repeatedly makes the point that this trade, this inoculation,
cannot be made except through addiction. The addict is not addicted to
junk, but to junk as a way of life, to habit. "The point of junk to a user is that
it forms a habit" (*Junky*, 99). Addiction removes the addict from real time
or, in VR terms, RL (Real Life), a removal that can only be effected, according to Burroughs, by the addict becoming of that alternate world, that is,
becoming junk.

> The kick of junk is that you have to have it. Junkies run on junk time and junk
> metabolism. They are subject to junk climate. They are warmed and chilled by
> junk. The kick of junk is living under junk conditions. (*Junky*, 97)

This isn't new. As Avital Ronell has noted, "Precisely due to the promise
of exteriority which they are thought to extend, drugs have been redeemed
by the conditions of transcendency and revelation with which they are not
uncommonly associated."[13] Robert Markley offers the cyberspace update
when he writes, "In cyberspace, the individual resolves the divisions within
her nature only by allowing herself to become an effect of the technology
that re-creates her" ("Boundaries," 73).

> And what exactly was (Keith) Richards' appeal? "Hey, man, look at him," says
> McKagan. (The Guns n Roses bassist and a former heroin user.) "He's cool,
> he's bad, he can get his blood transfused."[14]

In two recent novels, Jeff Noon's *Vurt* and Kathleen Ann Goonan's *Queen
City Jazz*, the main characters are "impure"; their bodies have permanently
incorporated technologies that give them special powers to merge with virtual worlds. Scribble, the protagonist of Noon's novel, has been bitten by a
dreamsnake, a creature of the Vurt, Noon's name for VR locales and their
virtual inhabitants. This bite, like the knowledge-giving snake of Garden of

Eden fame, contaminates Scribble's cells with traces of Vurt, enabling him to access its powers and pleasures directly without mediation. For the poor, low-level, government-produced feathers provide access to game worlds that substitute for real-world entitlements. Higher-level "knowledge feathers" are reserved for mysterious wealthy classes who, true to their less embodied state, never appear in the book. Those who use knowledge feathers may opt never to return from the Vurt; they may exchange "death for life," gaining a measure of immortality and supposedly transcendent knowledge via subsumption of the biological body by Vurt. However, this transcendence is governed by Hobart's rule, a law of exchange that says: R = V ± H. "Any given worth of reality can only be swapped for the equivalent worth of Vurtuality," plus or minus Hobart's Constant, "H," which is, not incidentally, slang for heroin (*Vurt*, 63). Noon, as does Burroughs, makes it clear: transcendence is for sale, and the price of admission is addiction.

In *Queen City Jazz*, because Verity's DNA has been replaced with tellingly named "Enlivenment," or nanotechnology, she may directly access and control virtual and material realms. In each of these narratives, access, and the knowledge and powers it brings, is paired with the rhetorics of addiction. The protagonists' choices to enter virtual worlds are never free from compulsion as they answer the call of their "permanent cellular alteration." In each novel, as in *Junky*, the protagonists seek fuller mergings with transcendent virtual worlds through penetration, repetition, immersion, and the replacement of the "natural" body with technologies of virtuality.

Verity's name is an obvious reference to the association of virtuality with transcendent knowledge. Initially, she lives in a community that forbids contact with Enlivenment. But Verity's cellular longing for the Enlivened city of Cincinnati pulls the narrative toward its denouement and her consumption/assumption of Enlivened systems. There, the binary code that has replaced or supplemented a portion of Verity's DNA becomes the vehicle for a direct, unmediated apprehension of new and powerful knowledges.

> You wanted power, she told herself. Now you must use it. . . . A binary code from deep within her surfaced. . . . A new scent filled the air, laden with information that went directly into her brain through her nose and was translated by her mind into knowledge bringing both dread and fierce exhilaration.[15]

Conversely, the Vurtually Immune are *Vurt's* "flightless birds," those who, for whatever reason, are not susceptible to the addicting, orally administered feathers that move human consciousness between RL and VR. Scribble says, "I had met one (of the Vurtually Immune) a few years ago and the look of despair in his eyes would never leave me" (*Vurt*, 26). In the remainder of this essay, I want to explore the question of why some of us want to be virtual, to ingest, to inject, to become binary code, in the light of another constitutive rhetoric that says we already are code: DNA.

EVERYTHING IS WRITING . . . BUT CODE IS THE MOTHER OF ALL

You can't wear the thongs of the cybernetic machine mask for long without feeling its seduction, knowing the grace that comes when the cyberlink between cortex and text becomes seamless and complete, feeling the code stamp itself upon the jelly of your flesh so that you metamorphose into a soft machine, knowing that it feels so . . . so right, and hurts so good.

PORUSH, *Out of Our Minds*

Welcome to the new world of point and click biology.

INCYTE PHARMACEUTICALS *advertisement, June 7, 1996*

It's a real floaty, godlike trip.

STEVEN TYLER, *Aerosmith singer, speaking of a heroin high*

Reprising Plato's opposition of writing to truth; of writing to presence; of writing to voice, Derrida says, "Writing is irresponsibility itself, the orphanage of a wandering and playing sign. Writing is not only a drug, it is a game."[16] In Plato's *Phaedrus,* the world of the simulacrum is fatefully linked to writing, to the *pharmakon,* a word signifying both drug and remedy. Writing contaminates; it weakens true, interior memory and substitutes rememoration and death for presence, memory, and life. Writing kills the father because it substitutes a nonliving representation for his living speech. In the Western logocentric tradition, only this speech carries the authority of logos: of presence, intellection, and reason. Thus, writing assumes a simulacrum of transcendent powers by representing the authoritative speech of the father. This substitution, this killing, intoxicates, effecting a release from authority, allowing the user to forget the artificiality of writing itself, to forget the simulacrum, to propagate the dangerously powerful effects of an errant technology.

Logos is living presence, unmediated intellection, "the hidden illuminating, blinding source."[17] This is the same blinding source that the escaped prisoner from Plato's cave approaches as he moves upward and away from enchainment and the shadows toward the sensible and the visible, and then, the sun.

> Whenever I'm feeling particularly paranoiac re: the God problem, I imagine that we're all just brains in bottles somewhere, thoughts in a void, . . . & this phenomenological world is some cheesy Total Recall vision we're renting from The Company who stays in business keeping us from the horrible ecstatic truth.[18]

Further on, Derrida notes that "Socrates' brand of magic is worked through *logos* without the aid of any instrument, through the effects of a voice without accessories. . . . When confronted with this simple, organless voice, one cannot escape its penetration by stopping up one's ears" (*Dissemination,* 118). Here, both voice and writing produce their effects through compulsion and penetration. In typically moralistic fashion, what Plato objects to is the slip of writing outside of the authority of the law, not to enthrallment itself. What we hold against the drug addict, Derrida claims, is that "he escapes into a world of simulacrum and fiction" ("Rhetoric of Drugs," 7). The addict body is an irresponsible, irrational body. Echoing Derrida's figuration of the addict, Istvan Csicsery-Ronay Jr., terms VR a "secessionist paraspace."[19] In the sense that cyberspace, a coded world, a simulacrum, a substitution, functions as a site of the production of a simulacrum of transcendent power, and that it does this via the rhetorics of addiction, cyberspace could be seen to threaten the metaphysics of responsible presence much as writing does in the *Phaedrus,* much as the figure of the addict threatens her responsible others. Yet for Plato, writing is a dangerous supplement of unlife because it simulates the living presence of the father with a dead thing, I want to suggest that largely due to the co-constitution of cybernetics and molecular biology, the signifier "life" is relocating to code, away from voice, phonetic language, and organisms.

During the 1970s, techniques for recombining and cloning DNA became available for the first time. Prior to this, as Evelyn Fox Keller notes, "The notion of 'genetical information' . . . was not literal, but metaphoric."[20] Once the four amino acid components of DNA were known, represented by the letters A, T, C, G, and sequences could be combined and cloned at will, the metaphorical association of DNA with "data" and "program" became an identity. As Richard Doyle writes:

> The conflation of what life "is" with the "action" of a configuration of molecules conventionally represented by an alphabet of "ATCG" produced an almost vulgarly literal translation of Jacques Derrida's famous remark, "il n'y a pas de hors-texte." Literally, the rhetoric of molecular biology implied, there is no outside of the genetic text. No body, no environment, no outside could threaten the sovereignty of DNA. (*Beyond Living,* 109)

Doyle writes that by the mid-twentieth century an invisible, unifying property, "aliveness," becomes located in the genome. But the notion of life as a hidden unity rendered molecular biology open to cybernetics, or information theory, and the "metonymic displacement of an organism by a code-script" (*Beyond Living,* 116). This displacement "plunges research ever deeper into the genome to a place beyond the molecule, the postvital." Today, "the postvital organism is nothing but coding" (*Beyond Living,* 17). Of the rhetorics of A-Life (Artificial Life), Doyle notes that the "conceptual move from the notion that life is a 'text' to the idea that 'information' can be 'life' is a short one" (*Beyond Living,* 110). Traditional A-Lifers look for the secret of life in emergent behaviors such as "flocking, schooling, and sex" (*Beyond Living,* 111). I think something quite different is happening in VR discourses. Here, the rhetoric of world-as-code, fully saturated with the idea that organisms are nothing but information, is conjoined with rhetoric of Platonic ontological hierarchies. In contrast to how noncarbon life is defined for A-Lifers, in VR discourses code does not have to exhibit any specific emergent behaviors in order to qualify as "life." Code is idealized life, life abstracted but actively engendering. DNA is no longer the Code of codes but has itself become a mere instance of information. Code as the transcendent, the extrahuman, is ontologically prior to DNA. Code is not unlife; it is the giver of life, the matrix of life.

Nicole Stenger, a computer animation artist, explicitly identifies herself as an "idealist" who has decided to "follow the light" ("Mind," 49). Transcendence is mapped in her essay along familiar lines: dis- or reembodiment into a "realm of pure feelings" ("Mind," 53), and the assumption of godlike powers of generation, which include the power to create and name new "cyberspace creatures." She speaks of "living twice" ("Mind," 52), that is, of producing binary-coded duplicates of herself and of her longing for "a D day when this substance (VR) would finally escape and invade what we call reality" ("Mind," 49). Of reembodiment, or becoming code, Stenger writes, "On the other side of our data gloves, we become creatures of colored light in motion, pulsing with golden particles. . . . In this cubic fortress of pixels that is cyberspace, we will be, as in dreams" ("Mind," 52). Finally, Stenger sees DNA-directed reproduction and evolution as a penultimate form of evolution and the ascendance to binary individuals as the more desirable state. "Wouldn't the drive for cyberspace be so irresistible that some of the basic functions of human life might fall off like ripe fruit? Human reproduction, for instance. . . . What if cyberspace were the final act of a natural evolution of a family? A mutation into the virtual cloning of individuals?" ("Mind," 56).

Other writers take a more critical, or at least a more quizzical, stance. Yet throughout VR discourses, the relationship of addiction to transcendence remains unexamined. This oversight leads to weirdly mutated versions of hyper-real transcendence that share foundational elements with logocentrism, even when it is logocentrism that is being critiqued. David Porush calls for "the re-assertion and re-adaptation of the genetic code (passion, imagination, the irrational) over the industrial one (rationality) that has tried to suppress it."[21] According to Porush, cybernetic code can never provide an adequate model for the metaphoricity, the nontotalizability of human consciousness. Postmodern literature, "the enduring attempt to model in words the activities of the mind in all its irrationality" ("Frothing," 259), provides more promising maps for evolving technology and ourselves ("Frothing," 247–49). Porush pays homage to "long habits of associating transcendence with essentializing beliefs" and to Derrida's derision of the "nostalgia" of the attempt to bring "the Word and the Spirit into perfect communion."[22] At the same time, he asks postmodern "antiessentialists" to reexamine the question of transcendence, arguing that "hyper-reality is a consequence of the human nervous system itself; the impulse to hyper-reality is hard-wired in our cognitive habits by the genetic code" ("Frothing," 247). Porush labels this "the urgent compulsion to exteriorize our nerve net" ("Hacking," 108) and a "metaphysical impulse" ("Hacking," 127). The metaphysical impulse expresses itself in "the tension between the word and spirit (which is) the fundamental creative impulse in humanity." This impulse can "help us transcend dualisms like rationality and irrationality, (and) is at the heart of postmodern literature" ("Hacking," 139). Transcendence here is figured in the classical terms of addiction, that is, as a "compulsion" toward exteriorization and, in addition, as an imperialism. Indeed, Porush writes that the "natural, biological necessity of the human nerve net is to imperialize nature through artifice" ("Frothing," 259).

The establishment of cyberspace as an exteriorized, irrational zone will be an accessory, Porush claims, to the death of logocentrism. Yet the zone is described, in its aims and effects, in largely Western logocentric terms. I am sympathetic to Porush's emphasis on the irrational, the passionate, the imaginative, and even the spiritual potentials of VR mediums. However, transcendence here still seems to require the reinstatement of mental voice and intellection as more "ideal" than writing and bodies; the apotheosis of godlike powers; and a mind-over-matter notion of imperialistic control. And while Porush denigrates the powerful, ubiquitous "industrial" Code, his version of transcendence still requires a relationship between humans and code of compulsion and substitution. The transcendee must become of the same substance as the drug: a synthesis requiring that genetic code and "industrial" code be commensurate, transparently commutable, translatable. Only this enables Porush to claim that once we are able to directly mindlink to the technology, cyberspace will become "an expression of pure cognition" ("Frothing," 260). "Logocentrism will be dead . . . the word will be obsolete."[23] Yet for Derrida, writing is the locus of the separation from the father, or logos, precisely because it threatens the ideality of pure intellection and its *pharmakeus:* the voice from the mind. So when Porush dreams of a world of "pure cognition" and asks, "why write when you can broadcast your thoughts?" ("Out of Our Minds," 234), he seems to be powerfully reinstating exactly the dualisms of which he wishes to rid us.

In the *Timaeus,* Plato writes of a "receptacle," a *chora,* a matrix, or a plane from which mimetic forms come and go. Plato likens this receptacle to a mother and the source or the spring to the father. The matrix is "an invisible and formless being which receives all things and in some mysterious way partakes of the intelligible."[24] Investing code with sublime life, VR becomes both receptacle and source. By ingesting code, the user "recovers" from the condition of mimesis. For those of us who indulge in it, the ongoing production of this transcendence demands the turning away from, the turning our backs on, alternative accounts of the status of biological bodies, on alternatives to the cultural and scientific narratives that read The Whole as code, on the ways in which the demands of biological reproduction might intersect with or disrupt notions of posthuman, postfemale generation, and particularly on any serious troubling of relationships to and among the nontranscendental yet global corporations that provide the materiel of VR and, indeed, capitalize on and serve as loci for these very rhetorics of transcendence.

Yet mortality anxieties contaminate the digitized subject as well. This substitution of the postvital mind for bodily presence, junk cells for mortal cells, Code for DNA, depends on repetition. The *pharmakon* is both drug and remedy. In order for it to "work," the user must become it; the user must become an addict. Theuth, the inventor of writing, claims that the *pharmakon*, writing, "enables us to repeat, and thus to remember" ("Rhetoric of Drugs," 6), a claim that the God-King rejects on the grounds that writing is irresponsible repetition that does not enhance authentic memory. In *Junky*, Burroughs writes that the junkie is addicted to habit, to repetition as the vehicle for substitution of junk cells for human cells, for transcendence of the "the aging, cautious, nagging, frightened flesh" (*Junky*, 152), for secession from Real Life. In VR discourses, the insistent rhetorics of addiction must work continually to reproduce hyper-real transcendence by repeatedly inoculating and intoxicating the anxious user with an idealized, vitalized, inFORMation Code.[25] There is no safety, no sure promise of resurrection. The fallible physical world and its machines haunt the ghosts.

I think it is possible, after the foregoing, to make two claims. First, that the connection between addiction and transcendence was clearly established in the Western tradition, within which I include Burroughs, and was available as a constitutive, founding rhetoric for discourses concerning VR. This tradition already connected writing and drug addiction to dis- or reembodiment, life extension, and special powers. As a thought-game, I suggest imagining that the program for "addiction," for bodily subsumption, ongoing intoxication, repeated supplementation, has been deleted from every or any particular VR text. My own experience attempting this has been that when the "addiction" program is deleted, the transcendence program stops making sense. The thrill is simply gone. For those who have read *Neuromancer*, imagine that for Case, jacking in is just another day at the job. Or even that he has cool, hallucinogenic experiences while in cyberspace, but, y'know, RL calls. Would anyone even want to read about it? A real question.

Second, for Plato, and for most of Western culture until quite recently, "life" was instantiated in presence, in voice, and particularly in the voice of the God-King, leaving the inter(inner)loper, the dangerous supplement, writing, to serve as a murderer. This attribution of life seems to be shifting so that the model of the model is both law and executor, the vitalized, idealized Code. And what could be more reproductive of Platonic notions of presence, and of the sovereign subject, than the longing to become a pixelated mind communicating with other pixelated minds through the unmediated medium of the Same? Thus, VR rhetorics that take Platonism as their standpoint or reference effect an end run around Baudrillard and others who predict the demise of transcendence, or around those who believe a change in medium, a change from phonetics to codonics, will change the message, which is still a conservative, logocentric promise of unity and presence while playing in the field of the hyper-real.

POSTCODESCRIPT

Allucquère Rosanne Stone has written that "software produces subjects."[26] Since subjects also produce software, I arrive at the idea that some of us desire to produce ourselves as addicted subjects, and that we also desire to be produced as addicted subjects. Stone terms virtual realities "spaces of transformation, identity factories in which bodies are meaning machines, and transgender—identity as performance, as play, as wrench in the smooth gears of the social apparatus of vision—is the ground state" (*War*, 180–81). While Nicole Stenger imagines herself as a "hermaphrodite" angel, able to produce binary clones of her "self," and cybernauts as gods of new entities they invent and name ("Mind," 52), Stone proffers various renditions of an unstable "New Creature" (*War*, 167) who practices "multiplicity," "fragmentation," and "liminality." Stone describes herself as happily "hooked on technology" (*War*, 3). As does Stenger, she participates in and relies on addiction software, on rhetorics of what she terms the cybersubject's "generous permeability, an electronic porosity" (*War*, 166). Stone's figure for this cyberprotean subject is the Vampire, a border creature of compulsion, regeneration, postvital, potentially immortal life. The question remains one that has been asked of the cyborg: How many ways does the addicted subject swing?[27] Neoplatonist or Queer? Virtual Mind Jockey or Transvampire and In Your Face?

Rather than choose, I notice that these questions begin to characterize the larger project for which this essay is profoundly preliminary. This larger project explores the manifold manifestations of the centralization of addiction in the production of subjectivity for certain late-twentieth-century folks. In her groundbreaking essay, "Epidemics of Will," Eve Kosofsky Sedgwick contemplates the "peculiarly resonant relations that seem to obtain between the problematics of addiction and those of the consumer phase of international capitalism."[28] Any form of human behavior may come under the purview of "addiction attribution," even those, or especially those, such as exercise, that

connote free will. But, of course, this freedom may never be fully and satis-
factorily possessed, only imperfectly exercised in the chase. Sedgwick proposes "reconstructing an 'otherwise' for addiction-attribution" ("Epidemics,"
591). She asks us to reflect on habit, "a version of repeated action that moves
not toward metaphysical absolutes but toward interrelations of action and
the self acting with the bodily habitus, the appareling habit, the sheltering
habitation" ("Epidemics," 591). I would like to take a different tack, one suggested to me by the French-Cuban writer Severo Sarduy. Sarduy writes of an
attenuated transcendence, a momentary release from linear time (but not
from mortality), from "the weight of one's self . . . (from) the punctual
watchfulness of the Other in the omnipresent shape of the Law."[29] This "irresponsibility" is a mode of self-re-creation, or even transubstantiation, and its
vehicle is compulsive repetition: intoxicated writing, chanting, painting,
casual sex (*Christ,* 84–88). Sarduy grieves for what "God denies . . . true
intoxication, true euphoria" (*Christ,* 11). Yet it is precisely this notion of weak
transcendence that fascinates me. Viewed as a temporary psychosensory
mode that renders demarcations between self and other undecidable, it
points toward an alternative to discussions that fatally oppose transcendence
to mortality, multiplicity, and bodies. Like habit, weak transcendence is
grounded in the body, bodies available to us here and now. However, weak
transcendence urges me to reflect on the ways in which the terms of addiction—penetration, repetition, and displacement—might become vectors
for reconsidering the question of intersubjectivity as *intrasubjectivity,* of "interrelations" as undecidably possessed and possessing *intrarelations.*

My essay suggests that in Western culture addiction has always served to
reproduce both the conservative law of the father with its Platonic notions
of transcendence and the sovereign subject; and the operations of multi-
ples, of models without originals, of the marginal, the monstrous, the
escapees. Some of the transformative effects of addiction softwares are
effects of desires that may always work against encounters with mortality,
multiplicity, and difference, regardless of who is writing the software. In this
case, those of us who have deemed transcendence deadly but who continue
to write ourselves as addicted subjects, may want to ask if and how we are
participating in the reproduction of what we have rejected. Or more in line
with my own desires, queer the conjunction of addiction and transcendence
and make it our own.

> Some call it a cerebral overhaul, others hypnotic. Some believe its 50,000 volts
> of immediate gratification while others dare whisper Anarchy.[30]
>   You can't swap death for life. Not even in the Vurt. . . . We're neither free
> nor safe, until we've earned it. (*Vurt* 310, 316)

If "Reality Is the Best Metaphor,"
It Must Be Virtual

Marguerite R. Waller

What is the search for the next great compelling application but a search for the human identity?
—DOUGLAS COUPLAND, *Microserfs*

We can look forward to a richly textured and complex cyberspace, where we are at all times human, and can become bits of pixel dust flying through a virtual landscape.
—3-D, multiuser, interactive, on-line virtual-reality producer

"Avatars are Next," the June 1996 issue of *Wired* announces on its cover, above a glossy foldout of Bill Gates in bathing trunks floating on a lemon yellow air mattress in a sensuous Hockney-blue swimming pool. "Mr. Bill goes Hollywood! Special Gatesfold Issue," reads the caption underneath the (photomontaged) naked torso. The U.S. Congress's attempt in February 1996 to conceptualize the Internet as an incitement to indecent sexual conduct (in Section 507 of the 1996 Telecommunications Act, the so-called Computer Decency Act) is clearly the lampooned subtext of this juxtaposition of sexualized body with the concept of the avatar. The antithesis of sensuous, avatars are bandwidth-conserving, virtual figures that take the place of users' physical bodies in the three-dimensional, interactive, multiuser virtual environments that software developers in 1996 insisted would be the telos of the development of the World Wide Web. The *Wired* cover implies that the nerd community finds Congress's association of digital media with sex ridiculous (however flattering they may find it to be constructed as sexually dangerous). Not unusually, sexuality is being invoked by the state as a justification for extending its own reach (and that of the corporate interests it represents).

But the sex/gender politics of Net free-speech advocates are not necessarily more progressive. As feminist commentator Laura Miller argues in "Women and Children First: Gender and the Settling of the Electronic Frontier," the metaphor of a frontier beyond the jurisdiction of Congress, deployed by opponents of federal regulation, draws on a conventional construction of gender that threatens to reinscribe women as victims, reinforcing "the power imbalance between the sexes, with its roots in the concept of women as property, constantly under siege and requiring the vigilant protection of their male owners."[1] The unintended consequence of this conceptualization, she worries, is that "the threat of regulation is built into the very mythos used to conceptualize the Net by its defenders" ("Women and Children," 50).

My worry, therefore, embraces both sides of the debate over free speech on the Net. The skirmish between Big Brother and the software pioneers seems to be shaping up rhetorically as a classic fraternal competition "between men."[2] We may read it as a contest between fundamentally congruent "male" subject positions, both of which incline to disempower "female" subject positions and both of which stand to increase their own political and economic capital by the appearance of a conflict. The power-producing relationality at play in this turf war, however, simultaneously threatens to *subvert* the claims of each position to its own, independent ontology. Both parties, therefore, can be expected compulsively to deny their relational status. John Perry Barlowe insists in his "Declaration of Independence in Cyberspace," "Your legal concepts of property, expression, identity, movement, and context do not apply to us. They are based on matter. There is no matter here."[3]

It is this more subtle metaphysical issue, the occlusion of relation, implicated in but not reducible to, the constructions of sexuality and gender deployed by both Netizens and Congresspeople, that I find the most pressing issue in designs, uses, and discussions of cyberspace. I will argue that, in fact, the current wave of Internet development (both practically and discursively) is in some sense driven by a desire to make cyberspace safe for essentialist subjectivities of whatever ideological/political persuasion. I will unfold this argument in terms of a certain notion of addiction. My interest is not "cyberaddiction" per se, in the sense of individuals who spend what they or their associates consider too much time on-line, but rather the construction of cyberspace—both rhetorically and electronically—as a clean, clear realm in which we can transcend positionality while remaining (or becoming more fully) "ourselves." I am not, that is, using "addiction" as the binary opposite of "free will," a tendency in popular discourse that Eve Sedgwick has brilliantly analyzed in her "Epidemics of the Will."[4] I am associating the term, instead, with the interdependent, contingent status of subject positions, themselves multiple and relational, and with strategies for denying or appearing to escape this relational status.

One further caveat: I want to make clear from the outset that I do not see this construction of, and relationship to, cyberspace as inevitable. In the press packet of one of the eight or ten companies currently specializing in the creation of the three-dimensional virtual environments I will focus on here, one article asserts that the electronic, multiuser virtual play space the company has designed to link seriously ill children in hospitals will allow the children to "rediscover the simple joys of childhood." The play space, called "Starbright World," developed by Worlds Incorporated working with Steven Spielberg's philanthropic Starbright Foundation, was intended to "empower the kids to be in a different environment than their hospital room" and to forget temporarily their illnesses. "It is not expected . . . that children will use the network in any type of support group fashion. In fact the kids may not talk about their medical conditions at all," the projects' managing director is quoted as saying.[5] The hospitalized children themselves have not all borne out this prediction. A recent article in *Wired* reports that the ill children using the network discuss everything from family dynamics ("brothers are always in your face") to the subtleties of their illnesses and treatments. "They tell each other just everything. We sit there in awe," Colette Case, a Starbright coordinator at Stanford University's Children's Hospital, is quoted as saying.[6] In other words, they are using their virtual environment to address what is happening to them physically and emotionally in the "real world." In this instance, users have not been colonized by the metaphysics of transcendence that the network was supposed to instantiate. Thus, despite my emphasis in the remarks that follow on amplifications and remystifications of the Western metaphysical subject—associated historically with a politics of domination, whatever its various idealisms—I also indicate ways in which properties of the medium could operate, and be read, otherwise. In German director Werner Herzog's film *Fitzcarraldo,* the European Fitzgerald's plan to transport a boat over a mountain and bring opera to the Amazon unpredictably intersects with his indigenous workers' plan to offer a gift to their gods. The result of this intersection is the failure, the success, or the unreadability, of the project, depending on how one looks at it. I share this suspicion that difference will out, whether happily, catastrophically, or illegibly.

A plethora of articles in the print media claim that three-dimensional, multiuser, on-line virtual environments, for which we may soon have to coin a shorter term, constitute a new medium—a communications "revolution," "a whole new metaphor for interaction and connectivity."[7] *Wired* strongly concurs that the development of these spaces could imply a cultural shift on the order of, though unlike, those associated with the invention and propagation of the cinema, the telephone, or television.[8] The developers of this medium take it to be the telos in an evolutionary process whose origin is said to be the immobile, black-and-white letters of the printed page. Print evolves into the interactive DOS command-line interface, which becomes the two-dimensional Macintosh-style interface, which leads, now, to much more "intuitive,' "immersive," "three-dimensional" (although one's eyes are still focusing on a two-dimensional computer screen) virtual environments—electronic rooms and landscapes, computed on the fly as user-avatars navigate through them, meeting and interacting with other users' avatars in real time.

This is not the occasion for a lengthy commentary on the implications of this linear, narrative, historiographical schema, but note that it both ontologizes the medium as "natural" and posits it as the successor mode to writing, the privileged arena of knowledge, politics, and so on in the First World nation-state. Such a medium would, indeed, be a fitting home for the universal(izing) subject familiar from Euro-American, masculinist political culture. Or, as I have heard graduate students say in irreverent response to the claim that computer users can escape "racegenderclass" in cyberspace, "On-line everyone is free—to be a white male." A more cross-cultural and historically ample narrative has been offered by French historian Roger Chartier, whose evocative genealogy of "reading revolutions" includes the move from scrolls to quires during the first centuries of the Christian era, the separation of words instituted by Irish and Anglo-Saxon scribes during the high Middle Ages, and the fall of book prices (due to piracy) in eighteenth-century England, France, and Germany.[9] And there is no reason to limit this genealogy to the culture of the codex. For Sue-Ellen Case, the interactive computer screen descends just as logically from theater, film, television, performance art, and the post–World War II American city.[10] I will include comics and cartoons in this mix of ancestral media.

Worlds Inc's prototype Worlds Chat, the first three-dimensional, multi-user, on-line environment made available to the public on the World Wide Web (in April 1995) is fairly typical of the medium. Worlds Chat first introduces users to an avatar gallery from which they may choose a figure (male/female human, animal, or inanimate object) that will serve as a visual representation of themselves to other users. After inventing a user name, which is displayed over the head of the avatar, the user finds herself looking at a screen depicting a large room, the hub of a fancifully designed space station, within which the closest dozen or so avatars of other users can also be seen. The avatar is controlled by the mouse, while conversations are typed in a chat box at the bottom of the screen. Using various keyboard commands, one can limit the range of these communications ("whisper") to designated interlocutors. To change locations, the user either "walks" her avatar through doors, up stairs and escalators, and around corners, or teleports directly to other parts of the space station by pointing and clicking on a schematic map. One particularly popular room includes a mirror in which the user can see her avatar's reflection. Crashing through the "glass," the avatar enters a labyrinth, and, negotiating that, encounters a minotaur at its center. The newest version of Worlds Chat has added features that make the space more varied and less Euclidean, but add persistence of on-line identity by encouraging the visitor to use the same name and avatar during repeated visits.

Whether persistent or not, the avatar is supposed to make negotiating the computer interface more like operating in the physical world, an objective I will say more about in a moment. It also works well from a technical standpoint that the avatar and the predownloaded environment economize bandwidth. Sending and receiving avatar images can be handled with a 14.4 modem, far less than video conferencing would require, while the Worlds Chat server needs to track only an avatar's position in order to make the user's computer display the appropriate visuals for that position at any given moment. As of spring 1996, Worlds Chat had been downloaded to more 200,000 PCs, and the company was registering 1,000 new downloads a day.

The same company's AlphaWorld began as a kind of programmer's hobby space. A flat plane of green, surrounded by mountains (bearing a remarkable resemblance to Palm Springs), AlphaWorld allows users to stake out property and build on it. The houses, gardens, trees, fountains, revolving globes, advertising pavilions, newspaper stands, and mailboxes with which users cover their lots persist over time and become part of the landscape that others log into. It is, in this sense, a highly interactive, user-designed environment. Users are again represented as avatars, all white and male when AlphaWorld first went on-line in fall 1995, but now more varied and, for those with programming skills, customizable. Conversations appear in comic-style bubbles over the heads of the avatars. Modes of locomotion include "walking," "flying," and "teleporting" and are controlled by combinations of keyboard command and use of the mouse. The user can also switch back and forth between first- and third-person points of view. Conversations, many feel, work best in third person, where the user sees her own avatar as well as those of others, as if from a camera somewhere behind the avatar's right shoulder (belying any simple assimilation of virtual to physical reality). In concert with the metaphor of homesteading, users "immigrate" to AlphaWorld, which involves sending the server an e-mail address and getting a visa number in return. The procedure tends to keep AlphaWorld personae consistent, which, along with the persistence of the user-constructed city-scape, seems to foster the growth of community. An AlphaWorld newspaper was quickly established, and one couple held their wedding there. By spring, 1996, AlphaWorld was growing at the rate of 500 new citizens a day, and had already reached a population of 60,000.

Directly inspired by the "Metaverse," the locale of much of the action in Neal Stephenson's cult cyberpunk novel *Snowcrash,* AlphaWorld also figures in the next large venture envisioned by virtual environment developers.[11] The plan is to link cyberspaces together—not only the worlds created by one company but also those introduced by a growing variety of enterprises, including Microsoft, Compuserv, Time-Warner, Disney, and various banks, businesses, and game manufacturers. A user can already send e-mail to other AlphaWorld users by clicking on the mailboxes in front of their houses. Clicking on a newspaper stand takes one to the text of the newspaper on the company's Web site. Soon an avatar may be able to walk through a door from AlphaWorld to Worlds Chat, shifting connections from one server to another without having to log off one and onto the other. The hybrid metaphor of the "home page" could give way to that of the "home," a virtual house furnished with objects linking it to other Web sites that may themselves increasingly be configured as three-dimensional, multiuser environments. The vision coming into focus in the summer of 1996 is that of an infinitely extensible, open platform—as opposed to a collage of separate spaces and kinds of space—on which increasing numbers of people would spend increasingly large portions of their lives.[12] Franz Buchenberger, president of Black Sun Interactive (a developer of virtual reality tools that takes its name from a cafe in the Metaverse), insists that within a few years all technical barriers to this vision will have disappeared and "everybody will walk around cyberspace as an avatar."[13] I would reiterate, though, that it has not always been obvious that this would be the direction in which three-dimensional, on-line, multiuser virtual environments were heading. When I began researching the medium in 1994, there was a decidedly ateleological sense that the technology was intrinsically fascinating while its possible applications were still to be imagined. Seamless extensibility (with its probable colonizing, homogenizing effects) assumed the status of manifest destiny only in 1996.

Contemporary with this "evolution" of the personal computer interface, a paradigm shift in scientific analysis has also been taking shape. Already used for simulations and modeling of various physical phenomena, three-dimensional computer visualization is now being developed as a means to synthesize and abstract—the more positivisitic metaphor used is that of "mining"—vast quantities of heterogeneous statistical data. That is, the data processing power of the computer is being linked with its graphical capabilities to create easily grasped, navigable, three-dimensional visuals out of data so complex and heterogeneous that they would not otherwise be accessible. Like images in Dante's *Paradiso*, these visuals do not refer mimetically to any physical reality, but rather are tailored to maximize the collaboration between computer memory and the human sensorium. For example, data sets acquired over twenty years of field experience in the Great Barrier Reef can be synthesized, or "mined," to visualize the interrelations of currents, weather, and fish populations leading, theoretically, to more accurate environmental impact assessments.[14] Not only can two-dimensional numbers and words be explored in a more intuitive three-dimensional visual form, but the three-dimensional images may be animated, allowing the interactive exploration of processes taking place over time. And furthermore, with multiuser technology, geographically separated investigators can meet together electronically in these data spaces, exploring them collaboratively—an uncanny instantiation of the "consensual hallucination" conceived of by cyberfiction writer William Gibson in his novel *Neuromancer.*

Howard Rheingold, early in his book on virtual reality, quotes Heinz Pagel explaining the epistemological implications of this new tool. Pagel reasons, in the epigraph opening a chapter Rheingold calls "Grasping Reality Through Illusion":

> The primary research instrument of the sciences of complexity is the computer. It is altering the architectonic of the sciences and the picture we have of material reality. Ever since the rise of modern science three centuries ago, the instruments of investigation such as telescopes and microscopes were analytic and promoted the reductionist view of science. Physics, because it dealt with the smallest and most reduced entities, was the most fundamental science. From the laws of physics one could deduce the laws of chemistry, then of life, and so on up the ladder. . . . The computer, with its ability to manage enormous amounts of data and to simulate reality, provides a new window on that view of nature. We may begin to see reality differently simply because the computer produces knowledge differently from the traditional analytic instruments.[15]

Scientists have characterized these techniques as "the biggest thing since the experiment," a remarkable claim, with potentially complex implications for the scientific and the public community's understanding of what constitutes scientific knowledge.

But at least one visualization project, proposed at a conference hosted by the California Institute of Technology, does not involve conceptually resituating diverse scientific knowledges according to their "instruments of investigation." The conference position paper proposes extrapolating "very precise information" otherwise "hidden" in large volumes of complex data to create detailed, long-range ecological scenarios. These scenarios would then be made available to a broad cross-section of people on the World Wide Web for interactive viewing, revising, interrogation, and debate. The proposers of the project hope that a large constituency of users—not only scientists but also farmers, environmentalists, urban dwellers, business people, long-range planners, policymakers, and educators—would become collectively involved in visualizing the terrifying future consequences of current developmental trends, leading to large-scale changes in patterns of human thought and desire. The dispersed but vital cyber community brought into being would become a significant new political force, a consensus-building power base, overseeing sustainable development locally and globally.[16]

The series of assumptions embedded in this proposal are internally consistent, and to an antiessentialist, alarming. First, knowledge or information is constructed as separate from the investigating subjects. This assumption makes plausible the idea that information can alter people's desires and behavior in the absence of any challenge to the political, economic, philosophical, and psychological vectors involved. The subject is reinscribed, that is, as the neutral, autonomous, self-determining entity one keeps encountering in more commercial pitches for virtual reality. This subject, in turn, accedes to power through participation in "consensus-building," a form of political discourse invented by the eighteenth-century European "man of reason," and closely related to the consensus-style protocols of conventional Western scientific discourse, without having to acknowledge that others are constrained or effaced by participation in its logic. This logic, as we have seen, reifies the relational differences that underwrite "identities" in terms of self and other, truth and untruth, and sets up the sense of danger and mess that the subject then yearns to transcend. Directly related to this issue of subject construction is the failure to recognize the contingent epistemological status, noted by Pagels, of computer-generated "information." However idealistically motivated one's use of "knowledge" may be, if it effaces the politics underwriting the production of "facts" and the use of "knowledge" to legitimate authority, then it, too, contributes to the construction and epistemological exploitation of disempowered "others." (Why do we need a computer image to argue against the testing of nuclear devices in the Pacific Islands when we have the evidence of the "jelly babies" that mothers there are giving birth to?) Epistemologically and politically, then, this plan would seem to encourage the construction or performance of homogeneous subjects predisposed to seek the "transcendence" that will take them out of relation with their diacritically related fellow humans.

A second idealistic application of three-dimensional multiuser virtual environments is the massive use of the technology to address the ills of public education in the United States. In congressional subcommittee and in a memo prepared for advisors to President Clinton, developers have suggested that students transcend their schools by going on-line. Students could not only see and hear, but interact with "top instructors" from anywhere. They could collaborate with each other in virtual groups on the construction of a virtual polis whose laws they could vote on and in whose evolution they could become participant observers. They could take field trips with friends to a virtual Smithsonian, role play life in colonial Boston. The medium would overcome students' alienation by giving them a community of peers and mentors, as well as interactivity with the best educational resources the world has to offer. The developers themselves place an epistemologically radical spin on this scenario, suggesting that learning would therefore take place, not by setting up subject/object relationships, but by "being and doing." "Knowledge," the students would learn, "is that which can be applied, shared, or tested."[17] I will return below to this claim and to what it overlooks.

Avatar. n. Hindu mythology, the descent of a deity to the earth in an incarnate form or some manifest shape; the incarnation of a god. 2. *an embodiment or concrete manifestation of an abstract concept.*

The Random House Dictionary of the English Language

Phone home.

E.T.

In the remainder of this discussion of subjectivity, the metaphysics of addiction/transcendence, and conceptualizations of cyberspace, I will focus on the growing appreciation of the immediacy (in both senses— speed and intimacy) with which users can apprehend and communicate information in a three-dimensional visual medium. Psychologists of vision and computer visionaries agree that a human driving a car down the street processes far more visual information, far better, than any computer could. According to cognitive scientists the human brain is faster than even the fastest supercomputer at pattern recognition, and, furthermore, we process pattern—even two-dimensional pattern—with the same tools we use to perceive three-dimensional space.[18] Inversely, humans process numbers and alphabetic text slowly and poorly relative to computers. The most efficient way to interact with the microprocessor, then, does seem to be to join the speed with which the computer can organize and process data with the speed and complexity of human, three-dimensional pattern recognition. The animated, three-dimensional graphical interface would, therefore, appear to be the optimal workspace and playground for any self-respecting human/computer cyborg, whatever her theoretical and political orientations.

But will this interface be the site of a seduction away from Western logo-centrism or of a more subtle, deep-seated entrenchment? Many first-wave commentators enthusiastically anticipate a painless metamorphosis of users into gracefully decentered Derridian subjects. Western desires for identity, self-sameness presence, and mastery will give way to the *jouissance* of multiple personalities, consciously performative and completely fluid sex/gender roles, the dissolution of binary opposition, of self/other, presence/absence.[19] I am suggesting that this interface also needs to be theorized in relation to a structure of addiction/transcendence associated with the denial of difference and the logic of the same.

Doing so, however, leads quickly to the realization that categories of all kinds tend to become slippery in the exploration of the properties of a new medium. Theories of the subject derived from and addressing the subject of text-based print culture, or even of cinema, for example, may be misleading in the attempt to theorize three-dimensional, interactive, multiuser, on-line virtual existence. Compounding this complication is the realization that the on-line virtual environment resembles nothing so much as one of our least studied, most marginalized entertainment media. What the developers, scientists, educators, and retailers are saying, in essence, is that large numbers people will be spending large amounts of their lives being represented as, and interacting with . . . CARTOONS!! Leaving aside for the moment the question of how "interacting" differs from both reading and being a spectator, cartoons themselves differ from both verbal texts and pictorial images, disrupting a commonplace distinction between the two. The miscegenating "comic book" has not been claimed by either literature or visual art in the traditional academic curriculum. Academic culture, which privileges the phonetic word over the image and makes "visual culture" a special departmental interest, has conditioned even film theorists to have little or nothing to say about the hieroglyphics of animation.

Computer avatars (animated figures, which are, by an apt semantic coincidence, controlled by and conceptually related to the "mouse") were devised to make interaction with other users and with the electronic environment more "intuitive." That is, they are intended to situate what the user sees on screen within an already naturalized human response loop that mimics "the sophisticated and nuanced response to environmental cues."[20] So "where" and "what" would a group of hypothetical students be as they take a field trip into the submicroscopic center of a helium nucleus deep in the heart of the sun, some dimension of themselves embodied in three-dimensional icons navigating through computer animations?[21] How will students, scientists, friends, and consumers come to know themselves, to think and behave, significantly differently in the mirror of this interactive graphical interface? And how will the experience be different for subjects situated differently (in terms of gender, race, class, age, and so on) in "Real Life?"[22]

Theoretician of comics Scott McCloud offers a provocative commentary on the ways we relate to the stripped down iconicity of cartoons (see Figure 2). A form of amplification through simplification, "cartooning isn't just a way of drawing," he maintains, "it's a way of seeing."[23] Intensity, liveliness, and focus are achieved by drawings in which every line counts as a signifier. McCloud goes on to attribute the peculiar attraction of the cartoon character to its likeness to the sketchy mind-pictures we carry around of ourselves. When you enter the world of the cartoon, you see yourself, he surmises, "The cartoon is a VACUUM . . . an empty shell that we inhabit that enables us to travel in another realm. We don't just observe the cartoon, we become it."[24] I would extrapolate that cartoons, as McCloud theorizes them, operate like anti-Oedipal rhizomes, drawing reader/viewers and cartoon images to form improvisational matrices of intensity. Gilles Deleuze and Felix Guattari figure this relationship through the mutual deterritorizations and reterritorializations of the orchid and the wasp:

The orchid deterritorializes by forming an image, a tracing of a wasp; but the wasp reterritorializes on that image. The wasp is nevertheless deterritorialized, becoming a piece in the orchid's reproductive apparatus. But it reterritorializes the orchid by transporting its pollen. Wasp and orchid, as heterogeneous elements, form a rhizome. . . . There is neither imitation nor resemblance, only an exploding of two heterogeneous series on the line of flight composed by a common rhizome.[25]

To borrow further from the terminology of Deleuze and Guattari, the human sensorium becomes nonstratified. "It is not space, nor is it in space; it is matter that occupies space to a given degree—to the degree corresponding to the intensities produced."[26]

I follow Deleuze and Guattari in distinguishing this relation from the Oedipal relations of "voyeurism" and "identification." The latter operations imply, inscribe, and depend on a hierarchically organized subject who either objectifies that which he looks at or heightens his own sense of mastery by eliding his consciousness/gaze with that of a character—an ego-ideal—whose own represented relation to the world is that of subject to object. "Identification," that is, implies a whole range of circumstances having to do with the construction of "identity" that leads us back to the subject of classical Western metaphysics. As Anne Friedberg succinctly puts it, "identification . . . replicates the very structure of patriarchy. Identification demands sameness, necessitates similarity, disallows difference."[27]

A second way in which comics are distinguished by McCloud from other kinds of text has to do with the continuum—what from a "stratified" perspective looks like miscegenation—they set up between words and pictures, between graphics we "read" and those we "look at." McCloud observes (and illustrates):

When pictures are more abstracted from 'reality' they require greater levels of perception, *MORE LIKE WORDS*. When words are bolder, more direct, they require lower levels of perception and are received faster, *MORE LIKE PICTURES*.[28]

McCloud is not an academic theoretician and seems not to be aware of the conceptual consequences of this failure to patrol the boundary between the phenomenal and the abstract. Jean Baudrillard, by contrast, has made a career of deploring such lapses:

Something has disappeared: the sovereign difference . . . that was abstraction's charm. . . . the difference which forms the poetry of the map and the charm of the territory, the magic of the concept and the charm of the real. . . . With it goes all of metaphysics.[29]

The "loss" of distinction between the map and the territory, like the loss of distinction between the word and the picture, subverts the system of binary

Figure 2. Scott McCloud, *Understanding Comics: The Invisible Art* (Northhampton, Mass.: Kitchen Sink Press, 1993), 49. Understanding Comics © and ™ Scott McCloud.

opposition upon which a certain understanding of signification depends. The old patriarch in Baudrillard, who finds this "loss" perverse, recognizes that when the binary opposition between concrete and abstract (not between signified and signifier or referent and sign, but between literal and figural) disappears, so does the possibility of mooring the movement of signification in a "real," however hypothetical or socially constructed. The problem becomes, as Baudrillard so quotably has written, that "there is no real ... that is not already a nonoriginal 'reproduction,' or, more accurately, an iteration of an abstract code or matrix, a simulacrum."[30] If the trick of Western Platonic structures of knowledge and authority, as Judith Butler has compellingly argued, is discursively to construct "matter" as a pre-discursive category that both grounds and is transcended by description, analysis, and other kinds of representation, then the "magic" and "charm" that Baudrillard complains of losing are the magic and charm of epistemic dominance, the same kind of dominance we saw figured in the proposed use of computer imaging.[31] It follows that, since the literalness of the receiving/perceiving subject is included in this loss, the question of transcendence is rendered completely moot. Baudrillard's residual nostalgia for transcendence then functions (with multiple-edged irony, I think) to index the impotence of theoretical knowledge relative to the powerful tides of political and emotional conditioning.

The scientists at the Caltech conference, the members of the U.S. Congress, and the capitalist marketplace are perhaps even less ready than Baudrillard to give up the panoptical position, the centered and centrally located subject, whose utopian desire is to transcend relation, to see universally, producing a version of "reality" that supports their kind of subject position. (This is not to be taken as a moral critique, which would merely put me in the same position. As science-fiction writer Octavia Butler compellingly suggests in the three novels of her *Xenogenesis* series, nonbinary, nonlogocentric forms of domination are just as conceivable as the binary forms we are more familiar with.[32]) We have seen how the shift to three-dimensional virtual reality potentially unmasks the authoritarian production of knowledge and other artifacts of the European episteme that have relied on a matter/mind, phenomenological/analytical dichotomy. Now I would like to consider how the flow of subjectivity into the "visual pixel dust" of cartoon avatars nevertheless permits us to carry on with business as usual, even to feel a sense of traveling home after a long exile. What is homelike about these virtual spaces—and for whom—and where does the importunate urge to phone such a home come from?

Dismantling the "biunivocality" of the "White Man" (their term) "is no mean affair," Deleuze and Guattari remark in their essay on faciality. "It is never a question of a return to the polyvocality of a semiotic in which the head is part of the body, a body that is already deterritorialized relatively and plugged into becomings spiritual/animal."[33] How, for example, to think non-Platonically about the relationship of avatars and their environments to physicality is a complicated question that needs to be framed diachronically as well as synchronically. Artist Judit Hersko, describing her own series of avatarlike shadow images, based on sixteenth- and seventeenth-century representations of witchcraft, comments:

> The contrast between the immaterial nature of the presentation and the strong physicality of the images expresses the shift that occurred in the human psyche during the transition from the middle ages to modernity when the bodies of actual women served as the battle ground. The process played out during this period of marginalizing the body by declaring its desires feminine vices and exorcising them at the stake seems to be intricately entangled with the . . . emergence of the sanitized body and the scientific mind fit for industrial production.[34]

In other words, Hersko reminds us, the body (as matter) has for some time been constructed as our premier arena of control, this body has been closely associated with women, and our experiences of our bodies are thoroughly and variously mediated by both these circumstances.[35]

Thus when A. R. Stone insists that "the physical/virtual distinction is *not* a mind/body distinction," I would partially agree, within a synchronic frame. One *could* think of the electronic avatar as a "narrow bandwidth extension" of the already marginalized, Cartesian body.[36] There is no reason not to believe, though, that even within contemporary computer culture the sense of physical extension varies greatly depending on the user's "real-life" sense of her/his physicality. What happens, for example, if one has a strong sense of the "to-be-looked-atness" that some feminist theorists have associated with being a young, white female? How does the avatar extend (or not) a racialized body?[37] What if one is used to sensing other people with the surface of the skin, through the soles of the feet, by smell? And this is to leave completely bracketed any question of the users' linguistic patterns.

If we read avatars and bodies diachronically, it becomes much harder to escape the conclusion that the physical/virtual distinction is deeply implicated in the mind/body split. Having outlived its usefulness as arena-of-control, the body of nineteenth-century science and industry becomes marginalized even further. The term avatar, significantly, comes from the Sanskrit word for the embodiment in human form of a Hindu deity. The human user in this analogy becomes a godlike, incorporeal being. The incorporeal electronic avatar, paradoxically corresponding to the god's physical embodiment as a human, is understood as a technical construct under the god's control. The human user, rewritten as "human spirit," is then "freed" to rove at will through the universe. The old nineteenth/twentieth-century (Euro-American) body, with its vestigial sensorium and markers of race, gender, mortality, and other "constraints" of identity and situation, is replaced by one or a series of new navigating entities, now obediently and flexibly *allied with,* rather than opposed to, spirit/mind, which is, it should be noted, more than ever in charge. This maneuver parallels developments in genetics and evolutionary science, where the rhetorical construction of DNA as the source and governor of life depends on abstracting genetic code from its physical instantiation, an abstraction that then permits computer scientists to attribute "life" to their on-screen simulations of genetic recombinations.[38]

Evelyn Fox Keller is highly critical of the first move, using the Nobel Prize-winning work of Barbara McClintock on the transposition of genes to discuss an alternative, nonhierarchical model in which DNA is just one element in a complex web of interactions among the nucleus, the rest of the cell, the cell's environment, and the organism's environment. Genes function "only with respect to the environment in which [they are] found," Fox Keller quotes McClintock as saying.[39] Ann Weinstone comments on Artificial Life, "Code is coming to function as the transcendental, unifying, and ideal substance of life—for the non-referential, the unmediated—while at the same time, it retains attributes, or the trace if you will, of writing, replacing the body with a less mortal letter."[40] N. Katherine Hayles has suggested that the desire expressed in the cybernetic construct of the body-plus-computer-plus-simulation is to leave the body and have it too—to use the human sensorium's pattern recognition faculties without having to deal with such reminders of geographical, temporal, and political situatedness as disease, pollution, commodification, and sociologically marked bodies.[41]

Read this way, the destabilization of binary opposition, subversion of ontology, and gender-bending encountered by/through the subject of "life" on the screen are all recuperated by a seductive new phallicism, even as they appear to decenter the old. An intoxicating phallicism that does not seek agency, stability, and identity by separating from and dominating bodies, objects, or physical territories, but by engaging in weightless, transparent interactivity, this "virtual reality" claims not the figurality of its literal, but the literalness of its figures. "Reality is the best metaphor," claim virtually all of the press releases from Worlds Inc. Diacritical difference, both the irreducible *différance* underwriting signification, and the contingent, historical manifestations of this *différance* that the rhetorical hype assumes we should want to "transcend," are rigorously effaced, visible at best as the recreational interests of a transcendental subject whose sovereignty and self-presence are never seriously in question. On-line graphical virtual reality seems to fulfill the old positivist dream of a common language in which noise, ambiguity, and misunderstanding are reduced to a minimum, and communication can aspire to transparency. We are "home free"—or finally at home for the first time—having triumphantly closed the alienating gap between representation and reality.

In criticizing this model of graphically based electronic communication, I do not mean to essentialize the body. It is, I have argued, the virtual reality rhetoric that perpetuates and intensifies the coding of a physical, material body separate from mind. My sense of the importance of physicality has more to do with a model of knowledge and communication as transparency. Biology, temporality, culture, gender—the kinds of differentiation that present themselves as obstacles to knowing and communicating within the logic of the same—constitute precisely the *via*, the means to know and to communicate, when meaning is understood to be metaphorical, contextual, and relational rather than ontological. It is by knowing that we do *not* understand, by encountering *aporias*, that we (incompletely) glimpse the contours and contingencies of our subjectivities and can begin to communicate otherwise than solipsistically or imperially. What Henri Lefebvre calls "the enigma of the body," the material body's ability, within the Western episteme of the last several centuries, to produce differences, to be the bearer of the new, including the supreme novelties of old age and death, has been one of the most effective means we have had to counter the depredations of the desire for transcendent transparency.[42] If instantaneous, transparent, mutual readability within a homogeneous or, to use Lefebvre's term, "abstract" space is the ideal result of three-dimensional interfaces, then, even before the very important question of access is broached, it would appear that the transcendence of difference being claimed for our avatars is a self-colonizing high.

"Transparency . . . is in fact the perfect boobytrap," writes Lefebvre. "Someone who knows only how to see ends up . . . seeing badly. The reading of a space that has been manufactured with readability in mind amounts to a sort of pleonasm."[43] Ted Nelson, who coined the term "hypertext" to describe what he imagined would be a heterogeneous space of nonrandom intertextuality, warns that the evolving paradigm of the World Wide Web, in which any location can be connected with any other, models thinking as an ultimately meaningless mass of logically circular "spaghetti code."[44] In physics, if all points are equally connectable to all other points, what is described is not a space at all, but a spatial singularity—a black hole—whose gravitational force compresses everything into a single point from which no light can escape.

NOTES

INTRODUCTION

1. A previous selection of essays from this conference has appeared as a special edition of *Diacritics*, edited by Marc Redfield. Two of those essays (Weinstone's and Waller's) are reprinted here. Readers interested in essays of a literary and philosophical cast will want to examine *Diacritics* 27, 3 (fall 1997), as well as the present collection.

2. See Raymond Williams, *Keywords: A Vocabulary of Culture and Society,* rev. ed. (New York: Oxford University Press, 1983 [1976], 87–93. The entries "Aesthetic," "Art," and "Civilization," among others, are also of interest in this context. The quotations that follow in this paragraph are from the "Culture" entry. For a fuller account of and reflection on the rise of modern aesthetics, see Marc Redfield, *Phantom Formations: Aesthetic Ideology and the Bildungsroman* (Ithaca, N.Y.: Cornell University Press, 1996); and *The Politics of Aesthetics: Nationalism, Gender, Romanticism* (Stanford, Calif.: Stanford University Press, 2002).

3. The *OED* does, however, record a case from 1779 in which Samuel Johnson speaks of an "addiction to tobacco"; it seems plausible that during the nineteenth century the word would occasionally have been used in a context in which its ancient sense of binding ("enslavement," "attachment," "devotion") was employed in relation to a substance we now call "addictive" (tobacco, alcohol, opium).

4. W. J. Rorabaugh, *The Alcoholic Republic: An American Tradition* (New York: Oxford University Press, 1998).

5. For histories of drug use and policies see, for example, Virginia Berridge and Griffith Edwards, *Opium and the People: Opiate Use in Nineteenth-Century England* (New Haven, Conn.: Yale University Press, 1987); H. Wayne Morgan, *Drugs in America: A Social History, 1800–1980* (Syracuse, N.Y.: Syracuse University Press, 1981); David F. Musto, *The American Disease: Origins of Narcotic Control* (New York: Oxford University Press, 1987); and for an excellent overview of changes in U.S. drug policies and the impacts on women, Stephen R. Kandall, *Substance and Shadow: Women and Addiction in the U.S.* (Cambridge, Mass.: Harvard University Press, 1996).

6. For a history of late-nineteenth-century legal interventions in private sexual behavior, see Janet Farrell Brodie, *Contraception and Abortion in Nineteenth-Century America* (Ithaca, N.Y.: Cornell University Press, 1994).

7. Among the fine historical studies of the development of addiction discourse, in addition to the studies cited above, see Barry Milligan, *Pleasures and Pains; Opium and the Orient in Nineteenth-Century English Culture* (Charlottesville: University Press of Virginia, 1995) for a study focused more sharply on the ideological link between opium and the "orient" in nineteenth-century Britain. For current official definitions of "addiction," see ICD-10 *Classification of Mental and Behavioral Disorders: Clinical Descriptions and Diagnostic Guidelines* (Geneva: World Health Organization, 1992); and the *Diagnostic and Statistical Manual of the American Psychiatric Association,* 4th ed. (Washington, D.C.: American Psychiatric Association, 1994).

8. Much important work on addiction discourse has been influenced by the work of Michel Foucault: for an account of disciplinary society, see especially Foucault's *Discipline and Punish: The Birth of the Prison,* trans. Alan Sheridan (New York: Pantheon Books, 1977); on the "invention of sexuality" and the pathologization of identity, see above all Foucault's *History of Sexuality, Volume I: An Introduction,* trans. Robert Hurley (New York: Random House, 1978). To varying degrees the work of Eve Sedgwick and Mark Seltzer cited below fall within the Foucaultian tradition.

9. The two wings of "culture" fold together in Richard Klein's *Cigarettes Are Sublime* (Durham, N.C.: Duke University Press, 1993), where the appeal of the cigarette, in both popular and elite contexts, is identified as "sublime"—the aesthetic category that, in the Kantian tradition, is associated with acculturated taste. See Immanuel Kant, *Critique of Judgment,* trans. Werner S. Pluhar (Indianapolis, Ind.: Hackett Publishing Co., 1987), section 29, "On the Modality of a Judgment about the Sublime in Nature": "In order for the mind to be attuned to the feeling of the sublime, it must be receptive to ideas. . . . It is a fact that what is called sublime by us, having been prepared through culture, comes across as merely repellent to a person who is uncultured and lacking in the development of moral ideas. Thus (as Mr. De Saussure relates) the good and otherwise sensible Savoyard peasant did not hesitate to call anyone a fool who fancies glaciered mountains" (124).

10. Eve Kosofsky Sedgwick, "Epidemics of the Will," in *Tendencies* (Durham, N.C.: Duke University Press, 1993), 132.

11. See Jacques Derrida, "Plato's Pharmacy," in *Dissemination,* trans. Barbara Johnson (Chicago: University of Chicago Press, 1981), 61–171.

12. Jacques Derrida, "The Rhetoric of Drugs," trans. Michael Israel, in *Points . . . Interviews,* 1974–1994, ed. Elisabeth Weber, trans. Peggy Kamuf et al. (Stanford, Calif.: Stanford University Press, 1995), 236.

13. Avital Ronell, *Crack Wars: Literature, Addiction, Mania* (Lincoln: University of Nebraska Press, 1992), 13, 40.

14. Sedgwick, 133–34.

15. Mark Seltzer, "Serial Killers (I)," *differences* 5, no.1 (spring 1993): 101.

16. Ronald Bayer and Gerald M. Oppenheimer, eds., *Confronting Drug Policy: Illicit Drugs in a Free Society* (Cambridge, Mass.: Cambridge University Press, 1993); various aspects of the global drug trade are discussed in Alfred W. McCoy and Alan A. Bock, eds., *War on Drugs: Studies in the Failure of U.S. Narcotics Policy* (Boulder, Col.: Westview Press, 1992).

17. For a rigorous reading of the trope of war in this context, see Ronell, esp.19; for a more recent study, see Dan Baum, *Smoke and Mirrors: The War on Drugs and the Politics of Failure* (Boston: Little, Brown, 1996).

18. William S. Burroughs, "Introduction: Deposition: Testimony Concerning a Sickness," in *Naked Lunch* (New York: Grove Press, 1966), xxxiv.

19. Karl Marx, *Capital*, trans. Ben Fowkes (New York: Vintage, 1977), 1:163. For the German, see Karl Marx and Friedrich Engels, *Werke* (Berlin: Dietz Verlag, 1960), 23:85.

20. "Morphine becomes a biologic need like water and the user may die if he is suddenly deprived of it. The diabetic will die without insulin, but he is not addicted to insulin. His need for insulin was not brought about by the use of insulin. He needs insulin to maintain a normal metabolism. The addict needs morphine to maintain a morphine metabolism, and so avoid the excruciatingly painful return to a normal metabolism" (Burroughs, 239–40). This quotation and the following one are taken from the appendix to the Grove edition of *Naked Lunch*, "Letter from a Master Addict to Dangerous Drugs."

21. Judith Butler, *Bodies that Matter: On the Discursive Limits of "Sex"* (New York: Routledge, 1993), xi.

22. See Donna Haraway, *Simians, Cyborgs, and Women: The Reinvention of Nature* (New York: Routledge, 1991).

CHAPTER 1: ADDICTION AND THE ENDS OF DESIRE

1. Sir Arthur Conan Doyle, "The Parasite," in *Dracula's Brood*, ed. Richard Dalby (New York: Dorset Press, 1987), 125. Further references appear parenthetically in the text.

2. In an anonymous pamphlet written in 1845, for example, a man who claims to be a mesmerist confesses to having used his powers to elicit desire in the attractive women he treated: "Reader, let me tell you that to be placed opposite a young and lovely female, who has subjected herself to the process for the purpose of effecting a cure of some nervous affection or otherwise, to look into her gentle eyes, soft and beaming with confidence and trust, is singularly entrancing. You assume her hands, which are clasped in your own, you look intently upon the pupils of her eyes, which as the power becomes more and more visible in her person, evince the tenderest regard, until they close in dreamy and as it were spiritual affection.—Then is her mind all your own, and she will evince the most tender solicitude and care for your good. Your will then becomes not only as law to her, but it is the greatest happiness to her to execute your smallest wish. . . . Self is entirely swallowed up in the earnest regard that actuates the subject, and they will stop at no point beyond which they may afford you pleasure should you indicate it by thought or word." See *The Confessions of a Magnetiser, Being an Expose of Animal Magnetism* (Boston, 1845), 9–10.

3. Robert C. Fuller, *Mesmerism and the American Cure of Souls* (Philadelphia: University of Pennsylvania Press, 1982), 149. Of course, this transition was neither simple nor absolute. As many historians have shown, mesmerism was originally presented as a form of "cure," while later manifestations of hypnosis (as practiced by Freud, for example) were often feared as a form of enslavement as much as they

were sought as therapy, especially for women who were, more often than men, the subjects of hypnosis. By the end of the century, however, there was clearly a shift in emphasis from a concern with coercion from outside the self to a concern with exposure of the self. For more on mesmerism and mind control, see Robert Darnton, *Mesmerism and the End of the Enlightenment in France* (New York: Schocken Books, 1970); Henri Ellenberger, *The Discovery of the Unconscious: The History and Evolution of Dynamic Psychiatry* (New York: Basic Books, 1970); Fred Kaplan, *Dickens and Mesmerism: The Hidden Springs of Fiction* (Princeton, N.J.: Princeton University Press, 1975); Alan Gauld, *A History of Hypnotism* (New York: Cambridge University Press, 1992); Adam Crabtree, *From Mesmer to Freud: Magnetic Sleep and the Roots of Psychological Healing* (New Haven, Conn.: Yale University Press, 1993); Nina Auerbach, "Magi and Maidens: The Romance of the Victorian Freud," in *Reading* Fin de Siècle *Fictions,* ed. Lyn Pykett (New York: Longman Addison Wesley Ltd., 1996), 22–38; and Alison Winter, *Mesmerized: Powers of Mind in Victorian Britain* (Chicago: University of Chicago Press, 1998).

4. It would be wrong to assume, however, that Doyle is simply drawing on a much earlier model of mesmerism in which the mesmeriser was imagined to "impress" his own desires on the victim, for the form of desire he invokes in "The Parasite" was, by century's end, already being linked to the emergent technology of drug addiction.

5. Nathan Beman, *Beman on Intemperance* (New York, 1829), quoted in Harry Gene Levine, "The Discovery of Addiction: Changing Conceptions of Habitual Drunkenness in America," *Journal of Studies on Alcohol* 39, no. 1 (1978): 156. See also Levine's essay, "The Alcohol Problem in America: From Temperance to Alcoholism," *British Journal of Addiction* 79 (1984): 109–19.

6. Virginia Berridge and Griffith Edwards, *Opium and the People: Opium Use in Nineteenth-Century England* (New Haven, Conn.: Yale University Press, 1987), 155.

7. Aside from the articles by Harry Gene Levine (note 5, above), see, for example, Mark Seltzer, "Serial Killers (I)," *differences* 5, no. 1 (spring 1993): 92–128, and Eve Sedgwick, "Epidemics of the Will," in *Tendencies* (Durham, N.C.: Duke University Press, 1993). Avital Ronell's reading of Emma Bovary's addiction as "a kind of crash economy, an exorbitant expenditure with no reserve" also relies on the addict-as-consumer model. See her *Crack Wars: Literature, Addiction, Mania* (Lincoln: University of Nebraska Press, 1992), 109. At the same time, a different school of criticism has claimed that addiction is not so much a generalizable pathology of market culture as it is a kind of utopian transcendence of the market. Derrida, for example, claims that what scares us about the addict is that he flouts the logic of the market by liberating desire from the rhythms of exchange, becoming in the process a kind of pure consumer who refuses to make desire productive of anything except more desire. In an interview on "The Rhetoric of Drugs," he argues, "We do not object to the drug user's pleasure per se, but we cannot abide the fact that his is a pleasure taken in an experience without truth. . . . The drug addict, in our common conception, the drug addict as such produces nothing, nothing true or real." As a consumer who produces nothing, the addict, according to Derrida, empties out the model of identity built on possession in order to find the "ideal" self or "perfect body" that could resist "social oppression, suppression, and repression." Similarly, David Lenson argues that "what one is purchasing when one buys drugs . . . is the

promise of a change in consciousness—and possibly an alternative to Consumerism." Of course, the fact that the addict in this model must purchase this "perfect body" with his endless desire for that body suggests that his desire is, in fact, quite productive. On this reading, then, the addict doesn't escape the market so much as he manages to inhabit a "perfect" market in which he engages only in unalienated forms of consumption. From the perspective of the market, in other words, this utopian refuge from consumerism looks less like transcendence and more like a purification of consumerist logic. See Jacques Derrida, "The Rhetoric of Drugs, An Interview," *differences* 5, no. 1 (spring 1993): 7–8, 14; and David Lenson, *On Drugs* (Minneapolis: University of Minnesota Press, 1995), 28.

8. Levine, "Discovery," 165.

9. Seltzer, 111–14.

10. Benjamin Ward Richardson, "The Physical Benefits of Total Abstinence or, Idiosyncrasy and Alcohol," in *Temperance in All Nations: Papers from the World's Temperance Congress*, vol. 2, ed. J. N. Stearns (New York: National Temperance Society Publications House, 1893), 217.

11. Henry Cole, *Confessions of an American Opium Eater* (Boston, 1895), 235.

12. In other words, even something as disruptive as the unconscious still depends on a basic notion of unity in which each desire, intention, and thought must be understood as originating in and thus defining the self, whether or not this self is imagined to be transparent to itself. After all, the unconscious always works to define what the individual "really" wants. Mikkel Borch-Jacobsen makes a version of this argument in *The Freudian Subject* when he claims that in Freud's theory of the unconscious "the *same* subject has and does not have access to a given representation, remembers and does not remember a given 'scene,' experiences and does not experience a given pleasure. In this sense, the cleavage or division of the subject that psychoanalysis keeps talking about takes place against a background of unity, a *unitary* subject." I am claiming that the model of addiction Doyle draws on in "The Parasite" explodes this presumed unity by describing a desire that literally comes from outside the self—a desire, therefore, that cannot define that self. See Mikkel Borch-Jacobsen, *The Freudian Subject*, trans. Catherine Porter (Stanford, Calif.: Stanford University Press, 1982), 6.

13. Moretti makes explicit the connection between his reading of *Dracula* and Marx's theory of how capital creates value: "'Capital is dead labour which, vampire-like, lives only by sucking living labour, and lives the more, the more labour it sucks.' Marx's analogy unravels the vampire metaphor. As everyone knows, the vampire is dead and yet not dead: he is Un-dead, a 'dead' person who yet manages to live thanks to the blood he sucks from the living. *Their* strength becomes *his* strength." See Franco Moretti, *Signs Taken for Wonders: Essays in the Sociology of Literary Forms*, trans. Susan Fischer, David Forgacs, and David Miller (New York: Verso, 1988), 91.

14. Jennifer Wicke, "Vampiric Typewriting: *Dracula* and Its Media," *ELH* 59 (1992): 476–79.

15. For an interesting history of the *Trilby* craze, see L. Edward Purcell, "*Trilby* and *Trilby*-Mania, The Beginning of the Bestseller System," *Journal of Popular Culture* 11, no. 1 (summer 1977): 62–76.

16. George Du Maurier, *Trilby* (New York: Oxford University Press, 1995), 78, 80, 63. All further references will be cited parenthetically in the text.

17. See Eve Kosofsky Sedgwick, *Epistemology of the Closet* (Berkeley and Los Angeles: University of California Press, 1990), 189, 194, 188.

18. Bram Stoker, *Dracula* (New York: Penguin Books, 1979), 37. Further references appear parenthetically in the text.

19. Moretti, 103.

20. Stephanie Demetrakopoulos, "Feminism, Sex Role Exchanges, and Other Subliminal Fantasies in Bram Stoker's *Dracula*," *Frontiers* 2, no. 3 (1977): 106. See also Kathleen L. Spencer, "Purity and Danger: *Dracula*, the Urban Gothic, and the Late Victorian Degeneracy Crisis," *ELH* 59 (1992): 197; Phyllis A. Roth, "Suddenly Sexual Women in Bram Stoker's *Dracula*," *Literature and Psychology* 27 (1977): 113–21; Judith Weissman, "Women and Vampires: *Dracula* as a Victorian Novel," *Midwest Quarterly* 18 (1977): 392–405; C. F. Bentley, "The Monster in the Bedroom: Sexual Symbolism in Bram Stoker's *Dracula*," *Literature and Psychology* 22 (1972): 27–34; and Anne Williams, "*Dracula*: Si(g)ns of the Fathers," *Texas Studies in Literature and Language* 33, no. 4 (winter 1991): 445–63. For readings that argue that the novel represents the repression of a specifically homosexual desire, see Christopher Craft, "'Kiss Me with Those Red Lips': Gender and Inversion in Bram Stoker's *Dracula*," *Representations* 8 (fall 1984): 107–33; Marjorie Howes, "The Mediation of the Feminine: Bisexuality, Homoerotic Desire, and Self-Expression in Bram Stoker's *Dracula*," *Texas Studies in Literature and Language* 30, no. 1 (spring 1988): 104–19; and Talia Schaffer, "'A Wilde Desire Took Me': The Homoerotic History of *Dracula*," *ELH* 61 (1994): 381–425. For a critique of the sexual repression model, see Robert Mighall, "Sex, History and the Vampire," in *Bram Stoker: History, Psychoanalysis, and the Gothic*, ed. William Hughes and Andrew Smith (New York: St. Martin's Press, 1998), 62–77.

21. Moretti, 104.

22. In the work of Deleuze and Guattari, the "body without organs" is imagined to be a circuit through which desire flows rather than desire's point of origin. Although I am certainly indebted to their claims, I am not interested in making similar arguments against a strict Oedipal model of subjectivity; I am arguing instead that this anti-identity model actually emerged at the same moment as the Freudian one and that it was not imagined to be an antidote to but to be in competition with this model. See Gilles Deleuze and Felix Guattari, *Anti-Oedipus: Capitalism and Schizophrenia*, trans. Robert Hurley, Mark Seem, and Helen R. Lane (Minneapolis: University of Minnesota Press, 1983).

23. Wicke, 478.

24. On *Dracula* and empire, see Stephen Arata, "The Occidental Tourist: *Dracula* and the Anxiety of Reverse Colonization," *Victorian Studies* 33, no. 4 (summer 1990): 621–45; Judith Wilt, "The Imperial Mouth: Imperialism, the Gothic, and Science Fiction," *Journal of Popular Culture* 14, no. 4 (spring 1981): 618–28; Judith Halberstam, *Skin Shows: Gothic Horror and the Technology of Monsters* (Durham, N.C.: Duke University Press, 1995); Daniel Pick, "'Terrors of the Night': *Dracula* and Degeneration in the Late Nineteenth Century," in *Reading Fin de Siècle Fictions*, ed. Lyn Pykett (New York: Longman Addison Wesley Ltd., 1996), 149–65; David Glover, *Vampires, Mummies and Liberals: Bram Stoker and the Politics of Popular Fiction* (Durham, N.C.: Duke University Press, 1996); and Wicke.

25. Frank Norris, "A Reversion to Type," *The Third Circle* (New York: Doubleday, Doran and Co., 1928), 44. Further references appear parenthetically in the text.

26. In some respects, this image of a man overwhelmed by passion looks like a typical Naturalist dynamic. But in the context of my argument, this power of desire to overwhelm the personality is linked specifically to the personality of the ancestor—a model of identity that Norris shares, in varying degrees, with writers as different as Pauline Hopkins and Henry James.

27. Henry James, *The Sense of the Past* (1917; reprint, Fairfield, N.J.: Augustus M. Kelley, Publishers, 1976), 97. Further references appear parenthetically in the text.

28. Pauline Hopkins, *Of One Blood; or, The Hidden Self,* in *The Magazine Novels of Pauline Hopkins* (New York: Oxford University Press, 1988), 551. Further references appear parenthetically in the text.

29. My reading of race at the turn of the century owes much to Walter Benn Michaels's account of racial identity in *Our America.* My argument differs from his, however, in that the model of possession I am describing is not uniquely racial, but rather is a technology for creating nonmarket identity in a variety of different ways. Indeed, race is only one example of a model that produces, among other things, addiction and celebrity. See Walter Benn Michaels, *Our America: Nativism, Modernism, Pluralism* (Durham, N.C.: Duke University Press, 1995).

30. Susan Gillman, "Pauline Hopkins and the Occult: African-American Revisions of Nineteenth-Century Sciences," *American Literary History* 8, no. 1 (spring 1996): 73, 78.

31. Thomas J. Otten, "Pauline Hopkins and the Hidden Self of Race," *ELH* 59 (1992): 229, 230, 248. Although Cynthia Schrager notes that Hopkins embraces a "deterministic notion of racial identity by the end of the novel," she suggests that this reliance on "blood" enables Hopkins to "reestablish a network of kinship ties to family and ancestors that at least potentially may enable the formation of a Pan-African community capable of collective resistance and change." See Schrager's "Pauline Hopkins and William James: The New Psychology and the Politics of Race," in *Female Subjects in Black and White: Race, Psychoanalysis, Feminism,* ed. Elizabeth Abel, Barbara Christian, and Helene Moglen (Berkeley and Los Angeles: University of California Press, 1997), 314, 322.

32. Benjamin Rush Davenport, *Blood Will Tell: The Strange Story of a Son of Ham* (New York: Books for Libraries Press, 1972), 50, 250, 301–2.

33. Otten, 255 n. 38.

34. W. E. B. DuBois, *The Souls of Black Folk* (New York: New American Library, 1969), 45.

35. For a more detailed discussion of the noncontractual subject of privacy, see my "The Public Life: The Discourse of Privacy in the Age of Celebrity," *Arizona Quarterly* 51 (summer 1995): 81–101.

CHAPTER 2: A TERMINAL CASE

1. Stanton Peele with Archie Brodsky, *Love and Addiction* (New York: Signet, 1975), 182. Further references appear in the text.

2. Widely cited estimates of the number of alcoholics in America, for instance, have ballooned from four to five million in the 1960s to more than twenty million by the 1980s—though these estimates have been questioned by some researchers (see Don Cahalan, *Understanding America's Drinking Problem: How to Combat the Haz-*

ards of Alcohol [San Francisco: Jossey-Bass, 1987], 16–19; and Joseph R. Gusfield, *The Culture of Public Problems: Drinking-Driving and the Symbolic Order* [Chicago: University of Chicago Press, 1981], 55–60). Other work has shown that increasing addict identification bears little resemblance to patterns of consumption, which are declining (Milan Korcok, "Alcohol Treatment Industry to Grow as Risk Group Matures," *U.S. Journal of Drug and Alcohol Dependence* [March 1987]: 1).

Speculative estimates are even more common in the new addiction treatment industries. According to Edward Armstrong, the executive director of the National Association on Sexual Addiction Problems, somewhere between 10 and 25 percent of Americans have "a sexual addiction that requires treatment" (quoted in Stanton Peele, *Diseasing of America: Addiction Treatment Out of Control* [Boston: Houghton Mifflin, 1993], 115). Accurate or not, such estimates have led to increased treatment. The percentage of Americans in treatment for alcoholism was twenty times higher in 1976 than in 1942 and it has increased steadily ever since (Peele, *Diseasing*, 49; C. M. Weisner and R. Room, "Financing and Ideology in Alcohol Treatment," *Social Problems* 32 [1984]: 167–84). As might be expected, the number of treatment facilities and support groups for both traditional problems such as alcoholism, and new pathologies like "shopping addiction" has increased dramatically (Peele, *Diseasing*, 46–52, 115–43).

3. As William S. Burroughs noted in 1956, "We speak of addiction to candy, coffee, tobacco, warm weather, television, detective stories, crossword puzzles" (William S. Burroughs, "Appendix," *Naked Lunch* [New York: Grove, 1959], 239).

4. David Foster Wallace, *Infinite Jest* (Boston: Little, Brown, 1996), 200–5.

5. Eve Kosofsky Sedgwick, "Epidemics of the Will," in *Incorporations,* ed. Jonathan Crary and Sanford Kwinter (Cambridge, Mass.: Zone/MIT Press, 1992), 584. For a similar discussion in the context of much larger questions about homosexuality and "homosexual panic," see Sedgwick's *Epistemology of the Closet* (Berkeley and Los Angeles: University of California Press, 1990), esp. 171–78.

6. "Possessive individualism," in C. B. Macpherson's classic account, derives from the political philosophy of Hobbes and Locke and rests on the notion that "every man is naturally the sole proprietor of his own person and capacities (the absolute proprietor in that he owes nothing to society for them)" (C. B. Macpherson, *The Political Theory of Possessive Individualism: Hobbes to Locke* [Oxford: Oxford University Press, 1962], 270). In this model, individuals owe nothing to an abstractly conceived society because they are "self-made" rather than socially constructed; they possess unique attributes in the form of internal "property"; and their autonomy is guaranteed by the ability to exchange property in the open market.

7. Richard H. Blum, "On the Presence of Demons," *Society and Drugs: Social and Cultural Observations,* ed. Richard Blum and Associates. (San Francisco: Jossey-Bass, 1969), 327.

8. Cultural historians have long argued that anxieties about individual liberty and self-control are enmeshed in U.S. culture. Richard Hofstadter's classic essay, "The Paranoid Style in American Politics," demonstrates that anxieties about hidden forms of corporate and government control have been a staple feature of American culture since the colonial period. "The distinguishing thing about the paranoid style," writes Hofstadter, "is not that its exponents see conspiracies or plots here and there in history, but that they regard a 'vast' or 'gigantic' conspiracy as *the motive force*

in historical events. History *is* a conspiracy " (*The Paranoid Style in American Politics and Other Essays* [New York: Alfred A. Knopf, 1965], 29). See Tony Tanner's pioneering accounts of the way this tendency manifests itself in post-World War II American literature, *City of Words: American Fiction 1950–1970* (London: Jonathan Cape, 1971). For more recent work on paranoia and American literature, see Patrick O'Donnell, "Engendering Paranoia in Contemporary Literature," *boundary 2* 19, no. 1 (1992): 181–204; David Porush, *The Soft Machine: Cybernetic Fiction* (New York: Methuen, 1985), 85–111; and Timothy Melley, *Empire of Conspiracy: The Culture of Paranoia in Postwar America* (Ithaca, N.Y.: Cornell University Press, 2000). For an essay that relates addiction to American Puritan origins, see Blum, "Presence of Demons," 323–41.

9. Peele, *Diseasing of America*, 232–33.

10. See David Riesman, Nathan Glazer, and Reuel Denney, *The Lonely Crowd: A Study of the Changing American Character* (New Haven, Conn.: Yale University Press, 1950).

11. F. C. [a.k.a. the "Unabomber"], "Industrial Society and Its Future" (online at http://wwfreepress.com/unaba.html, rev. online 15 May 1999 at http://readroom.ipl.org/bin/ipl/ipl.books-idx.pl?type = entry&id = 3638.), 203. In 1996, the so-called Unabomber—whom the FBI suspected of a series of mail-bombings against industrialists and scientists—published a "manifesto" in *The Washington Post* on Sept. 19, 1995, under the pen name "F.C." This monograph consists of 230 numbered paragraphs. My references denote these paragraphs, not page numbers. Much of the Unabomber manifesto, which the mainstream press often described as the work of an antisocial lunatic, is squarely in the tradition of American individualism that begins roughly with Thoreau and runs through recent critiques of technological rationalization, bureaucracy, and social control. When the Unabomber suggests that "too much control is imposed by the system through explicit regulation or through socialization, which results in a deficiency of autonomy" (85), he could be quoting a number of popular postwar texts. Herbert Marcuse's conclusion, for instance—that individuals suffer a deficiency of autonomy and become "one-dimensional"—is similar to the Unabomber's complaints about the "oversocialized" subjects of postindustrial America. It is worth noting, too, that Marcuse's concept of social "introjection" relies on the same metaphysics of internal and external control that underwrites the rhetoric of addiction. See Herbert Marcuse, *One-Dimensional Man: Studies in the Ideology of Advanced Industrial Society* (Boston: Beacon, 1964), 9.

12. This term comes from Richard Slotkin's classic study of the American frontier, *Regeneration Through Violence: The Mythology of the American Frontier, 1600–1860* (Middletown, Conn.: Wesleyan University Press, 1973).

13. Scott Bukatman's excellent study of postmodern science fiction (*Terminal Identity: The Virtual Subject in Postmodern Science Fiction* [Durham, N.C.: Duke University Press, 1993]) centers on radically reimagined forms of human (and humanoid) subjectivity. The term "terminal identity" itself comes from Burroughs's *Nova Express* (New York: Grove Press, 1964), 19.

14. Burroughs, *Naked Lunch*, vi. Further references appear parenthetically in the text.

15. *The Letters of William S. Burroughs, 1945–1959*, ed. Oliver Harris (New York: Viking, 1993), 365. Further references appear parenthetically in the text.

16. As Tony Tanner points out, "'We are all agents,' is one of Burroughs's sayings" (116).

17. Philosopher Charles Taylor's account of human agency often mobilizes the traditional opposition between human agency and addiction. See "What Is Human Agency?" in *Human Agency and Language: Philosophical Papers I* (Cambridge: Cambridge University Press, 1985), esp. 21–22.

18. Karl Marx, *Capital: A Critique of Political Economy*, vol. I, trans. Samuel Moore and Edward Aveling, rev. Ernest Untermann (New York: Modern Library, 1906), 81–82. In Marx's view, the commodity is "a mysterious thing, simply because in it the social character of men's labour appears to them as an objective character stamped upon the product of that labour" (83). To illustrate this point, Marx personifies commodities (81–82) and imagines what would happen "could commodities themselves speak" (95).

19. William S. Burroughs, *Junky* (1953; reprint, New York: Penguin, 1977), 22. Further references appear parenthetically in the text.

20. Jacques Derrida, "The Rhetoric of Drugs," trans. Michael Israel, *differences: A Journal of Feminist Cultural Studies* 5, no. 1 (1993): 7.

21. Jean Cocteau, *Opium: The Diary of a Cure,* trans. Margaret Crosland and Sinclair Road (French original, 1929; English trans., London: Peter Owen, 1957), 73.

22. Avital Ronell, *Crack Wars: Literature, Addiction, Mania* (Lincoln: University of Nebraska Press, 1992), 45.

23. Martin Heidegger, *Being and Time,* trans. John Macquarrie and Edward Robinson (German original, 1927; English trans., New York: Harper and Row, 1962), 196.

24. Derrida, "Rhetoric," 6.

25. William S. Burroughs, "The Invisible Generation," in *The Ticket that Exploded* (New York: Grove, 1967), 213. Further references to both *Ticket* and "Invisible" appear parenthetically in the text.

26. Jacques Derrida, "Plato's Pharmacy," in *Dissemination,* trans. Barbara Johnson (Chicago: University of Chicago Press, 1981), 101. On the notion of writing as "organism," see 79 in the same volume.

27. Derrida, "Rhetoric," 14–17.

28. On the cut-up technique and Burroughs's control theories, see Barry Miles, *William Burroughs: El Hombre Invisible* (New York: Hyperion, 1993), 111–28; Ted Morgan, *Literary Outlaw: The Life and Times of William S. Burroughs* (New York: Henry Holt and Company, 1988), 321–23, 338–41; Timothy Murphy, *Wising Up the Marks: The Amodern William Burroughs* (Berkeley and Los Angeles: University of California Press), 103–7, 135–41; David Porush, *The Soft Machine,* 101–4; and Tanner, 131–40.

29. In a 1963 interview, Burroughs claimed that large organizations such as *Time/Life* magazines and the CIA controlled a powerful hoard of "words and images" that even their human heads (Henry Luce, for instance) had "no control over" (quoted in Miles, 130).

30. William S. Burroughs, *The Soft Machine* (1961; rev. ed., New York: Grove, 1966), 89.

31. William S. Burroughs, *Exterminator!* (New York: Penguin, 1973), 6.

32. William S. Burroughs, "Appendix," *Soft Machine* (1961; rev. ed., London: Calder, 1968). Quoted in Miles, 120.

33. Donna Haraway sets out the distinctions between "postmodern" biology and previous models of the self in "A Cyborg Manifesto: Science, Technology, and Socialist-Feminism in the Late Twentieth Century," in *Simians, Cyborgs, and Women: The Reinvention of Nature* (New York: Routledge, 1991), 149–81.

34. Donna Haraway, "The Biopolitics of Postmodern Bodies," in *Simians, Cyborgs, and Women: The Reinvention of Nature* (New York: Routledge, 1991), 212, 207.

35. See Marvin Minsky, *Society of the Mind* (New York: Simon and Schuster, 1985). For commentary on this model, see Daniel Dennett, *Consciousness Explained* (Boston: Little, Brown, 1991); and Francisco Varela, Even Thompson, and Eleanor Rosch, *The Embodied Mind: Cognitive Science and Human Experience* (Cambridge, Mass.: MIT Press), esp. chap. 6. The latter text offers a positive alternative to Minsky's view and to the problems I am tracing here.

36. Gilles Deleuze and Félix Guattari, *Anti-Oedipus: Capitalism and Schizophrenia*, trans. Robert Hurley, Mark Seem, and Helen R. Lane (Minneapolis: University of Minnesota Press, 1983), 283, 20. Scott Bukatman offers an interesting discussion of the relation between Burroughs's fiction and the notion of "the body without organs" in *Terminal Identity* (see esp. 325–28).

37. Haraway, "Biopolitics," 215, 212.

38. Richard Dawkins, *The Extended Phenotype: The Gene as the Unit of Selection* (Oxford: Oxford University Press, 1982), 264, 254, 210, 39.

39. Haraway, "Biopolitics," 217.

40. William S. Burroughs, *Queer* (New York: Penguin, 1985), xxii. Further references appear parenthetically in the text.

41. For several eyewitness accounts of this event, see Morgan, 194–97.

42. The misogynist strain of these writings is nowhere so evident as when Burroughs attempts to defend himself against charges of misogyny. See, for instance, his short essay, "Women: A Biological Mistake?" in *The Adding Machine: Selected Essays* (New York: Arcade, 1985), 125–27. For a more detailed account of Burroughs's misogyny than I can give here, see Murphy.

43. Sigmund Freud, *The Psychopathology of Everyday Life,* trans. and ed. James Strachey, vol. 6, *The Standard Edition of the Complete Psychological Works of Sigmund Freud* (German original, 1904; English trans., London: Hogarth, 1953–74), 259.

44. Freud, 258.

45. William S. Burroughs, "On Coincidence," in *The Adding Machine: Selected Essays* (New York: Arcade, 1985), 99. Further references appear parenthetically in the text.

46. Gregory Bateson, "The Cybernetics of 'Self': A Theory of Alcoholism," *Steps to an Ecology of Mind* (New York: Ballantine, 1972), 329.

47. Bateson, "Cybernetics," 331.

48. Gregory Bateson, "Conscious Purpose Versus Nature," *Steps to an Ecology of Mind* (New York: Ballantine, 1972), 461.

49. William S. Burroughs, "The Limits of Control," in *The Adding Machine: Selected Essays* (New York: Arcade, 1985), 117. Further references appear parenthetically in the text.

50. William S. Burroughs, "Sexual Conditioning," in *The Adding Machine: Selected Essays* (New York: Arcade, 1985), 87.

51. See *Letters of William S. Burroughs*, 68–69, 85–86, 88–89, and 115–16.

52. Sedgwick, "Epidemics of the Will," esp. 589. See also Michel Foucault, *The History of Sexuality: An Introduction*, trans. Robert Hurley, vol. 1 (New York: Vintage, 1978), esp. 42–43.

53. Vance Packard, *The Hidden Persuaders* (New York: David McKay, 1957), 239–40.

54. Quoted in Packard, 239–40.

55. Packard, 240.

56. Packard, 239. Like Riesman, though more melodramatically, Ellul suggests that psychological collectivization, which is epitomized by advertising, will "implant in [the individual] a certain conception of life" (Jacques Ellul, *The Technological Society*, trans. John Wilkinson [New York: Vintage, 1964], 406).

57. Packard, 107.

58. Packard, 107.

59. Packard, 107–8. Citations from Packard here are chapter titles. Others chapters with similar implications include "Babes in Consumerland," "Back to the Breast, and Beyond," "The Engineered Yes," and "The Packaged Soul?" Stanton Peele draws the same kind of connection between drugs and large social institutions. Drugs, he says, "also drew the ire of the bureaucratic institutions which were growing up alongside of opiates in America—institutions which exercised a similar type of power psychologically to that of the narcotics, and with which, therefore, the drugs were essentially competing" (Peele, *Love and Addiction*, 37).

60. Tanner, 118.

61. Norbert Wiener, *The Human Use of Human Beings: Cybernetics and Society* (New York: Da Capo, 1950), 11–12. Further references appear parenthetically in the text.

CHAPTER 3: NARRATING NATIONAL ADDICTIONS

1. Thomas De Quincey, "The English-Mail Coach," in *The Collected Writings of Thomas De Quincey*, 14 vols., vol. 13, ed. David Masson (New York: AMS, 1968), 13:270–330, 322. Further references appear parenthetically in the text.

2. Claudia L. Johnson, *Equivocal Beings: Politics, Gender, and Sentimentality in the 1790s—Wollstonecraft, Radcliffe, Burney, Austen* (Chicago: University of Chicago Press, 1995), 105.

3. See my "Techniques of Terror, Technologies of Nationality: Ann Radcliffe's *The Italian*" (*ELH* 61 [1994]: 853–76) for an extended consideration of the connection between Gothic fictions of the 1790s and English nationality.

4. Thomas De Quincey, "Suspiria de Profundis," in *The Collected Writings of Thomas De Quincey*, 14 vols., vol. 13, ed. David Masson (New York: AMS, 1968), 13:331–69, 352. Further references appear parenthetically in the text.

5. For other literary models from which De Quincey borrowed, see especially the remarkable passage in "Suspiria de Profundis" in which De Quincey makes an extended analogy between a palimpsest and the human mind. The palimpsest features a "Grecian tragedy" overwritten by a "monkish legend," which is in turn overwritten by a "knightly romance." These three genres—tragedy, legend, and

romance—also characterize the development of the individual mind, for when death, sickness, or opium bring to light the "mysterious handwritings of grief or joy" that have been inscribed there, these genres appear in succession: "The romance has perished that the young man adored; the legend has gone that deluded the boy; but the deep, deep tragedies of infancy, as when the child's hands were unlinked forever from his mother's neck, or his lips for ever from his sister's kisses, these remain lurking below all" ("Suspiria," 13:348, 349).

6. For a representative journal entry, consider this excerpt from 1803: "Last night I imagined to myself the heroine of the novel dying on an island of a lake. . . . Last night too I image myself looking through a glass. 'What do you see?' I see a man in the dim shadowy perspective and (as it were) in a dream. . . . There is something gloomily great in him; he wraps himself up in the dark recesses of his own soul. . . . I image too a banquet or carousel of feodal magnificence—such as in Schiller's Ghost-Seer, in ye. middle of which a mysterious stranger should enter, on whose approach hangs fate and the dark roll of many woes, etc." (quoted in V. A. De Luca, *Thomas De Quincey: The Prose of Vision* [Toronto: University of Toronto Press, 1980], 4). For an extensive list of De Quincey's early reading in the Gothic, see his *Diary*, ed. Horace A. Eaton [1803; reprint, London: Noel Douglas, 1927], 215–52).

7. Eve Kosofsky Sedgwick, *The Coherence of Gothic Conventions* (New York: Methuen, 1986), 7.

8. Sedgwick, 44. As in Radcliffe and Lewis, for instance, De Quincey had an obsession with secret murders and societies for accomplishing them (see Alethea Hayter, *Opium and the Romantic Imagination* [Berkeley and Los Angeles: University of California Press, 1968], 245–46). As in Maturin's *Melmoth the Wanderer,* De Quincey frequently expresses a terror of crowds ("the human face tyrannized over my dreams" [*Confessions*, 1822, 81]). The full catalog of "Gothic conventions" listed by Sedgwick may be found throughout De Quincey's writings.

9. Sedgwick, 49.

10. Nigel Leask discusses the medicalizing and pathologizing of biographical subjects in De Quincey. See his *British Romantic Writers and the East: Anxieties of Empire* (Cambridge: Cambridge University Press, 1992), 178–79.

11. On Russ's use of the term "Shadow-Male," see Tania Modleski, *Loving with a Vengeance: Mass-Produced Fantasies for Women* (1982; reprint, New York and London: Routledge, 1988), 79.

12. As F. S. Schwarzbach has argued, such a vision reveals a sense of London as quite literally foreign, an unknown and threatening *terra incognita*. (See "'Terra Incognita'—An Image of the City in English Literature, 1820–1855," in *The Art of Travel: Essays on Travel Writing*, ed. Philip Dodd [London: Frank Cass, 1982], 65–67.) Later, scenes of architectural terror would come to dominate De Quincey's opium dreams. As he writes, "With the same power of endless growth and self-reproduction did my architecture proceed in dreams" (*Confessions*, 1822, 106). J. Hillis Miller calls the sensation evoked by scenes such as this one the "Piranesi effect" after Piranesi's *Carceri* sketches, which were apparently known to De Quincey through Coleridge's description of them (Miller, *The Disappearance of God: Five Nineteenth-Century Writers* [1963; reprint, Cambridge, Mass.: Harvard University Press], 67; see also Hayter, 248).

13. On mass society, see John Barrell, *The Infection of Thomas De Quincey: A Psychopathology of Imperialism* (New Haven, Conn.: Yale University Press, 1991), 4–5.

14. This is, in essence, J. Hillis Miller's understanding of De Quincey. Miller, however, attributes a source for this sense of catastrophe: the death of De Quincey's sister, Elizabeth, which, writes Miller, "colors all his existence thereafter" (19). My focus is not on the supposed origin of De Quincey's inevitable narrative of catastrophe (which is also a narrative of inevitable catastrophe), but on the uses to which such a narrative was put in providing a plot both for De Quincey himself and for the English nation.

15. Michelle A. Massé, *In the Name of Love: Women, Masochism, and the Gothic* (Ithaca, N.Y.: Cornell University Press, 1992), 40–72.

16. Perhaps the most resonant use of "pariah" occurs in a footnote that De Quincey appended to the second part of "Suspiria," entitled "Levana and Our Ladies of Sorrow," when it appeared in *Blackwood's Magazine* in June 1845: "The reader who wishes at all to understand the course of these Confessions ought not to pass over this dream-legend. . . . Its importance to the present Confessions is this,— that it rehearses or prefigures their course. This FIRST Part belongs to Madonna. The THIRD belongs to the 'Mater Suspiriorum,' and will be entitled *The Pariah Worlds*" ("Suspiria," 13:369n).

17. As De Quincey writes of himself in the 1856 version of *Confessions,* it is as if he were possessed by "some overmastering fiend, . . . some oestrus of hidden persecution that bade [him] fly when no man pursued" (338).

18. That the Sphinx should pose the question of the Incommunicable, and that a lion should conquer him without a struggle, is perhaps of a piece with De Quincey's intense phobia of large cats. For an extended treatment of this phobia, see the chapter in Barrell entitled "Tigridiasis: Tipu's Revenge" (48–66). Barrell fails to mention a remarkable coincidence involving tigers in the First Opium War. After hostilities had begun, the first large Chinese counterattack was carried out by troops wearing "tiger-skin caps": "The timing of the Chinese attack—a night assault on 10 March 1842—was decided in the event . . . by War Magic: the twenty-eighth day of the first Chinese month (a Tiger month) and at the hour of the tiger (between 3 and 5 a.m.)" (Jack Beeching, *The Chinese Opium Wars* [New York: Harcourt, 1975], 144).

19. Barrell's *Infection of Thomas De Quincey* treats De Quincey's fear of this pollution or "infection" compellingly and at great length.

20. As Joshua Wilner observes, "The drug's effect is to cut across or suspend the historical or organic continuity of the subject and institute in its place a depersonalized and detemporalized machinery of imaginative production" ("Autobiography and Addiction: The Case of De Quincey," *Genre* 14 [1981]: 493–503, 493). But, like the *pharmakon* that it is, opium also promises to avert such destabilization. Alina Clej notes: "His [De Quincey's] emphasis on 'the most exquisite order, legislation, and harmony' brought by the opium rapture is an attempt to preempt any danger of dissemination and dissipation of the self through the contagious influence of the (feminine, proletarian, or oriental) Other" (*A Genealogy of the Modern Self: Thomas De Quincey and the Intoxication of Writing* [Stanford, Calif.: Stanford University Press, 1995], xi). (On the *pharmakon,* see Jacques Derrida, "Plato's Pharmacy," in *Dissemination,* trans. Barbara Johnson [Chicago: University of Chicago Press, 1981]).

21. Virginia Berridge and Griffith Edwards, in *Opium and the People: Opiate Use in*

Nineteenth-Century England (New Haven, Conn.: Yale University Press, 1987), establish that "the majority of descriptions at this time [the late eighteenth century] still saw opium eating or smoking as a peculiarly Eastern custom" (xxv).

22. Barrell, *Infection of Thomas De Quincey*, 21. Such a logic of the simultaneous plausibility of opposed possibilities is typical of De Quincey. Note the rhetorical gymnastics of the following sentence, in which guilt is at once denied and admitted: "But, on the one hand, as my self-accusation does not amount to a confession of guilt, so, on the other, it is possible that, if it *did*, the benefit resulting to others, from the record of an experience purchased at so heavy a price, might compensate, by a vast overbalance, for any violence done to the feelings I have noticed, and justify a breach of the general rule" (*Confessions*, 1822, 30).

23. Barry Milligan observes in *Pleasures and Pains: Opium and the Orient in Nineteenth-Century British Culture* (Charlottesville: University of Virginia Press, 1995): "Coleridge laid the foundation for a conception of opium as the medium of a retributive Oriental infection-invasion that not only threatens to dissolve the national identity of its user but also clouds some basic reference points for individual identity" (12). The peculiarly powerful anxieties and desires surrounding opium he attributes to the fact that "not only was it literally ingested by British bodies . . . but it also had a reputation for altering the consciousness of its user, and it is this dual force that prepares the ground for a cultural context in which to interpret opium and its attendant transformations as various forms of foreign invasion, invasions that are imagined in nineteenth-century British culture as simultaneously pleasurable and painful" (30). Berridge and Edwards locate the association of opium use in England with "moral as well as physical descent" in the antiopium movement of the last quarter of the nineteenth century (193); both Coleridge and De Quincey, however, betray a similar anxiety more than half a century earlier.

24. Marilyn Butler, *Romantics, Rebel and Reactionaries: English Literature and its Background 1769–1830* (Oxford: Oxford University Press, 1981), 74–75.

25. As Michael Cochise Young points out, such a displacement of blame is characteristic of De Quincey (55, 57); see also Maniquis, who argues that for De Quincey "the 'real' self floats within a stream of discontinuous selves, and it is always this real self that is innocent. Discontinuous selves mark the presence of guilt, which is always alien, never *his*" ("Lonely Empires: Personal and Public Visions of Thomas De Quincey," in *Literary Monographs*, vol. 8, ed. E. Rothstein and J. Wittreich [Madison: University of Wisconsin, 1976], 58).

26. I am grateful to Peter Stallybrass for calling my attention to Mulready's *Train Up a Child;* for a deft reading of the painting as well as an account of various contemporary reactions to it, see his essay, "Marx and Heterogeneity: Thinking the Lumpenproletariat," *Representations* 31 (1990): 69–95, 78.

27. See Nancy L. Paxton, "Mobilizing Chivalry: Rape in British Novels about the Indian Uprising of 1857," *Victorian Studies* 36 (1992): 7–8.

28. Stallybrass, 78.

29. On the linguistic implications of this scene, see also Leask, 209–13.

30. J. Elliot Bingham, *Narrative of the Expedition to China, from the Commencement of the War to its Termination in 1842; with Sketches of the Manners and Customs of that Singular and Hitherto Almost Unknown Country* (1st ed., 1843; 2d ed., 2 vols., Wilmington, Del.: Scholarly Resources, 1972), xiii.

31. By 1821 there had been two official missions to China from the British Crown. Both missions had been sent by George III. The first, in 1793, was led by Lord Macartney; the second, in 1816, was led by Lord Amherst. Neither was particularly successful at convincing the Chinese to deal directly with the British Crown—though De Quincey believed that both managed at least to convey British refusal to submit to the Chinese view of them as "barbarians" bearing tribute. Despite these political contacts, relations between the two countries were, from the start, almost entirely mercantile.

32. Maurice Collis, *Foreign Mud: The Opium Imbroglio at Canton in the 1830s and the Anglo-Chinese War* (1946; reprint, New York: W. W. Norton, 1968), 80.

33. Some indication of the volume of opium imported into China is provided by Collis, who writes that at the end of the eighteenth century two thousand chests of opium (each chest weighing 150 pounds) were sold to the Chinese annually; by 1825, the number had risen to nearly ten thousand chests; in 1836, to more than twenty-six thousand (64).

34. Beeching, 1–12; Jean Chesneaux, Marianne Bastid, and Marie-Claire Bergère, *China from the Opium Wars to the 1911 Revolution*, trans. Anne Destenay (New York: Pantheon, 1976), 53–56; Collis, 13–91; and Brian Inglis, *The Opium War* (London: Hodder and Stoughton, 1976).

35. Beeching, 36.

36. Chesneaux, Bastid, and Bergère, 62.

37. Beeching, 74–81; Chesneaux, Bastid, and Bergère, 63.

38. Collis, 295.

39. Beeching, 152–56; Chesneaux, Bastid, and Bergère, 65; and Inglis.

40. Arthur Cunynghame, *The Opium War: Being Recollections of Service in China* (1845; reprint, Wilmington, Del.: Scholarly Resources, 1972), 37.

41. J. Elliot Bingham, *Narrative of the Expedition to China* (1843; reprint, 2 vols., Wilmington, Del.: Scholarly Resources, 1972), I:159. These comments, as well as De Quincey's, perhaps owe much to Reverend Sydney Smith's 1803 account. According to Smith, Malays are "the most vindictive and ferocious of living beings. . . . We cannot help thinking, that, one day or another, when they are more full of opium than usual, they will run *amock* from Cape Cormorin to the Caspian" (quoted in Leask, 209–10).

42. Peter Ward Fay, *The Opium War 1840–1842* (Chapel Hill: University of North Carolina Press, 1975), 366.

43. David Masson, ed., *The Collected Writings of Thomas De Quincey*, vol. 14 (New York: AMS, 1968), 346.

44. Nigel Leask, John Barrell, and Robert Maniquis all discuss De Quincey's writings on the Opium Wars; see Leask, 208–28; Barrell 147–56; and Maniquis, 96–106.

45. The essay was published in June 1840 under the title "The Opium and the China Question." It was reprinted in the *Collected Writings* as "The Opium Question with China in 1840."

46. Beeching, 56.

47. Collis, 178.

48. As Leask writes, "The most disturbing element of De Quincey's dream

life . . . is the way that it is quite literally materialized in his later writings about China, Ceylon and the Indian Mutiny" (216).

49. This nexus appears in various guises throughout the essay. In arguing that the Chinese are not to be believed when they claim that they seek to stop the opium trade for the benefit of their citizens, for instance, De Quincey proclaims: "This sudden leap into the anxieties of parental care is a suspicious fact against the Chinese government" ("The Opium Question," 14:167–68). The suggestion that the Chinese, as a nation, are not good parents is echoed in a later essay on China in which Chinese mothers are attacked: the one duty of such a mother, writes De Quincey, is to "teach to her children, as her earliest lesson in morality, some catechism of vengeance" (quoted in Barrell, 154).

50. Beeching, 16.

51. See also Beeching, 81. The incident involving the *Lady Hughes* also figures in an 1833 article in the *Chinese Repository*. The article's anonymous author, who Collis suggests was probably Jardine of Matheson, Jardine, and Co., concludes his discussion of the incident thus: "Has not the Chinese commerce of Great Britain been purchased with the blood of the gunner of the *Lady Hughes?* Has not his immolation up to this day remained unavenged? There is the smell of blood still" (quoted in Collis, 97).

52. On De Quincey's sense of the inevitable, eternal iteration of atrocities, see De Quincey, "The English Mail-Coach" 304; Miller, 193; Robert Lance Snyder, "Introduction" to *Thomas De Quincey: Bicentenary Studies,* ed. R. L. Snyder (Norman: University of Oklahoma Press, 1985), xvii–xxiv, xix.

53. James Hogg, "Introduction: The English in China," in *The Uncollected Writings of Thomas De Quincey,* ed. James Hogg, vol. 2 (1890; reprint, Freeport, N.Y.: Books for Library, 1972), 7.

54. Interestingly, as John Barrell has noted, some of De Quincey's predictions did, in fact, come true (152). There was the case of Captain Stead, who landed on the island of Chou-san, which had been seized by the British early in the First Opium War. Stead did not know when he landed, however, that the island had since been returned; he was killed by angry Chinese (Beeching, 128). There were also two ships captured on Formosa (present-day Taiwan): one, a troop transport named the *Nerbudda,* is referred to by De Quincey in "The Chinese Question in 1857" (14:365; see also Barrell, 152); a second, which goes unmentioned, was named—eerily enough in light of *Confessions*—the *Ann* (Beeching, 137–38).

55. In the words of Alina Clej, "To posit and assert itself the subject has to exceed or lose itself." This consolidation of subjectivity by way of excess and transgression constitutes for Clej the principal instance of De Quincey's anticipation of modernity: "This prodigality, the extended play of defiance and impossible redemption, informs De Quincey's confessions and the texts of many of his modernist successors" (11).

56. The constellated concerns of opium, subjectivity, empire, and the Gothic recur frequently in texts throughout the nineteenth century, from Wilkie Collins's *The Moonstone* (1868) and Dickens's *The Mystery of Edwin Drood* (1870) to Oscar Wilde's *The Picture of Dorian Gray* (1891) and Arthur Conan Doyle's "The Man with the Twisted Lip" (1901).

57. Note the privileged position occupied by tea in the domestic idyll that De Quincey, immediately before embarking on the section of *Confessions* titled "The

Pains of Opium," invokes as an emblem of all that his addiction to opium rendered irretrievable: "From the latter weeks of October to Christmas-eve, therefore, is the period during which happiness is in season, which, in my judgment, enters the room with the tea-tray: for tea, though ridiculed by those who are naturally of coarse nerves, or are become so from wine-drinking, and are not susceptible of influence from so refined a stimulant, will always be the favourite beverage of the intellectual" (*Confessions*, 1822, 94).

58. Inglis, 198.

59. Leask, 5.

60. It was in India rather than China that the national victimization De Quincey anxiously predicted finally took place. Sepoy troops stationed at Meerut mutinied on May 10, 1857, firing on their British officers and looting European homes before fleeing toward Delhi: the Indian Rebellion (or Sepoy Mutiny, as the British called it at the time) was underway. Of the various confused accounts of the rebellion that reached England in the weeks and months following the initial action, most electrifying were rumors of atrocities committed against Englishwomen and their children. On September 17, 1857, for instance, *The Times* reported: "Children have been compelled to eat the quivering flesh of their murdered parents. . . . Men in many instances have been mutilated and, before being absolutely killed, have had to gaze upon the last dishonour of their wives and daughters previous to being put to death" (quoted in Graham Dawson, *Soldier Heroes: British Adventure, Empire and the Imagining of Masculinities* [London and New York: Routledge, 1994], 87). Such scenes of carnage quickly assumed the shape of a veritable iconography, a collection of anecdotes and illustrations whose depictions of the rebellion focused with horrified fascination on the spectacle of white women and children menaced, tortured, or hacked to bits by swarthy sepoys. The suppression of the rebellion—which involved no small share of its own atrocities—was conceived less as a military solution to the politico-military crisis of a colony in revolt than as the only appropriate answer to the savaging of English innocents. In the aftermath of the rebellion, the Englishness De Quincey constructed in the pages of *Confessions of an English Opium-Eater* and in his essays on the Opium Wars, aggressive because fragile, grips the public imagination and shapes official policy toward India. As in the opium-eater's tableaux of victimization, depictions of the rebellion as Indian violation of English daughters, sisters, and mothers evoke by way of response a justly vengeful masculinity. To De Quincey himself such depictions were more than simply the vindication of his predictions, for his daughter Florence, her husband Colonel Richard Bairdsmith, and their young child were living in Delhi when it was captured by rebel troops (Grevel Lindop, *The Opium-Eater: A Life of Thomas De Quincey* [New York: Taplinger, 1981], 379, 383; Masson, 131). The boundaries between personal and national, textual and historical waver and collapse; the subject position demanded of the public by the iconography of the rebellion—that they witness outrages upon women as if they were those women's sons, brothers, or fathers—is precisely reproduced in De Quincey's relation toward his own daughter and grandchild. Inevitably, De Quincey draws on his private torment in order to fashion a public call to action in the form of a series of essays on the situation in India, all published in James Hogg's *Titan:* "Hurried Notices of Indian Affairs" (September 1857), "Passing Notices of Indian Affairs" (October 1857), and "Suggestions upon the Secret of the Mutiny" (January 1858). (On the Indian Rebel-

lion of 1857–58, see Wayne G. Broehl Jr., *Crisis of the Raj: The Revolt of 1857 through British Lieutenants' Eyes* [Hanover and London: University Press of New England, 1986]; C. Hibbert, *The Great Mutiny, India 1857* [Harmondsworth: Penguin, 1978]; F. G. Hutchins, *The Illusion of Permanence: British Imperialism in India* [Princeton, N.J.: Princeton University Press, 1967]; Sir Penderel Moon, *The British Conquest and Dominion of India* [London: Duckworth, 1989], 676–781; Jenny Sharpe, *Allegories of Empire: The Figure of Woman in the Colonial Text* [Minneapolis and London: University of Minnesota Press, 1993], 57–82; and Eric Stokes, *The Peasant Armed: The Indian Revolt of 1857,* ed. C. A. Bayley [Oxford: Claredon, 1986]; and Paxton, cited above.)

CHAPTER 4: VICTORIAN HIGHS

1. M. P. Shiel, "The House of Orven," in *The Eighteen-Nineties,* ed. Martin Secker (London: The Richards Press, 1948), 447.

2. Arthur Conan Doyle, *The Sign of Four* (New York: Penguin Books, 1982), 7.

3. Arthur Conan Doyle, "The Man with the Twisted Lip," in *The Adventures of Sherlock Holmes,* ed. Richard Lancelyn Green (Oxford: Oxford University Press, 1993), 124.

4. Arthur Conan Doyle, "The Yellow Face," in *The Memoirs of Sherlock Holmes,* ed. Christopher Roden (Oxford: Oxford University Press, 1993), 53.

5. Hugh C. Weir, "The Man with Nine Lives," in *Crime on Her Mind,* ed. Michele B. Slung (New York: Pantheon Books, 1975), 140.

6. Shiel, 448.

7. Doyle, *Sign of Four,* 94.

8. Wilkie Collins, *The Moonstone* (Harmondsworth: Penguin Books, 1969), 67.

9. Ashish Roy, "The Fabulous Imperialist Semiotic of Wilkie Collins' *The Moonstone,*" *New Literary History* 24 (1993): 658.

10. Unlike Barry Milligan (*Pleasures and Pains: Opium and the Orient in Nineteenth-Century English Culture* [Charlottesville: University Press of Virginia, 1995], 93), Nigel Leask distinguishes between pollution from the outside and homeopathic defense (like "Chinoiserie") which he deploys in an inoculation model of culture (Leask, *British Romantic Writers and the East: Anxieties of Empire* [Cambridge: Cambridge University Press, 1992], 8).

11. Collins, 420.

12. Milligan, 68.

13. Sax Rohmer, *Tales of Chinatown* (New York: A. L. Burt Company, 1922), 14–15.

14. Charles Dickens, *The Mystery of Edwin Drood* (London: Oxford University Press, 1956), 3. Further references are cited parenthetically in the text.

15. Doyle, "Man with the Twisted Lip," 123, 140–41.

16. Robert Crooks has noted the curious isolation of all colonial traces in detective fiction that suspend them from our ideological attention. He finds the situation of the Hindus in *The Moonstone* to be paradigmatic ("Reopening the Mysteries: Colonialist Logic and Cultural Difference in *The Moonstone* and *The Horse Latitudes,*" *Lit* 4, no. 3 (1993): 215–28, 217, 226).

17. Edgar Allan Poe, "A Tale of the Ragged Mountains," in *Collected Works,* ed.

Thomas Ollive Mabbott (Cambridge, Mass.: Harvard University Press, 1978), 940. Further references are cited parenthetically in the text.

18. John W. Bilsland, "De Quincey's Opium Experience," *Dalhousie Review* 55 (1975): 421.

19. Thomas Burke, *The Ecstasies of Thomas De Quincey* (London: George G. Harrap & Co. Ltd., 1928), 22.

20. Marek Kohn, *Narcomania: On Heroin* (London: Faber and Faber, 1987), 28.

21. Geoffrey Harding, *Opium Addiction, Morality and Medicine* (New York: St. Martin's Press, 1988), 24.

22. Edgar Holt, *The Opium Wars in China* (London: Putnam, 1964), 101.

23. Karl Marx quoted in Colin Mackerras, *Western Images of China* (New York: Oxford University Press, 1989), 114.

24. Leigh Hunt, "Tea-Drinking," in *Inspired by Drink*, ed. Joan and John Digby (New York: William Morrow and Company, Inc., 1988), 335.

25. Holt, 36–37.

26. Samuel Johnson quoted in David Sanctuary Howard, *New York and the China Trade* (New York: The New York Historical Society, 1984), 22.

27. Zhang Longxi, "The Myth of the Other: China in the Eyes of the West," *Critical Inquiry* 15 (1988): 125.

28. Hugh Honour, *Chinoiserie: The Vision of Cathay* (London: John Murray, 1961), 201.

29. John Keay, *The Honorable Company: A History of the English East India Company* (London: HarperCollins, 1991), 359.

30. Virginia Berridge and Griffith Edwards, *Opium and the People: Opiate Use in Nineteenth-Century England* (London: A. Lane, 1981), 173–74.

31. Karl Marx and Frederick Engels, *On Colonialism* (New York: International Publishers, 1972), 220.

32. Michael Greenberg, *British Trade and the Opening of China 1800–1840* (Cambridge: Cambridge University Press, 1951), 104.

33. Holt, 64. See also Brian Inglis, *The Opium War* (London: Hodder and Stoughton, 1976), 74. This was all in keeping with Britain's central role in the drug trade generally, because "by the late seventeenth-century over 95% of drug imports came through London" (Terry M. Parssinen, *Secret Passions, Secret Remedies: Narcotic Drugs in British Society, 1820–1930* [Manchester: Manchester University Press, 1983], 15).

34. Holt, 143. For recent accounts of the complexities of Anglo-Chinese relations leading to the Opium Wars, see Marshall Sahlins, "Cosmologies of Capitalism: The Trans-Pacific Sector of 'The World System,'" in *Culture/Power/History: A Reader in Contemporary Social Theory*, ed. Nicholas B. Dirks et al. (Princeton, N.J.: Princeton University Press, 1993), 412–55; and Cannon Schmitt, *Alien Nation: Nineteenth-Century Gothic Fictions and English Nationality* (Philadelphia: University of Pennsylvania Press, 1997), 65–75.

35. Holt, 152. "Along the China coast itself the traffic was conducted with a guardedness that was little short of stealth. The word 'opium' disappeared from the instructions Matheson sent his skippers. When he absolutely had to specify types and quantities, he clothed them in the nomenclature of the cotton textile trade, Patna becoming 'whites,' Benares 'greys,' and Malwa 'chintzes.' Correspondents in Eng-

land were advised that the whole subject was 'under the rose'" (Peter Ward Fay, *The Opium War: 1840–1842* [New York: W. W. Norton, 1976], 168).

36. Nathan Allan, *The Opium Trade; Including a Sketch of Its History, Extent, Effects, etc.* (Lowell, Mass.: James P. Walker, 1853), 51. A curious instance of this disappearing act is found in De Quincey who single-handedly transformed opium-eating from an Oriental to an English vice. He wrote on opium twice: first in *The Confessions* in 1821 where he praises opium as a miracle substance and again in 1840 in an essay on the Opium Wars. In his treatment of the causes of the war he makes the opium disappear by proving that there can be no population of addicts in China as popularly supposed because coolies are too poor to buy the drug ("The Opium Question with China in 1840," in *The Collected Writings of Thomas De Quincey*, vol. 14, ed. David Masson [New York: AMS, 1968], 168).

37. Allan, 96; De Quincey, quoted in John Barrell, *The Infection of Thomas De Quincey: A Psychopathology of Imperialism* (New Haven, Conn.: Yale University Press, 1991), 153. The Emperor Napoleon I, however, "viewing the whole affair from the neutral ground of St. Helena, thought that the British envoy's refusal to kowtow was a great deal of fuss about very little" (Holt, 42).

38. John King Fairbanks, *Trade and Diplomacy on the China Coast: The Opening of the Treaty Ports, 1842–1854* (Cambridge, Mass.: Harvard University Press, 1953), 59.

39. Holt, 25.

40. Milligan, 100–1.

41. Daniel Defoe, *The Farther Adventures of Robinson Crusoe*, vol. III (Oxford: Basil Blackwell, 1927), 109.

42. Charles Dickens, *Our Mutual Friend* (London: Oxford University Press, 1962), 318.

43. Arthur Conan Doyle, "The Bruce-Partington Plans," in *His Last Bow*, ed. Owen Dudley Edwards (Oxford: Oxford University Press, 1993), 37.

44. Ronald R. Thomas, "Minding the Body Politic: The Romance of Science and the Revision of History in Victorian Detective Fiction," *Victorian Literature and Culture* 19 (1991): 239.

45. Collins, 112; Roy, 662, 670–71. In *Dorian Gray*, the drugs are in a "large Florentine cabinet, made out of ebony, and inlaid with ivory and blue lapis" in a "Chinese box of black and gold-dust lacquer, elaborately wrought" (Oscar Wilde, *The Picture of Dorian Gray* [Harmondsworth: Penguin Books, 1985], 218–19).

46. Mark M. Hennelly Jr., "Detecting Collins' Diamond: From Serpentstone to Moonstone," *Nineteenth Century Fiction* 39 (1984): 33.

47. Ronald Knox, "Detective-Story Decalogue," in *The Art of the Mystery Story*, ed. Howard Haycraft (New York: Biblio and Tannen, 1976), 195.

CHAPTER 5: THE RHETORIC OF ADDICTION

1. Robyn Warhol and Helena Michie, "Twelve-Step Teleology: Narratives of Recovery/Recovery as Narrative," in *Getting a Life: Everyday Uses of Autobiography*, ed. Sidonie Smith and Julia Watson (Minneapolis: University of Minnesota Press, 1996), 327–50. Our point resembles David Rudy's contention that early-stage alcoholics are "converted" to their belief in their own alcoholism through their contact with AA.

See David Rudy, *Becoming Alcoholic: Alcoholics Anonymous and the Reality of Alcoholism* (Cardonbale: Southern Illinois University Press, 1986).

2. These terms achieved currency for narratologists through Nancy K. Miller's application of them to eighteenth- and nineteenth-century British and French novels with female central characters, or "feminocentric" texts. In the euphoric plot pattern, the heroine marries at novel's end; in the dysphoric pattern, she dies. See Nancy K. Miller, *The Heroine's Text: Reading in the French and English Novel, 1722–1782* (New York: Columbia University Press, 1980).

3. *Big Book: Alcoholics Anonymous* 3d ed. (New York: A.A. World Services, Inc.), 1976. Further references are cited parenthetically in the text.

4. Vibeke Steffen explains that the metaphorical substitution of "disease" for "sin" is grounded in the terminology of the Oxford movement, the primary religious influence on the founders of AA. See "Alcoholism and Soul-surgery: Disease Concepts and Metaphors in the Minnesota Model," *Folk: Journal of the Danish Ethnographic Society* 35 (1993): 127–46.

5. Norman S. Miller, M.D., and John N. Chappel, M.D., "History of the Disease Concept," *Psychiatric Annals* 21 (1991): 196–205.

6. Miller and Chappel, 197.

7. George Eliot, *Janet's Repentance,* ed. David Lodge (Harmondsworth: Penguin Books, 1977), 334–35. Further references appear parenthetically in the text.

8. Anne Brontë's novel is one fictional account of alcoholism that has received interesting analysis from narrative-centered critics. See Edith A. Kosta, "Narrative Experience as a Means to Maturity in Anne Brontë's *The Tenant of Wildfell Hall,*" *Connecticut Review* 14 (1992): 41–47; Marianne Thormählen, "The Villain of Wildfell Hall: Aspects and Prospects of Arthur Huntingdon," *Modern Language Review* 98 (1993): 831–40; and on narrative embedding, text, talk, and alcoholism in *The Tenant of Wildfell Hall, see* Catherine MacGregor, "'I Cannot Trust Your Oaths and Promises: I Must Have a Written Agreement': Talk and Text in *The Tenant of Wildfell Hall,*" *Dionysos: The Literature and Addiction Triquarterly* 4, no. 2 (fall 1992): 31–39.

9. Charles Dickens, *Hard Times,* ed. George Ford and Sylvère Monod (New York: W. W. Norton, 1966), 52. Further references appear parenthetically in the text.

10. Charles Dickens, *Our Mutual Friend* (Harmondsworth: Penguin Books, 1971), 291–92. Further references appear parenthetically in the text.

11. Anthony Trollope, *Dr. Thorne* (1858; reprint, Harmondsworth: Penguin Books, 1982), 371.

12. D. A. Miller, *Narrative and its Discontents: Problems of Closure in the Traditional Novel* (Princeton, N.J.: Princeton University Press, 1981); Marianna Torgovnick, *Closure in the Novel* (Princeton, N.J.: Princeton University Press, 1981).

CHAPTER 6: FIREWATER LEGACY

1. D. H. Lawrence, *Studies in Classic American Literature* (New York: Penguin, 1971), 40. On Indian and white commentary regarding alcohol, especially the fallaciousness of firewater myths of Indian biological predisposition to alcohol abuse, see Joy Leland, *Firewater Myths: North American Indian Drinking and Alcohol Addiction* (New Brunswick, N.J.: Rutgers Center for Alcohol Studies, 1976); Dwight B. Heath, "Alcohol Use Among North American Indians: A Cross-Cultural Survey of Patterns

and Problems," in *Research Advances in Alcohol and Drug Problems,* ed. Reginald G. Smart et al. (New York: Plenum Press, 1983), 343–96; Craig MacAndrew and Robert Edgerton, *Drunken Comportment: A Social Explanation* (Chicago: Aldine Press, 1969); and Peter C. Mancall, *Deadly Medicine: Indians and Alcohol in Early America* (Ithaca, N.Y.: Cornell University Press, 1995).

2. Roy Harvey Pearce, *Savagism and Civilization: A Study Of the Indian and the American Mind* (Baltimore, Md.: Johns Hopkins University Press, 1965), vi, 53.

3. Quoted in Pearce, 6.

4. MacAndrew and Edgerton, 115.

5. William Apess, *On Our Own Ground: The Complete Writings of William Apess, A Pequot,* ed. Barry O'Connell (Amherst: University of Massachusetts Press, 1992), 28.

6. Simon Ortiz, *From Sand Creek* (New York: Thunder's Mouth Press, 1981), 48.

7. Alan R. Velie, ed., *American Indian Literature* (Norman: University of Oklahoma Press, 1979), 256.

8. Increase Mather, *Wo to Drunkards,* 2d ed. (Boston: Timothy Green, 1712), 35.

9. Mancall, 169–70.

10. Margaret Fuller Ossoli, *At Home and Abroad,* ed. Arthur B. Fuller (Boston, 1856), 90.

11. Quoted in Mancall, 27.

12. Benjamin Franklin, *The Works of Benjamin Franklin,* ed. John Bigelow, vol. 1, *The Autobiography of Benjamin Franklin* (New York: G. P. Putnam's Sons, 1904), 244.

13. James Fenimore Cooper, *The Pioneers,* ed. James D. Wallace (Oxford: Oxford University Press, 1991), 33. Further references cited parenthetically in text.

14. Alan Taylor, *William Cooper's Town: Power and Persuasion on the Frontier of the Early American Republic* (New York: Alfred A. Knopf, 1995), 54.

15. In relation to the question of sentimentality and of Chingachgook's role in *The Pioneers,* Geoffrey Rans observes that it is "astonishing" that Cooper "should choose the least admirable stereotype [of those available to him]—the Indian degraded by liquor—and use it to convey so searing a critique of the entire ethos upon which the novel is founded." See Rans's *Cooper's Leather-Stocking Novels* (Chapel Hill: University of North Carolina Press, 1991), 260, n. 28.

16. James Fenimore Cooper, *The Last of the Mohicans,* ed. James Franklin Beard (Albany: State University of New York Press, 1983), 156. Further references cited parenthetically in text.

17. On the relation of alcohol to visionary aspects of Native American religions, see Heath; Mancall; and Eleomire Zolla, who criticizes the "Enlightenment pettiness" with which Cooper oversimplified Native American shamanism into "a jumble of coarse rituals," in *The Writer and the Shaman: A Morphology of the American Indian,* trans. Raymond Rosenthal (New York: Harcourt Brace Jovanovich, 1973), 93.

CHAPTER 7: SMOKING, ADDICTION, AND THE MAKING OF TIME

My thanks to Jill Matthews, Barbara Sullivan, and the editors of this volume for valuable comments on earlier versions of this essay, and to Christine Owen and Simon Philpott for assistance with the final draft.

1. Anti-Cancer Council of Victoria, "Smoking: Your Questions Answered," in

Deadly Habits?, ed. Kaye Healey (Wentworth Falls, Australia: Spinney, 1992), 11–12, 12.

2. Diane DuCharme, "The Cigarette Papers," in *Recoveries: True Stories by People Who Conquered Addictions and Compulsions,* ed. Lindsey Hall and Leigh Cohn (Carlsbad, Calif.: Gurze, 1987), 83–101, 87.

3. Richard Klein, *Cigarettes Are Sublime* (Durham, N.C.: Duke University Press, 1993), 8. Further references are cited parenthetically in the text.

4. While the preferred style is to use the plural subject to avoid the gender specificity of the singular form, at some points I felt it was important to retain the singular construction of "the smoker" or "the nicotine addict" to stress that a textually produced identity is being referred to, rather than all the smokers or nicotine addicts in the world. In these cases I have used male and female pronouns interchangeably.

5. U.S. Department of Health and Human Services, *The Health Consequences of Smoking: Nicotine Addiction: A Report of the Surgeon General* (Washington, D.C.: GPO, 1988). Interestingly, the analogy with cocaine has not gained the currency of the heroin comparison. Perhaps this difference is related to the debate over whether cocaine can, in fact, cause "genuine" physical addiction.

6. Jeffrey E. Harris, *Deadly Choices: Coping with Health Risks in Everyday Life* (New York: Basic, 1993), 154.

7. John W. Farquhar and Gene A. Spiller, *The Last Puff: Ex-Smokers Share the Secrets of Their Success* (New York: W. W. Norton, 1990), 28.

8. Rachelle Unreich, "Local Hero," *Mode* [Australia], Feb.–Mar. 1996, 28.

9. At a broader level, the discourse of nicotine addiction can be located within a trajectory of medicalization in which human conduct and experiences are increasingly understood and explained in medical terms. As Nikolas Rose has argued, the subjection of ethical judgments to the logic of health is part of the modern experience of medicine. He states, "As the secular value of health replaces older non-corporeal or theological virtues and becomes one of the principal dimensions according to which we seek to compose a style of life for ourselves, the remit of medicine extends beyond the dimension of illness and cure and into the management of normality itself." See "Medicine, History and the Present," in *Reassessing Foucault: Power, Medicine and the Body,* ed. Colin Jones and Roy Porter (London: Routledge, 1994), 48–72, 67. The construction of smoking as a health issue is one example of the authority of medical knowledge in social life.

10. This discourse can certainly can have unlikely effects. A newspaper reported that at one English girls' school, pupils who register as addicts are issued two cigarettes a day from the school nurse, to be smoked in her presence. See A. McIlroy, "School Lets Girls Smoke if it Is a Habit," *The Daily Telegraph* [UK] on-line. Reuters Newsbriefs Health List (March 9, 1995).

11. Renée Bittoun, *Stop Smoking!: Beating Nicotine Addiction* (Milsons Pt., Australia: Random House Australia, 1993), 2, 99. Further references are cited parenthetically in the text.

12. Robert Matthews, "Some Are Born to Be Smokers Say Scientists," *The Sunday Telegraph* [UK] on-line. Reuters Newsbriefs Health List (June 11, 1995). The simplistic genetic determinism that generates concepts like "smoking genes" and gives credence to the idea that genetic codes cause specific behaviors has been convincingly challenged by critics. See Evelyn Fox Keller, "Master Molecules," in *Are Genes*

Us? The Social Consequences of the New Genetics, ed. Carl F. Cranor (New Brunswick, N.J.: Rutgers University Press, 1994), 89–98; and Steven Rose, Leon J. Kamin, and R. C. Lewontin, *Not in Our Genes: Biology, Ideology and Human Nature* (Harmondsworth: Penguin, 1984). However, the power of the gene in popular narratives of selfhood remains undiminished. Nelkin and Lindee have argued that DNA now functions as the secular equivalent of the Christian soul: the basis of human identity and the locus of the self (see Dorothy Nelkin and M. Susan Lindee, *The DNA Mystique: The Gene as a Culture Icon* [New York: Freeman, 1995], 40–41). In this cultural context, it makes sense that a vulnerability to addiction should be marked by an indelible flaw in the genetic makeup.

13. A discourse of smokers' rights, which couches the debate in exactly these terms, has gained prominence at the same time that the smoker as addict has become a common figure. In smokers' rights discourse, smokers' freedom is threatened not by the tyranny of addiction, but by the Puritanical and fascistic forces of anti-smoking. There are a number of comprehensive smokers' rights sites on the World Wide Web, maintained both by organizations and by individuals (National Smokers Alliance; The Freedom Organisation for the Right to Enjoy Smoking Tobacco [UK]); and Joe Dawson, "Essays on the Anti-Smoking Movement," Smoker's Web site [http://www.tezcat.com/~smokers/issues1.html] (March 10, 1997). Much more could be said about the relationship between the discourses of rights and of addiction, but such a discussion is beyond the scope of this essay.

14. Although Nicotine Anonymous, founded in the 1980s, is a relatively small organization without the public recognition and prominence of Alcoholics Anonymous, a visit to its Web site suggests that it is experiencing some success. Regular meetings throughout North America are listed, with almost one hundred established in California alone. Australia, the United Kingdom, the Netherlands, Spain, Poland, Hong Kong, Pakistan, and Argentina are among the other countries in which NicA has a presence, albeit a limited one. Even France has three NicA groups, and Internet meetings are available for those in need who are unable to attend a "live" gathering. NicA publishes a basic text called *The Book,* a range of pamphlets and a quarterly journal. Prolific publisher of "recovery" titles, Hazelden, also produces books and materials for smokers using the Twelve-Step approach to quitting.

15. Jay L., "Nicotine Anonymous," in *The Clinical Management of Nicotine Dependence,* ed. James Cocores (New York: Springer Verlag, 1991), 326–36, 329.

16. Nicotine Anonymous, "How Nicotine Anonymous Works," Nicotine Anonymous [http://www.slip.net/~billh/nicworks.html] (January 15, 1996).

17. It should be noted that writers like Bittoun, who have a narrower and more "scientific" view of addiction, understand it as a state of physical and psychological dependence. Bittoun is an enthusiastic advocate of nicotine replacement therapy for "strongly dependent smokers," and she contrasts its "scientifically evaluated" effectiveness with the unscientific advice and tips offered by group therapy. Her only comment specifically on Smokers Anonymous (*sic*) is that it has been "singularly unsuccessful, mainly due to the physical and social differences between alcohol and nicotine" (Renée Bittoun, *You Can Quit!* [Rushcutters Bay, Australia: Gore & Osment, 1995], 34).

18. Elizabeth Hanson Hoffman, *Recovery from Smoking: Quitting with the 12 Step*

Process (Center City, Minn.: Hazelden 1991). Further references are cited parenthetically in the text.

19. Ellen Walker, *Smoker: Self-Portrait of a Nicotine Addict* (San Francisco: Harper, 1990), 108. Further references are cited parenthetically in the text.

20. Strictly speaking, the correct description of Hazelden authors is people "in recovery," rather than people who have recovered. In Twelve-Step discourse and practice, addiction is controllable but incurable and recovery is a life-long process.

21. Sid Farrar, "Foreword" to *Smoker: Self Portrait of a Nicotine Addict* (San Francisco: Harper. 1990), v.

22. Farrar, vi.

23. See Michael A. H. Russell, "Nicotine Intake and Its Regulation by Smokers," in *Tobacco Smoking and Nicotine: A Neurobiological Approach*, ed. William R. Martin et al. (New York: Plenum, 1987), 25–50, 43–47. Smoking has been identified as improving concentration, memory, and performance of cognitive tasks, in part because of the actions of nicotine in the brain (Keith Wesnes, "Nicotine Increases Mental Efficiency: But How?" in *Tobacco Smoking and Nicotine: A Neurobiological Approach*, ed. William R. Martin et al. [New York: Plenum, 1987], 63–79; and David Warburton, "The Appetite for Nicotine," in *Appetite: Neural and Behavioural Bases*, ed. Charles R. Legg and David Booth [Oxford: Oxford University Press, 1994], 264–84, 271–72). It is also related to decreased risk of Parkinson's disease, Alzheimer's disease, Tourette's Syndrome, endometrial cancer, and ulcerative colitis (Bittoun, *Stop Smoking*, 100; and Barry J. Ford, *SmokeScreen: A Guide to the Personal Risks and Global Effects of the Cigarette Habit* [North Perth, Australia: Halcyon, 1994], 129; further references to Ford are cited parenthetically in the text).

24. Some commentators have called for the production of low-tar, high-nicotine cigarettes as a way of reducing the harm of smoking, without depriving smokers of the drug effects they seek (Wesnes, 77). Others have speculated about long-term self-administration of purer forms of nicotine as a future alternative to smoking (Russell, 47). These ideas themselves reflect and support the view of smoking as basically a question of nicotine dependence.

25. The logic of substitution can lead to contestation of the boundary between good drug and bad drug. Oral pathologist Brad Rodu has developed a smoking cessation strategy that encourages smokers to switch to smokeless tobacco products, which he states are "98% safer than smoking"(Oral Pathology Dept., University of Alabama). Oral Pathology Dept., University of Alabama at Birmingham, "A Smoking Cessation Strategy," For Smokers Only [http://www.dental.uab.edu/www/oralpath/FSO.html] [Jan. 21, 1996]).This advice is contrary to public health policy, which is to counter the perception of smokeless tobacco as a safe alternative to smoking, stressing its connection with oral lesions and the possibility that it is "highly addicting" (Barbara S. Lynch and Richard J. Bonnie, eds. *Growing Up Tobacco Free: Preventing Nicotine Addiction in Children and Youths* [Washington, D.C.: National Academy Press, 1994], 155–59, 39).

26. Arden Christen and James McDonald Jr., "Safety of Nicotine-Containing Gum," in *Nicotine Replacement: A Critical Evaluation*, ed. Ovide F. Pomerleau and Cynthia S. Pomerleau (New York: Pharmaceutical, 1992), 219–35, 230.

27. Bittoun, *You Can Quit*, 20.

28. Harris, *Deadly Choices*, 172.

29. Gilles Deleuze and Felix Guattari, *A Thousand Plateaus: Capitalism and Schizophrenia,* trans. Brian Massumi (Minneapolis: University of Minnesota Press, 1987), 89–90, 158–62. My use of Deleuze and Guattari is indebted to the interpretations of Paul Patton, "Metamorpho-Logic: Bodies and Powers in A Thousand Plateaus," *Journal of Behavioral and Social. Phenomenology* 25 (1994): 157–69; and Elizabeth Grosz, *Volatile Bodies: Toward a Corporeal Feminism* (St. Leonards, Australia: Allen & Unwin. 1994), 166–73.

30. Deleuze and Guattari, 256–57.

31. Whorf cited in Barbara Adam, "Perceptions of Time," in *Companion Encyclopedia of Anthropology,* ed. Tim Ingold (London: Routledge, 1994), 503–26, 514.

32. Norman Denzin, *The Alcoholic Society: Addiction and Recovery of the Self* (New Brunswick, N.J.: Transaction, 1993), 97–101.

33. Public health discourse usually assumes that people underestimate the risks of smoking and are not aware of the extent of the dangers, thus "accurate" information is taken to mean information that stresses the magnitude of the risks, in order to raise risk perception. However, there is evidence that consumers' estimates of the effects of smoking on mortality and life expectancy tend to exceed "scientific" estimates (W. Kip Viscusi, *Smoking: Making the Risky Decision* [New York: Oxford University Press, 1992], 7, 83). This overestimation of risk is particularly pronounced in the case of lung cancer. Therefore, it could be argued that a concern with accuracy would be best served by information reassuring the public that the risk of smokers developing lung cancer is probably less than they imagine.

34. One reason put forward to explain why smokers do not want to quit, despite knowing the dangers, is that they labor under particular "cognitive defects." One of these is "time discounting," the tendency to attach too little importance to the future relative to the present (Robert Goodin, "The Ethics of Smoking," *Ethics* 99 [1989]: 582).

35. Mary Douglas, "Risk as a Forensic Resource," *Daedalus* 119 (1990): 3.

36. Douglas, 1.

37. Bittoun, *You Can Quit,* 9.

38. Nelkin and Lindee, 166.

39. Helga Nowotny, *Time: The Modern and Postmodern Experience,* trans. Neville Plaice (Cambridge: Polity, 1994), 51–52. Further references are cited parenthetically in the text.

40. Harris, *Deadly Choices.*

41. Hilary Graham, "Surviving by Smoking," in *Women and Health: Feminist Perspectives,* ed. Sue Wilkinson and Celia Kitzinger (London: Taylor & Francis, 1994), 102–23, 116–20.

42. Bobbie Jacobson, *Beating the Ladykillers: Women and Smoking* (London: Pluto, 1986), 119.

43. See Neales on the "urban myth" of the smoking and boozing "New Australian Woman" (Sue Neales, "The Ultimate Equality: Die Like a Man," *Age* [Melbourne, Australia], March 27, 1993, 20).

44. As Nowotny discusses in detail, this kind of "self-time" is unequally distributed, with access depending on the hierarchies of power and income in which individuals are located (133).

45. Most famously and succinctly by Oscar Wilde, "A cigarette is the perfect type

of a perfect pleasure. It is exquisite, and it leaves one unsatisfied. What more can one want?" (Oscar Wilde, *The Picture of Dorian Gray* [London: Oxford University Press, 1974], 79).

46. Roland Barthes, *A Lover's Discourse: Fragments,* trans. Richard Howard (Harmondsworth: Penguin, 1990), 31.

47. Another difficulty, downplayed by health promotion discourse, is the possibility of conflict between different health-related goals. The healthy lifestyle it promotes is presented as an interconnected set of practices that logically fit together into a harmonious whole: exercising, eating well, maintaining a desirable weight, and not smoking. But many smokers who quit smoking gain weight, and one of the factors in the increasing prevalence of overweight in the United States is the decline in smoking (Katherine Flegal et al., "The Influence of Smoking Cessation on the Prevalence of Overweight in the United States," *The New England Journal of Medicine* 333 [1995]: 1165–70).Therefore, one trend that is welcomed as the source of significant health benefits is linked to another trend that is regarded as a major threat to public health. By obscuring the tension between exhortations to stop smoking and encouragement to stay slim, health discourse suggests that individuals who fail to realize both goals are the problem, rather than questioning the feasibility or desirability of its utopian dream of health.

CHAPTER 8: AN INTOXICATED SCREEN

1. Terry Eagleton, *Literary Theory: An Introduction* (Minneapolis: University of Minnesota Press, 1983), 194–217. See also Pierre Bourdieu, *Ce que parler veut dire* (Paris: Fayard, 1982), 11–95.

2. Albert Gross and David Duke, *America's Longest War* (Durham, N.C.: Duke University Press, 1993), 78. Further references are cited parenthetically in the text.

3. David Musto, *The American Disease: Origins of Narcotic Control* (Oxford: Oxford University Press, 1987), 32.

4. See Musto; and also Stephen Kandall, *Substance and Shadow: Women and Addiction in the United States* (Cambridge, Mass.: Harvard University Press, 1996).

5. See Musto; David Courtwright, *Dark Paradise* (Cambridge, Mass.: Harvard University Press, 1982); and Clarence Lusane, *Pipe Dream Blues* (Boston: South End Press, 1991).

6. Kenneth Anger, *Hollywood Babylon* (New York: Dell, 1975); Kevin Brownlow, *Behind the Mask of Innocence: Films of Social Conscience in the Silent Era* (Berkeley and Los Angeles: University of California Press, 1990); and Michael Starks, *Cocaine Fiends and Reefer Madness* (East Brunswick, N.J.: Cornwall Books, 1982).

7. Because they were produced outside of the major studios, and within the exploitation circuit, these films were, strictly speaking, neither Hollywood nor hegemonic. However, insofar as exploitation films bypassed the Hays Code and did, cheaply and unpretentiously, what the studios themselves would have liked to do, the exploitation market revealed the worst sides of hegemonic discourse. For a superb treatment of the American exploitation drug films, see Eric Schaefer, *"Bold! Daring! Shocking! True!": A History of Exploitation Films, 1919–1959* (Durham, N.C., and London: Duke University Press, 1999), 217–52.

8. See Musto; Jack Herer, *The Emperor Wears No Clothes* (Seattle: Queen of Clubs Publishing Co., 1985); and Larry Sloman, *Reefer Madness* (New York: Grove Press, 1979).

9. See Lusane, 38–39.

10. See Starks, 165–94.

11. Dan Baum, *Smoke and Mirrors: The War on Drugs and the Politics of Failure* (Boston: Little, Brown & Co., 1996), 253.

12. Quoted in Baum, 253.

13. Harm Reduction designates a policy that tries to minimize the damage done by drug use instead of making things worse in the unrealistic attempt to reach a "drug-free America." The Netherlands are a good example of a country that implements Harm Reduction. The Dutch virtual legalization of cannabis has succeeded in separating the soft drugs (hemp and its derivatives) market from the hard drugs. It is worth noting that the number of people using soft drugs in Holland has not increased significantly. On the contrary, availability defuses the "forbidden fruit syndrome," so much so that the average age for youthful experimentation is calculated to be twenty, whereas in the United States it is sixteen! (DPF newsletter, fall 1997).

14. Herer, 20.

15. Herer, 22.

16. Another telling, if ludicrous, link between homosexuality and drug use was provided by drug czar Carlton Turner in 1987. The nation's foremost authority on marijuana (he studied it for years in the only legal pot farm in the United States) once quipped that "pot can make you gay."

17. Eve Kosofsky Sedgwick, *Tendencies* (Durham, N.C.: Duke University Press, 1993), 130.

18. Eve Kosofsky Sedgwick, *Epistemology of the Closet* (Berkeley and Los Angeles: University of California Press, 1990), 172.

19. According to Thomas Szasz's *Ceremonial Chemistry,* drugs and drug users are the modern-day equivalents of ancient Greece's *pharmakoi,* the "official" scapegoats sacrificed in the name of the well-being of the community. Of course, the *pharmakos'* (scapegoat) etymological proximity with *pharmakon* (drug) adds spice to Szasz's forceful argument. See his *Ceremonial Chemistry* (Holmes Beach, Fl.: Learning Publications, 1985).

20. Avital Ronell, *Crack Wars: Literature, Addiction, Mania* (Lincoln: University of Nebraska Press, 1992), 3.

21. Craig MacAndrew and Robert Edgerton, *Drunken Comportment* (Chicago: Aldine, 1969), 88.

22. Alfred Lindesmith, *Addiction and Opiates* (Chicago: Aldine, 1947).

23. Howard Becker, *Outsiders* (Toronto: McMillan, 1963).

24. Norman Zinberg, *Drug, Set, and Setting: The Basis for Controlled Intoxicant Use* (New Haven, Conn.: Yale University Press, 1984).

25. Andrew Tudor, "On Alcohol and the Mystique of Media Effects," in *Drunken Comportment,* ed. Craig MacAndrew and Robert Edgerton (Chicago: Aldine, 1969). Jim Cook and Michael Levington, *Images of Alcoholism* (London: BFI, 1979), 12.

CHAPTER 9: WELCOME TO THE PHARMACY

Thanks to Karen Cadora, Istvan Csicsery-Ronay Jr., Niklas Damiris, Richard Doyle, Diana Fuss, Sarah Jain, Marc Redfield, Jeffrey Schnapp, Sha Xin Wei, the Stanford University Graduate Women's Reading Group, Marguerite Waller, and Michael Wood for comments and critical feedback.

1. Nicole Stenger, "The Mind Is a Leaking Rainbow," in *Cyberspace: First Steps*, ed. Michael Benedikt (Cambridge, Mass.: MIT Press, 1991), 49–58, 57. Further references are cited parenthetically in the text.

2. Michael Benedikt, "Introduction" to *Cyberspace: First Steps*, ed. Michael Benedikt (Cambridge, Mass.: MIT Press, 1991), 1–25, 1. Further references are cited parenthetically in the text.

3. Niculae Asciu, "The Lure and Addiction of Life on Line" [cartoon], *New York Times*, March 8, 1995, B1.

4. Robert Markley, "Boundaries: Mathematics, Alienation, and the Metaphysics of Cyberspace," in *Virtual Realities and Their Discontents*, ed. Robert Markley (Baltimore, Md.: Johns Hopkins University Press, 1996), 55–78, 56. Further references are cited parenthetically in the text.

5. Jean Baudrillard, "Two Essays," trans. Arthur B. Evans, *Science-Fiction Studies* 18 (1991): 309–10.

6. Jacques Derrida, *Of Grammatology*, trans. Gayatri Chakravorty Spivak (Baltimore, Md.: Johns Hopkins University Press, 1976), 10. Further references are cited parenthetically in the text.

7. Richard Doyle, *On Beyond Living: Rhetorical Transformations of the Life Sciences* (Stanford, Calif.: Stanford University Press, 1997), 3, 4. Further references are cited parenthetically in the text.

8. Scott Bukatman, *Terminal Identity: The Virtual Subject in Postmodern Science Fiction* (Durham, N.C.: Duke University Press, 1993), 45–46.

9. Michael Heim, "The Erotic Ontology of Cyberspace," in *Cyberspace: First Steps*, ed. Michael Benedikt (Cambridge, Mass.: MIT Press, 1991), 60–80, 64. See also Heim's *The Metaphysics of Virtual Reality* (New York: Oxford University Press, 1993).

10. William Burroughs, *Junky* (New York: Penguin, 1977), xv–xvi. Further references are cited parenthetically in the text.

11. Jeff Noon, *Vurt* (New York: Crown, 1995), 339. Further references are cited parenthetically in the text.

12. "Burn:Cycle" [Philips Media VR game advertisement], *Wired*, Dec. 1994, 36.

13. Avital Ronell, *Crack Wars: Literature, Addiction, Mania* (Lincoln: University of Nebraska Press, 1992), 61.

14. John Colapinto, "Rock & Roll Heroin," *Rolling Stone*, May 30, 1996, 18.

15. Kathleen Ann Goonan, *Queen City Jazz* (New York: Tor, 1994), 253–54.

16. Jacques Derrida, "The Rhetoric of Drugs. An Interview," trans. Michael Israel, *differences* 5 (1993): 6. Further references are cited parenthetically in the text.

17. Jacques Derrida, *Dissemination*, trans. Barbara Johnson (Chicago: University of Chicago Press, 1981), 82. Further references are cited parenthetically in the text.

18. Tim Holmes, CD insert. Glenn Branca Symphony Nos. 8 & 10. Atavistic, 1994.

19. Istvan Csicsery-Ronay Jr., "Antimancer: Cybernetics and Art in Gibson's Count Zero," *Science-Fiction Studies* 22 (1995): 70.

20. Evelyn Fox Keller, "The Body of a New Machine: Situating the Organism Between Telegraphs and Computers," *Perspectives on Science* 2 (1994): 313.

21. David Porush, "Frothing the Synaptic Bath: What Puts the Punk in Cyberpunk?" in *Fiction 2000: Cyberpunk and the Future of Narrative,* ed. George Slusser and Tom Shippey (Athens: University of Georgia Press, 1992), 246–61, 256. Further references are cited parenthetically in the text.

22. David Porush, "Hacking the Brainstem: Postmodern Metaphysics and Stephenson's *Snow Crash,*" in *Virtual Realities and Their Discontents,* ed. Robert Markley (Baltimore Md.: Johns Hopkins University Press, 1996), 107–41, 14. Further references are cited parenthetically in the text.

23. David Porush, "Out of Our Minds," *ANQ: A Quarterly Journal of Short Articles, Notes and Reviews* 5 (1992): 234. Further references are cited parenthetically in the text.

24. Plato, *The Collected Dialogues,* ed. Edith Hamilton and Huntington Cairns (Princeton, N.J.: Princeton University Press, 1963), 1178.

25. Heim, "Erotic Ontology," 64–65.

26. Allucquère Rosanne Stone, *The War of Desire and Technology at the Close of the Mechanical Age* (Cambridge, Mass.: MIT Press, 1995), 167. Further references are cited parenthetically in the text.

27. Carol Mason, "Terminating Bodies," in *Posthuman Bodies,* ed. Judith Halberstam and Ira Livingston (Bloomington: Indiana University Press, 1995), 225–43, 228.

28. Eve Kosofsky Sedgwick, "Epidemics of Will," in *Zone 6: Incorporations,* ed. Jonathan Crary and Sanford Kwinter (New York: Urzone, 1992), 582–95, 587. Further references are cited parenthetically in the text.

29. Severo Sarduy, *Christ on the Rue Jacob,* trans. Suzanne Jill Levine and Carol Maier (San Francisco: Mercury House, 1995), 12.

30. "The Groove Thing" [Big Top Productions VR game advertisement], *Wired,* April 1995, 173.

CHAPTER 10: IF "REALITY IS THE BEST METAPHOR," IT MUST BE VIRTUAL

1. Laura Miller, "Women and Children First: Gender and the Settling of the Electronic Frontier," in *Resisting the Virtual Life: The Culture and Politics of Information,* ed. James Brook and Iain A. Boal (San Francisco: City Lights Books, 1995), 49–57, 53.

2. Eve Kosofsky Sedgwick, *Between Men: English Literature and Male Homosocial Desire* (New York: Columbia University Press, 1985).

3. John Perry Barlow, "Declaration of Independence of Cyberspace," e-mail forward from barlow@eff.org (February 9, 1996).

4. Eve Kosofsky Sedgwick, "Epidemics of Will," in *Zone 6: Incorporations,* ed. Jonathan Crary and Sanford Kwinter (New York: Urzone, 1992).

5. Tamara Bennett, "Starbright: Best of Broadband," *Convergence* (Dec. 1995): 36–41.

6. Susan McCarthy, "The Good Deed," *Wired,* Sept. 1996, 170–75, 230–31.

7. Laurie Flynn, "Prototypes of Virtual Shoppers: 'Avatars,' With Your Head on Their Shoulders, Navigate Cyberspace," *The New York Times*, March 4, 1996, C3; and Rob Schmults, "Issho Iwai, Toppan Printing, and Worlds Inc. Announce Sweeping Alliance, Move to Rapidly Accelerate the Spread of Online Multiuser 3-D in Japan," Worlds Inc. Press Release (March 11, 1996): 2.

8. Robert Rossney, "Metaworlds," *Wired*, June 1996, 142–46, 202–12; and Marc Laidlaw, "The Egos at Id," *Wired*, Aug. 1996, 122–27, 186–89.

9. Roger Chartier, "Representations of the Written Word," in *Forms and Meanings: Texts, Performances, and Audiences from Codex to Computer* (Philadelphia: University of Pennsylvania Press, 1995), 1–24.

10. Sue-Ellen Case, *The Domain-Matrix: Performing Lesbian at the End of Print Culture* (Bloomington and Indianapolis: Indiana University Press, 1996), 189–231.

11. Neal Stephenson, *Snowcrash* (New York: Bantam Books, 1992).

12. Rossney, 210; Laidlaw, 188.

13. Flynn, C3.

14. Duncan Galloway, Patrick Collins, Eric Wolanski, Brian King, and Peter Doherty, "Visualization of Oceanographic and Fisheries Biology Data for Scientists and Managers," *Communique: Data Explorer Newsletter* 3 (1995): 1–3.

15. Howard Rheingold, *Virtual Reality* (New York: Simon and Schuster, 1992), 13. See also Heinz Pagels, *The Dreams of Reason* (New York: Simon & Schuster, 1988).

16. "New Information Technology for Collective Visualization of the Future," conference handout. Informal conference convened at California Institute of Technology, spring 1996.

17. Dave Gobel et al., "Worlds Incorporated—Education Position Statement," Aug. 1995 (unpublished), 2.

18. Leland Wilkinson, *Sygraph: The System for Graphics* (Evanston Ill.: Systat, Inc., 1989), 45.

19. Allucquère Rosanne Stone, *The War of Desire and Technology at the Close of the Mechanical Age* (Cambridge, Mass.: MIT Press, 1995); and Sherry Turkle, "Artificial Life as the New Frontier," in *Life on the Screen: Identity in the Age of the Internet* (New York: Simon and Schuster, 1995).

20. N. Katherine Hayles, "The Seductions of Cyberspace," in *Rethinking Technologies*, ed. Verena Andermatt Conley (Minneapolis and London: University of Minnesota Press, 1993), 173–90, 177.

21. Gobel et al., 3.

22. Anne Balsamo, *Technologies of the Gendered Body: Reading Cyborg Women* (Durham, N.C., and London: Duke University Press, 1996), 144–45.

23. Scott McCloud, *Understanding Comics: The Invisible Art* (Northampton, Mass.: Kitchen Sink Press, Inc. 1993), 30–32.

24. McCloud, 36.

25. Giles Deleuze and Felix Guattari, *A Thousand Plateaux: Capitalism and Schizophrenia*, trans. Brian Massumi (Minneapolis: University of Minnesota Press, 1987), 10.

26. Deleuze and Guattari, 153.

27. Anne Friedberg, "A Denial of Difference: Theories of Cinematic Identification," in *Psychoanalysis and Cinema*, ed. E. Ann Kaplan (New York and London: Routledge, 1990), 36–45, 36.

28. McCloud, 49.

29. Jean Baudrillard, *Simulations* (New York: Semiotext(e), 1983), 2–3.

30. Baudrillard, 11.

31. Judith Butler, *Bodies that Matter: On the Discursive Limits of "Sex"* (New York and London: Routledge, 1993).

32. Octavia Butler, *Dawn* (New York: Popular Library, 1987); Octavia Butler, *Adulthood Rites* (New York: Popular Library, 1988); and Octavia Butler, *Imago* (New York: Popular Library, 1989).

33. Deleuze and Guattari, 189–90.

34. Judith Hersko, "Artist's Statement," *Europe: Creation and Recreation* at LA Artcore, Los Angeles, 1995 (unpublished handout).

35. J. Butler, 27–55.

36. Stone, 40, 93.

37. Balsamo, 144.

38. Evelyn Fox Keller, *Reflections on Gender and Science* (New Haven, Conn., and London: Yale University Press, 1985), 167–72; Turkle, 149–74.

39. Fox Keller, 168.

40. Ann Weinstone, "Welcome to the Pharmacy: Addiction, Transcendence, and Virtual Reality," (this volume), 163.

41. Hayles, 173–83.

42. Henri Lefebvre, *The Production of Space*, trans. Donald Nicholson-Smith (Oxford and Cambridge, Mass.: Blackwell, 1984), 396.

43. Lefebvre, 313.

44. Ted Nelson, e-mail correspondence with the author (August 17, 1995).

ABOUT THE CONTRIBUTORS

Janet Farrell Brodie is the chair of the Department of History at Claremont Graduate University. She is currently working on a book, entitled *Cultures of Secrecy in Early Cold War Los Angeles,* about the institutionalization of the national security state.

Helen Keane is assistant professor at the Australian National University. She is the author of *What's Wrong with Addiction?* (2002).

Stacey Margolis teaches English at the University of Utah. She is currently completing a book entitled *The Novel Effect.*

Timothy Melley is an associate professor of English at Miami University in Oxford, Ohio. He is the author of *Empire of Conspiracy: The Culture of Paranoia in Postwar America* (2000).

Marc Redfield is Chair of the Department of English at Claremont Graduate University. He is the author of *Phantom Formations: Aesthetic Ideology and the Bildungsroman* (1996) and *The Politics of Aesthetics: Nationalism, Gender, Romanticism* (2003).

Marty Roth is a professor of American literature and film studies at the University of Minnesota. He has worked for the past ten years in the field of cultural intoxication and addiction studies.

Cannon Schmitt teaches English at Duke University. He is the author of *Alien Nation: Nineteenth-Century Gothic Fictions and English Nationality* (1997). His current book-in-progress is titled *Savage Mnemonics: South America, Victorian Science, and the Reinvention of the Human.*

Maurizio Viano teaches in the Cinema and Media Studies Program at Wellesley College.

Marguerite R. Waller is a professor of English and women's studies at the University of California, Riverside, where she also teaches in the Film and Visual Culture Program. She is the author of *Petrarch's Poetics and Literary History,* coeditor with Jennifer Rycenga of *Frontline Feminisms: Women, War, and Resistance,* and coeditor with Frank Burke of *Contemporary Perspectives on Federico Fellini.*

Robyn R. Warhol is a professor of English and the chair of the Department of English at the University of Vermont. She is the author of *Having a Good Cry: Effeminate Feelings and Popular Forms* (2003); *Gendered Interventions: Narrative Discourse in the Victorian Novel* (1989), and coeditor with Diane Price Herndl of *Feminisms: An Anthology of Literary Theory and Criticism* (1991 and 1997).

Nicholas Warner, professor of English and comparative literature at Claremont McKenna College, is the author of *Spirits of America: Intoxication in 19th Century American Literature* (1997) and of numerous articles on English, American, and Russian literature.

Ann Weinstone is an assistant professor of comparative literature and radio, television, and film at Northwestern University. Her first book, *Avatar Bodies: A Tantra for Posthumanism,* is forthcoming from University of Minnesota Press. She is currently at work on a cross-cultural study of concepts of media.<v1.70><e1>

INDEX

Compositor:	BookMatters
Text:	10/12 Baskerville
Display:	Baskerville
Printer and Binder:	Maple-Vail Manufacturing Group

Top Buzzer

- Angry Scotsman, crazy is - eggy
- Close ups of dumpster